The Hunters
and
The Hunted

The Hunters
and
The Hunted

Jochen Brennecke

Translated by

R. H. Stevens

BLUEJACKET BOOKS

Naval Institute Press
Annapolis, Maryland

Naval Institute Press
291 Wood Road
Annapolis, MD 21402

First Bluejacket Books printing, 2003

Library of Congress Cataloging-in-Publication Data
Brennecke, Jochen.
    [Jäger-Gejagte! English]
    The hunters and the hunted / Jochen Brennecke; translated by R. H. Stevens.
    p. cm. — (Bluejacket books)
    Originally published: New York: Norton, 1958.
    ISBN 1-59114-091-9 (alk. paper)
    1. World War, 1939–1945—Naval operations, German. 2. World War, 1939–1945—Naval operations—Submarine. I. Title. II. Series.
    D781.B713 2003
    950.54'51'0943—dc21

                                                                    2003050120

Printed in the United States of America on acid-free paper ∞
10 09 08 07 06 05 04 03   9 8 7 6 5 4 3 2 1

CONTENTS

PART ONE 1939

CHAPTER   PAGE

   I   Battleships or U-boats?   9
  II   Unexpected Success   22

PART TWO 1940

  III   Mining Exploits, Silent Heroism . . .   32
  IV   Operation Weseruebung   40
  V   The U-boat and its Unwritten Laws . . .   58

PART THREE 1941

  VI   Otto Kretschmer and Guenther Prien . .   66
  VII   Muetzelburg and Lueth, U-boat Aces . .   79
  VIII   *U.74* and the Tragedy of the *Bismarck* . .   88
  IX   The Hessler Convoy and the Betrayal of the St.
        Antoa Rendezvous   94
  X   *U.81* Sinks an Air Squadron. *U.331* Destroys the
        Battleship *Barham*   103
  XI   New British Defensive Tactics   121
  XII   The Drama of the U-boats and *Atlantis* . .   128

PART FOUR 1942

  XIII   War with U.S.A.   140
  XIV   In the Caribbean—Dynamite   152
  XV   More Inexperienced Americans . . .   161
  XVI   *U.134* Out of the Fridge into the Oven . .   173
  XVII   *Laconia*   178
  XVIII   The Experiments of Helmuth Walter . .   191
  XIX   Another "Paukenschlag" off Cape Town . .   197

PART FIVE 1943

CHAPTER		PAGE
xx	The Break-up of the U-boat Force . . .	202
xxi	Dysentery Aboard!	213
xxii	"Dr. Fug"—Dr. Cauer, Professor of Chemistry .	224
xxiii	How Brandi, the Cruiser King, Lost his U-boat .	228
xxiv	U-boats in Far Eastern Waters	237
xxv	*U.792*, the Wonder U-boat	244
xxvi	A Sombre Prospect	249

PART SIX 1944

xxvii	Doenitz and the Walter U-boats . . .	258
xxviii	Emergency in the Indian Ocean Too . . .	263
xxix	Escape from 200 Feet Below the Surface. *U.763* in Portsmouth Harbour	267
xxx	A Lame U-boat Flees from Bordeaux . .	279
xxxi	A Petty Officer Saves *U.178* . . .	289
xxxii	Alongside a British Destroyer in the Arctic . .	293

PART SEVEN 1945

xxxiii	New Equipment for Old and New U-boats . .	298
xxxiv	Chivalrous to the Bitter End	301
xxxv	The U-boats Surrender	309
xxxvi	Where is Professor Walter? Where are the German Wonder U-boats?	314

LIST OF ILLUSTRATIONS

FACING PAGE

U-boat in construction 16

U-boat in dock 16

A lesson on construction 17

Instruction on Diesel motors 17

Demonstrating the attack on a convoy 17

U-boat aces, Brandi, Hardegen, Lueth and Kretschmer . 32

Old names for new boats; the Weddigen Flotilla . . 33

In all weathers; sunrise, storm in the Atlantic, a patrol in
the Atlantic with high seas 96

"Shooting" the sun 97

Taking a torpedo aboard at sea 97

Air attack on a U-boat 97

A merciless war; a torpedo striking home, the last man to
leave a sinking destroyer, survivors 112

In the Mediterranean; *U.77* off the coast of Palestine, *Ark
Royal*, *Malaya* and *Renown*, *Ark Royal* after she had been
torpedoed 113

After an attack; the commander at the periscope, waiting
for orders, crash dive, operating the hydrophones. . 192

Depth charges, the Diesel compartment . . . 193

From the other point of view; depth charges exploding as
seen by the enemy, motor launches to combat U-boats . 208

A rammed U-boat arrives safely home 209

A sinking U-boat in a Norwegian fjord 209

The first Walter U-boat. *V.80* in the Baltic . . . 256

The control room of *V.80* 256

A British aerial photograph of a convoy in the North
Atlantic 257

A tanker blows up 257

FACING PAGE

The next morning, burning wrecks mark the passage of
the convoy 257

Bombproof pens in St. Nazaire harbour . . . 272

A pen in Heliogoland in which U-boats could be repaired
and refitted 272

The end; U-boats found by the Allies in the shipbuilding
yards, British troops in the Blohm and Voss yards,
surrendered U-boats on Loch Ryan 273

Part One

1939

―――――

CHAPTER I

BATTLESHIPS OR U-BOATS?

Situation Report—August.

In August 1939 the German Navy had fifty-one* submarines in commission at its disposal. Not all of them, of course, were available for operations, for some, and more now than ever before, were required as training ships. Between 19 and 21 August, twenty-one submarines sailed from their home bases and took up the positions of readiness assigned to them. The sealed operation orders of the Naval High Command reposed snugly in the safes of their commanders. Among these officers were men whose names were destined a few months later to be blazoned on the front pages of the world's press and whose praises were to be sung by the German Broadcasting Service—Prien, Kretchmer, Schepke, Frauenheim, Schultze, Schuhardt and others.

*　　　　*　　　　*

Lieut.-Commander Schultze, called "Vaddi" for short, commander of *U.48*, turned to his Chief Petty Officer.

"Bo'sun," he said, "see to it that the ship's number is painted out; and while you're about it, you'd better have the bird taken down from its perch, too,"—this latter being the somewhat disrespectful but generally accepted name given to the eagle surmounting the national emblem on the submarine's conning-tower.

A few days previously, on 18 August, 1939, *U.48*, in company with others had sailed out into the North Sea. Her slim bows, with serrated net-cutter and gaping bull ring, giving the appearance of some horned reptile, were pointed northwards.

It was a day of early autumn sunshine, and the sea, sometimes referred to with a shiver by those who inhabit its coast as the frozen North Sea, was now calm and friendly. Only a barely perceptible swell swung lazily across the grey-green waters.

*British sources quote fifty-seven.

"Sniffing the powder a bit previous-like, aren't you, Sir?" grunted the C.P.O., abandoning in his astonishment the more normal response of "Aye, aye, Sir."

"War will only disappear when we find we've no more use for it, or when mankind really deserves peace," said Schultze philosophically. "That's true, you know—unfortunately; so it's no use making a face like a startled hen!" Slowly he turned aside, raised his binoculars and started to scan the open sea around him.

That put an end to the discussion of a thorny subject. "Gangway below!" shouted the C.P.O. into the dark cavern of the conning-tower, as a warning to anyone who at that moment might be thinking of coming up. For in the narrow shaft there was but one slim, cold, iron ladder, and on it there was only room for one man at a time. Like a weasel, the C.P.O. vanished below. An acrobat would have looked clumsy in comparison with him.

Before passing on the orders he had received he crept off to the engine-room, to his buddy, the chief artificer. "Damn dirty weather ahead. The old man has even ordered the ship's number to be painted out. That, my lad, means war!"

"Tripe! Tell that to the marines! There isn't going to be a war. A matey little shooting match with the Poles, perhaps. And what the hell do we here care about that! No fear, the Limeys aren't going to let themselves be mucked about."

"Half a minute! Don't forget, it's only the other day the British said they would stand by their obligations to Poland. Another thing—the cancellation of the naval agreement and the Reichstag declaration on 28 April that we no longer considered ourselves bound in any way by any limitations on naval construction—they won't lap that up like mother's milk. And it's not just for fun that we're sculling about in the North Sea at a time of crisis, instead of being in the Baltic off the Polish coast, where the balloon's just going up."

"Precautionary, purely precautionary. These islanders will take jolly good care of their own skins. Don't forget these." As he spoke, the chief artificer slapped the welded, pressurised body of *U.48*. "The British had a pretty bitter experience last time that nearly drove them to despair. And then, mark you, we only had a very few craft at the outbreak of war. This time there are fifty of us."

"You're far too mechanically minded. You think and reckon only in numbers and assume that engines and weapons are in-fallible. Don't let's lay too great a store on what happened in the last war. The enemy, too, has new methods, new weapons. And that reminds me—they do say that the British claim to have invented a completely new type of submarine-locating gear."

"I'd like to know what they've got that's better than ours! Anyhow, we've got better boats; we've got better technicians and we've got more guts."

"What you mean is—we've made improvements on the things we had in the last war. But so have they. The thing we really lack is U-boats, more U-boats and yet more U-boats. Raeder, however, has set his heart on battleships. But a battleship can't be built in a closed-in back-yard. A U-boat can."

"And you can only see things from your own angle. All you say may be true from the submariner's point of view. But the battleship is certainly still the back-bone of the fleet. For the time being, anyhow."

"True enough—in a powerful fleet. But the weaker side must learn to use the weapons weakness imposes. The U-boat—that's the weapon of the weaker side. And at sea the weaker side is—ours."

"If you go on thinking along those lines you'll give yourself the willies—and your men."

"Not a bit. I'm simply facing things soberly as they are, in exactly the same way as you regard your engines as soberly, as mathematically constructed entities."

*   *   *

More U-boats or more battleships? That was the problem which exercised the mind of even the humblest member of the navy. He had a feeling that behind the closed doors of Naval High Command in the Tirpitz-Ufer many a hard-fought scrap had been taking place. The submariners, fanatical in their belief in their own weapon, pinned their faith on the lion of their service, "their" Doenitz, who was far more to them than merely their own special commander. The little man in the submarine service summed things up in his own way when he said bitterly: "Our Commander-in-Chief (Admiral Raeder) doesn't want any U-boats and for why? Because we can't put a band on the upper deck and receive 'im with trumpets and drums!"

The young and enterprising U-boat officers, whom Doenitz described as the cream of the navy, expressed their rejection of Raeder's balance of power policy a little less drastically. But for all that they stood unreservedly and to a man behind "their" Doenitz and his demands.

A few months before the Polish crisis, Raeder, who was well aware of the opposition of the submarine officers to his surface vessels programme, took the opportunity of speaking pretty bluntly to a gathering of senior naval officers:

"I know that some of you gentlemen, and some of you in authoritative positions, hold views with regard to our new building programme which differ from my own. It is therefore very painful to me when I am reproached, sometimes implicitly and sometimes quite openly, with failure to appreciate the importance of a numerically strong, well-trained and enterprising submarine force. It would be the height of foolishness not to develop this new weapon which proved itself in the First World War, and I think, therefore, that the time has come for me to disillusion those who think that the Naval High Command does not realise it."

Raeder went on to explain what classes of ships should in his opinion be given priority of construction, in view of the political and military situation as a whole and the assurance, given to him by Hitler, that war with Britain was out of the question.

The irony of the thing is that both Raeder and Doenitz, each from his own respective point of view, were right. The only difference was that Raeder had to take everything into consideration as one corporate whole, whereas Doenitz, responsible solely for submarines, could take a one-sided view. Nor, of course, must it be assumed that history will judge Doenitz to have been more clear-sighted. Such an assumption would be as unjust as it is incorrect.

As an exponent of historic methods, Raeder adhered firmly to the principles of classical maritime strategy. He had made a scientific examination of all previous operations and of all the various factors which had contributed towards success or failure in the First World War. The experience gained in the battle of Jutland had shown the extent to which the fighting power of the German battleships was superior to that of the British. Their degree of invulnerability to sinking greatly exceeded anything that had been believed practically possible. Now, Raeder knew that Plan Z was producing new types of battleships, which could confidently engage any class of ship in the British Navy or in any other fleet in the world.

And when all is said and done, it was thanks to Raeder's wise policy in the selection of personnel that, in picking the officers to be entrusted with the formation of the new German U-boat weapon, the choice had fallen on Karl Doenitz.

In spite of all his enthusiasm, his drive and his tremendous initiative, Doenitz could not but admit that against his own conception of a numerically strong and technically highly-trained submarine fleet there were not a few grave and unknown factors in the scales. Britain, for example, claimed that with the invention of the so-called Asdic apparatus—a new type of underwater locating gear—she had mastered the U-boat problem. "It's possible, of course, that this is just a typical bit of British bluff," Raeder conceded; "but we don't know the apparatus, and so, if bluff it is, we can't call it. We're groping in the dark."

Face to face with such uncertainty, should he have staked his all on one card—on the U-boat? That, surely, was something that he, as Commander-in-Chief, and the man with overall responsibility, neither could nor should have done.

It was only later, after Doenitz had evolved his pack tactics and proved their efficiency in exercises under all kinds of conditions, that the need for more U-boats became automatically apparent. In the spring of 1939 these tactics proved their worth in a large-scale exercise between Cape Vincent and Ushant, in which twenty U-boats attacked a "convoy". In spite of this success the great, unanswered query regarding the enemy's anti-submarine defences still remained. Furthermore, at that time the German U-boat types were constantly developing. It therefore seemed both pointless and inadvisable to place mass orders, even for the bigger types, while size and performance had not yet reached the limits of practical perfection.

Even so, Doenitz, a lean, wiry figure, full of energy, was in no mood to capitulate tamely in the face of Raeder's reasoned policy. He continued to plead and warn and he proved beyond doubt that the number of U-boats available was not great enough to constitute a decisive factor in the event of war at sea with Great Britain. He was also quite convinced that Raeder's naval policy would come into conflict with the basic British principle of the balance of power.

"Simply to hope that Britain won't make a move on account of a frontier conflict with Poland just isn't good enough," he declared.

On the technical side, too, Doenitz became a dynamic force in his efforts to gain his object. To him, ruthless but methodical seeker that he was, the available U-boats represented only an interim solution.

*   *   *

All these worries and struggles were not, of course, noticed overmuch by the officers and men. Even among the submariners themselves there was little more than a feeling that fundamental differences of opinion on naval strategy existed which were retarding the programme of U-boat construction so passionately advocated by Doenitz.

In an attempt to reconcile means, objective and course of action, Raeder, with his wide historical knowledge, had ventured into the ticklish domain of speculation. He sought for the comforting sheet-anchor of certainty, and he believed implicitly in the Fuehrer's assurance that, while she would certainly protest, Britain would never intervene if the Polish dispute were eventually to develop into armed conflict.

All this seems to be particularly tragic, because Raeder possessed so exceptional a knowledge of British mentality, was so outstanding an assessor of their probable reactions and, indeed, did, in fact, introduce many very wise measures, which were based on his great knowledge of the Anglo-Saxon mind.

Right up to the time of the Polish crisis there had still been time to reverse the policy and to devote the whole capacity of those shipbuilding yards, which were at the disposal of the German Navy, to the construction of U-boats.

But Raeder was once again obstinately assured by Hitler: "There will be no war with Britain."

*   *   *

Autumn, 1939. . . .

At 04.45 on the morning of 1 September, German troops crossed the Polish frontier.

During the night of 2/3 September the lights were extinguished round the coasts of the British Isles and France, in the Bermudas and along the coasts of Canada. It was the darkest night since the First World War.

At 12.56 the radio-operators of the lurking U-boats received this message from their Commander-in-Chief:

"Commence hostilities against Britain forthwith."

Two hundred miles to the west of the Hebrides the British liner, *Athenia*, was pounding her way across the Atlantic. When news of the outbreak of war was received the passengers became very nervous and the captain did his best to calm them. There were more than a thousand souls aboard, many of them women and children.

Fervently they prayed to the grey, overcast heavens to bring them safely to the protecting arms of their port of destination. "According to international law, passenger ships may not be attacked unless they are sailing in convoy. We are sailing alone," declared the captain of the *Athenia*, trying to console his passengers.

Like a blood-red eye the sun sank below the western horizon, but for long afterwards passengers and members of the crew not on duty lingered on the upper deck—not to gaze in wonder at the ever impressive sight of sunset at sea. . . .

Very soon the canopy of stars spread itself above the ship. They were ready as always to serve friend and foe alike as staunch and ever-ready pointers across the wilderness of the boundless ocean. In the brilliantly lighted dining saloon there were many empty seats that evening. Only in the smoke-room a few, hard-bitten cases were to be found, propping up the bar and discussing with the help of much whisky the prospects of the powers now locked in conflict.

*   *   *

In the middle of that fateful night the radio operator of the *Bremen* passed a message up to the bridge, an SOS from the vicinity of the Hebrides. Commodore Ahrens noted its contents and—did nothing. But a day or two before he would have leapt into action and alerted the whole ship. The controls on the bridge would have clanged for full speed and the great ship would have swung instantly to a course bearing on the position whence the SOS had come. With a shake of his head and a gesture of bewilderment to his watch-keeper, Ahrens stuffed the SOS signal into his pocket.

It was the *Athenia* asking for help. She shrieked that she had been torpedoed by a German U-boat. The British destroyers *Electra* and *Escort* had acknowledged receipt of her signal and were steaming to her assistance. The Norwegian freighter, *Knute Nelson* and the yacht *Southern Cross* flashed signals to say they were on their way.

Thirteen hundred passengers and crew were saved; one hundred and twenty lost their lives.

At 10.40 the next day the *Athenia* sank by the stern. For a few seconds her bows hung like a tombstone poised above the water before she sank into the greenish-blue twilight of the eternal depths, the first victim of this new war.

U.30, however, under Lieut.-Commander Lemp, had logged his first success. The ship which she had sunk in the darkness of the night was described as a troop transport, proceeding alone at high speed. Only a few hours previously Lemp had received by radio the news of the declaration of war against Britain. His excitement can well be imagined as he broke open his sealed orders and read the instructions which were to govern the conduct of submarine warfare. It was already night when Lemp sighted a dark silhouette and he was sure this was not a passenger ship, but, without any shadow of doubt, a troop transport.

Nine hours after the outbreak of war with Britain and France, the first torpedoes hissed out of the tubes of *U.30*.

They found their mark well. Only too well. They could just as easily have hit the *Bremen*, whose position was unknown to Lemp.

*   *   *

U.48 had just sighted its first steamer.

Vaddi Schultze ordered the guns on deck to be cleared for action and fired a shot across the stranger's bows. The freighter stopped and sent a boat across. Schultze examined the papers which showed the vessel to be the Swedish ship *Aberdan*.

U-boat in construction. The framework of a U-boat pressure hull

U-boat in dock showing the forward hydroplanes. It is through the rectangular openings visible here that water is supplied to the diving tanks

The chief engineer gives a lesson
on construction

The chief engine-room artificer gives instruction on the
Diesel motors

Demonstrating the attack on a convoy

"All in order," declared Schultze, when he had rapidly skimmed through the papers.

The Swedish vessel continued its journey, dipping the blue flag with its yellow cross in friendly salute.

The next day another vessel was sighted. Once again a warning shot flew across the stranger's bows. But this time the captain did not stop. On the contrary. A thick, bubbling cloud of black smoke belched from the funnel. The stokers were raising steam and it was obvious that the ship was going to try to escape at high speed.

"Well—if that's the way you want it," muttered Schultze, "we, too, can talk quite differently—more directly, more plainly and much, much louder."

The next round from the 8·8 cm. gun was aimed in earnest and found its mark.

The stranger blew off steam and stopped. But her radio kept up a ceaseless chatter, repeating her SOS again and again. A British land station picked up the message and passed the signal on. Meanwhile the crew had been taking to the boats.

Schultze did not fire again. He did not want to risk hitting one of the lifeboats bobbing up and down at the freighter's side. Fire from a heaving submarine, whose guns have no automatic fire control, could not be accurate enough to ensure that a shot would not land among the survivors struggling their way into the lifeboats.

At last the crew were all safely in the boats and at a reasonable distance from their ship.

At 12.28 a torpedo rent asunder the body of the ship that bore so proud a name. The *Royal Sceptre* sank into the depths, and down with her went her faithful radio operator.

"Caps off, men!" ordered Schultze, deeply moved. "Now you know who our real enemy is. His name is Courage, when the flag's at stake. And since he's ready to face any danger and, if need be, to die, he won't spare us, either."

The youthful faces of the U-boat's crew, which but a moment before had been radiant with joy and pride, now became grim and earnest.

＊　　　＊　　　＊

U.48 had no time to bother about the survivors, for already two needle-like points and a wisp of smoke had become visible on the

17

horizon. Schultze got under way. His object was to try and cut off the unknown and still invisible freighter.

"Couldn't we have done something first to help the ship's company, Sir?" ventured the officer of the watch to his commanding officer. His tone voiced distaste, and he made no attempt to conceal his disapproval.

"Quite so," replied Schultze firmly, giving his subordinate a friendly nod. But strangely enough he made no move to change his last order to steer at once on the other freighter. And the latter in all innocence continued to steam straight into the U-boat's path.

A warning shot. An order: "Stop!"

The British ship obeyed at once. Instead of awaiting the advent of a prize crew, the whole ship's company tumbled head over heels into the hastily lowered boats. The radio, too, appeared to be silent.

U.48 approached to within hailing distance of the boats. Schultze told the British captain that the crew of a ship he had just sunk had taken to their boats and were close at hand.

"Go and help your countrymen, Captain. Pull back to your own ship and steam to the spot where she sank."

The captain was bewildered. He stood up in his boat and hesitated. It seemed as though he were expecting some trick.

"Damn it, man, I'm telling you to go and pick up the crew of *Royal Sceptre*. I've just sunk her, over there, I tell you!" yelled Schultze angrily and waved his arm in the appropriate direction. "Nothing will happen to you—or your ship."

At last they understood. Swiftly they pulled away and went aboard their own ship again, aboard the British freighter *Browning* of 5,000 tons.

That happened on the same day as the sinking of the *Athenia*, the same day on which the world press, ignorant of what had really happened, chastised the Germans for their inhuman manner of waging war and thundered about the violation of international agreements.

*   *   *

Lieut.-Commander Liebe already had not a few successes to his credit, when one day his chief quartermaster, Bruenninghaus, excitedly raised his binoculars to his eyes. He had seen mast-heads. And beneath those mastheads was a juicy prize. A tanker. Her captain's reaction to the warning shot was instantaneous.

"Don't blame him—do the same thing myself, if I had a few thousand tons of oil waiting to burst into flame under my behind!" said Lieutenant Lueth, watch-keeper and torpedo officer.

A boat came pulling towards the submarine. In it sat the captain with a bundle of papers under his arm. He need not have bothered, for even while he was on his way across, the activities of his radio operator, who had remained aboard, constituted a hostile act which justified the immediate sinking of the ship.

A torpedo flashed from its tube and sped towards its target. Like an erupting volcano the tanker burst asunder in one huge sheet of fire. With incredible speed the burning oil spread across the surface of the water. In their lifeboats the tanker's crew, pulling for their lives, sought desperately to escape the wall of fire. Menacingly, however, the juggernaut of burning oil began, bit by bit, to gain on some of the boats. Nobody aboard Liebe's U-boat bothered about the British captain. They were all enthralled and horrified by the spectacle before them, by the greedy flames licking avidly at the desperate men. The British captain, erect and dignified, stood motionless on the deck of the German U-boat. But his face was as white as a sheet.

Meanwhile, Liebe had reacted swiftly. Crisply he told his chief engineer, Lieut.-Commander Mueller—known on account of his invincible good humour as Smiler Mueller—what he proposed to do. He intended not only to close with the burning patch of sea, but to try and tow the lifeboats out of its flaming hell to safety. Slowly the U-boat went ahead. But an unpleasantly heavy sea was running and this and the smoke and mist made accurate manœuvring impossible. The life-boats threatened to capsize at any moment. And so, those who were right in the middle of the conflagration were swiftly grabbed and hauled aboard. Among them were some Chinese and two or three Irishmen.

Scarcely had Liebe got out of the danger zone than the Irishmen gave tongue and began to curse. It wasn't Liebe they cursed, or the German U-boat; it was England. And, for all the world as though the hour had brought them a fine gift, they slapped the bearded German submariners on the back. Instead of being thankful for their salvation from certain death, they were expressing their joy at the German success.

"Now what shall we do?" muttered Liebe. "Here we are in the

19

middle of the Atlantic, we can't tow the boats to the shore, and if we put the survivors into the boats that are still seaworthy we'll swamp them—and that won't do either."

"P'raps we'll sight a neutral," suggested Lueth. "Or another Britisher, for all I care. The great thing is—somehow or other we've got to get rid of these fellows."

A little later they sighted another tanker, an American, returning empty from England to America. Liebe fired a long-range shot across her bows and at the same time made directly towards her at full speed.

Suddenly the British survivors standing on the U-boat's deck became very agitated. The bridge look-out saw that the men were gesticulating and pointing at the horizon astern. The British captain cupped his hands. "Destroyer, Sir—a British destroyer!"

Liebe was inclined to agree with Lueth that it could easily have been a small cloud. "If it isn't, then all the more reason to catch that Yank as quickly as possible!"

"Smiler! Get some revs on your diesels and let her rip!" Liebe called down to the control. His voice was completely calm and matter-of-fact. "Cool as a cucumber, that bloke," thought Lueth to himself. "Wish I was like that. It pays like hell when things get sticky!"

Then a thought struck him. "If it is a destroyer, we'll have to dive. And then what about those poor devils on deck? There's no room for them in the boats, and the captain hasn't even got a lifebelt!"

Lüth was still thinking that one out, when he saw that on the Commander's orders a life-jacket—and aboard the U-boat there were exactly one for each man of the crew, no more and no less—was being handed down to the Englishman.

The British captain had now become more excited than the German crew. Imploringly he raised his hands. "Dive, Sir! For God's sake, dive!"

He need not have worried.

The 'smoke' had turned out to be a small cloud, after all.

In the meantime, the American vessel stopped. Her crew, in lifejackets, had lined the guard rail. The hails of the German crew seemed to be ignored. The British survivors spread themselves along the whole length of the U-boat's deck, waving their caps, such as had them, and shouting in chorus: "Send a boat! We're British sailors!"

That did the trick. The Americans sent over a boat. The departing Britishers waved from the American cutter to Liebe and his crew. Lüth took a few snapshots. Two of the Irishmen furtively gave the Nazi salute.

"I'm glad we've got a picture of that show," said Lueth. "No one would take our word for it!"

* * *

And what of Herbert Schultze when, on 11 September, 1939, he was compelled to shell the 4,869-ton British freighter *Firby*, which refused to stop, went on madly sending out the SOS signal and cut and ran for it?

Like Liebe and other commanders, he, too, tended the wounded. He, too, saw to it that their wounds were bandaged. He gave them food and water when he found that the lifeboat's provisions were scanty. He helped them with his charts to ensure that they would reach the neighbouring coast in safety.

He sent a signal to the British Admiralty, giving the position of the sunken freighter and her struggling lifeboats.

CHAPTER II

UNEXPECTED SUCCESS

Situation Report—Autumn 1939.

The British have reverted to the proven Churchillian convoy system of the First War. On 7 September the first convoy in the Battle of the Atlantic sailed from England. Destroyers and two hundred escort vessels stood by to guard the convoys two hundred miles to the west of Ireland. On the German side the pack-tactics evolved by Doenitz could not yet be put into practice, since the number of U-boats, which were now operating on a roster system, was still too small. But Raeder had in the meanwhile transferred the main shipbuilding effort from capital ships to U-boats. This step was encouraged by the first great successes achieved, and in particular by the sinking of the aircraft carrier Courageous *and Guenther Prien's exploit in Scapa Flow. He was now hoping to produce between twenty and thirty U-boats per month, instead of the current production of 12·5. The most difficult bottleneck occurred not merely in the acquisition of raw materials, but also in the building of Diesel engines and the manufacture of periscopes. Raeder's demand to be given his own air reconnaissance arm had been ignored by Hitler and Goering. Such few U-boats as there were often exhausted their supplies of fuel oil in fruitless searches for convoys and fast ships sailing independently. After the war, the French Admiral, Bajot, declared that even in 1942/43, the German U-boats could have won the Battle of the Atlantic if the Navy had been provided with adequate air reconnaissance.*

*   *   *

In the first weeks of the war the British stationed their aircraft carrier *Courageous* in Irish waters.

Not far away, was the liner *Veendamm*. She belonged to the Dutch Reederei Nederland-Amerika Stroomwart. Even the passengers noticed that she had increased speed. Ahead, in the rosy light of evening sunshine, plumes of smoke had first been sighted, and then, a little later, four men-of-war became visible.

The excitement among the passengers died down quickly when the bridge gave the comforting news that they were a British aircraft carrier and three escorting destroyers.

The carrier's aircraft swept round the *Veendamm*. They swooped low over the vessel, and the passengers delightedly claimed that they could see the smiling faces of the pilots. The White Ensign of the Royal Navy, too, could be discerned flying from the stern of the *Courageous*, upon whose flight deck the aircraft were coming in one by one to land in the rapidly gathering gloom.

Suddenly, directly alongside the carrier there rose a gigantic white cloud. It looked like fog, and for a moment the passengers and crew aboard the Dutchman thought it was some new type of smoke screen. But almost before these thoughts had passed through their heads, the sound of two terrible explosions reached them. Through the mist they saw swirling pieces of wreckage, bits of iron, of lead, of dismembered aircraft; and as the "mist" cleared—it was in reality composed of gigantic columns of water—great clouds of dense smoke became visible.

Tongues of flame started to dart through the black smoke. The projecting deck of the carrier had burst asunder. The huge ship began to capsize. At first slowly, and then ever more swiftly, she listed to port. Men could be seen sliding down the decks and leaping into the sea. A moment later, the *Courageous* was lying keel-upwards on the waters.

All around the scene of the catastrophe the surface was covered with a thick film of fuel oil. In the midst of it men threshed frantically, striving to get free of it and to escape from the biting, poisonous fumes given off by the oil.

The eye-witnesses aboard the *Veendamm* were alert, eager to do something, yet condemned to helplessness; they watched as those who had survived the explosion and reached the water one by one suffocated and, robbed of their strength by the gases, slowly sank and disappeared. The *Veendamm* went to the rescue. The captain ordered the boats to be lowered with all possible speed. The destroyers, too, came rushing up and hurtled into the vast oil patch. The British freighter, *Collingworth*, picked up the SOS and she, too, came hastening to the scene. But for the sailors struggling in the water the help came too late.

Of the ship's company, 682 officers and ratings were saved. 578 lost their lives.

The attack on the *Courageous* had been carried out by Lieut.-Commander Schuhardt, *U.29*. He had approached with the sun behind him. The small portion of his periscope which had been above water had not been noticed by the British in the fading light. The depth-charges dropped by the destroyers after the catastrophe were quite ineffective. They hurled all they had into the sea, seemingly without plan. Whole patterns were rolled overboard. But Asdic, apparently, had not been working very accurately. The attacker had long since left the spot where he should have been as calculated by this new submarine locating gear.

Courageous was the first warship to be sunk in the conflict. She was a carrier of 25,000 tons and carried 52 aircraft.

It was about this time that the German Navy lost the first U-boat.

U.39 was lost 150 miles west of the Hebrides while delivering a vain attack on one of the most modern of the British aircraft carriers, H.M.S. *Ark Royal*. The destroyers *Falconer*, *Foxhound* and *Firedrake* succeeded in concentrating their attack on the estimated position of the U-boat. *U.39* was surrounded and overwhelmed by a carpet of depth charges.

On the same day *Ark Royal* all but scored a second success. Three of its aircraft sighted a U-boat which shortly before had torpedoed a British freighter, whose SOS signals had been picked up. During the attempts of the British airmen to plant their bombs exactly on the target there occurred one of the strangest happenings of the whole war. Two of the attacking aircraft were destroyed by the blast of their own bombs as they dived steeply towards their target. The third, surviving aircraft reported that the U-boat had been severely damaged and probably destroyed. The boat—it was *U.30*—returned safely home, however, for in this attack the bombs used by the British airmen proved to be too weak in explosive power to tear asunder the pressure hull of the German U-boat. Actually, *U.30* survived through the whole war, only to be scuttled by her own crew in the Flensburg Bight in May 1945.

The great hopes that the British had set on their Asdic had not, apparently, been fully realised. It is true that anti-submarine craft equipped with the device were able to detect the presence of a submerged U-boat, but they could not give an accurate bearing. This was proved by the drama of the *Courageous*, whose escorting destroyers had obviously been led astray by faulty bearings.

Of itself, this Asdic apparatus is nothing more than an electric echo sounder. The only important difference is that the impulses do not only go downwards, as in the case of a fixed echo sounder, but can be transmitted in any direction desired. In U-boats which have been detected by Asdic the crew themselves have been able to hear the echo. The impact of the impulses on the outer casing causes a typical and quite unmistakable pinging noise.

The reports of U-boat commanders were evaluated and these led later to the development of an anti-Asdic gadget, which was called Bold.

In the first phase of the submarine war, however, Bold had not yet been born. This defensive apparatus was just being developed, as were many other defensive and offensive weapons, for which the war came too quickly.

*   *   *

A great deal has already been written about Prien's exploit. In none of these accounts, however, has due credit been given to the men in the engine-room. Without them and without that genius for improvisation which enabled them to remedy sudden technical defects with such aids and means as were to be found on board, Guenther Prien would never have got into Scapa Flow, and he certainly would never have returned.

Here in the words of the chief engineer, Wessels, is the story of this madcap enterprise as seen through the eyes of the engine-room.

According to instruction Prien was to break into Scapa Flow, that Holy of Holies of the Home Fleet, during the night of 12/13 October. In the evening *U.47* was lying close inshore. While there the chief engineer received a disturbing report from his senior engine-room artificer. The lubricating oil in the motors was showing an unusually high content of sea water.

"Bloody hell!" swore Wessels and rushed off to report to Prien, ending his remarks with a warning: "We shall have to postpone the Scapa Flow show, Sir. At the high speed which we expect there's a danger that the bearings will no longer be lubricated or even that the sea water will evaporate."

"I don't know much about that kind of thing, Wessels. But I've a sneaking feeling that you technicians are always a bit too cautious. Later, when we get back to port we can always have the old machines tinkered up again. But I'm sure they'll stick it and do what's asked of them now. They've got to hold out, Chief!"

"I could never accept the responsibility, Sir. It's far too dangerous. If the sea water evaporates, crystallised salt remains; and if salt crystals get in, we'll be running hot bearings in no time and if that happens in Scapa Flow then we've had it. Leave me out of it, Sir. But you can't trust just to luck and chance."

Prien, the imperturbable who drove himself as relentlessly as he did others, bowed his head. Wessel was right, of course. Well—he'd have to try and trace the defect.

And trace it Wessels did. It was a bad leak in the cylinder liner of the port diesel. The dismounting of the heavy cylinder liner was a job that could take hours. Wessels found the answer—an improvised but superb solution. Under his instructions his men got to work. They knocked up a thing rather like an ordinary house gutter and fixed it round the defective cylinder liner. The water caught by it was then led out through two tubes into the engine-room bilges. The improvisation was so successful that gutters of this kind were later supplied as standard equipment. The day on which the die was cast, was a Friday in October. Not only a Friday, but also the 13th. It would be!

As darkness fell, *U.47* made for the eastern entrance to Scapa Flow. Prien sailed on the surface. He had expected a dark night with a new moon. Instead of which he found a night with exceptionally bright Northern Lights shining. "Damn this crazy Friday! . . ."

In the control room Wessel calmly awaited events. And all through the boat, not a word was spoken.

Alarm! A passing ship forced *U.47* to dive. After a few minutes the noise of the stranger's propellers gradually died away. *U.47* rose to the surface again. Prien lounged on deck with Endrass and Varendorff, his watchkeeping officers. The chief boatswain was also on the bridge.

Wessels and Spahr were in the control room plotting the course on the chart. From time to time Spahr passed some alteration of course to the bridge. He was a first-class navigator, conscientious, and trained to think for himself. Prien had great confidence in him. Any moment now *U.47* was due to reach the entrance to Scapa Flow. Any moment now the boat would have to turn to port, to hug close to the small island of Lamb Holm.

There was only one narrow passage open as a few sunken ships obstructed their course and into it *U.47* steered. The tidal stream threatened to swing the boat off course. It was only by getting every possible ounce out of the engines that she managed to get through the narrow channel, with little room to spare on either side.

"Commander to ship's company. We're in!"

The next thing was to find a worth-while prize—and to attack it! For the rest of the way to the well-known anchorage of the British fleet Wessels on his own responsibility had switched both diesels over to charge and both were now driving the propellers and at the same time charging the batteries. Later, the batteries would be required to work to the point of exhaustion.

The bay was almost empty. Only a few tankers were lying at anchor, and for the moment nothing more was to be seen. But there, away back in the distance, those silhouettes, those queer three-decked constructions—those could only be battleships. There were two of them, *Royal Oak* and behind her, without a shadow of doubt, *Repulse*. The great bows of *Repulse*, protruding well beyond her consort offered the first target. . . . Hit!

It is the duty of the torpedo men in the bows to reload the tubes after each spread salvo, and they went about their work with a will. The rear door of one of the torpedo tubes suddenly sprang open. In a broad stream the water poured into the bow torpedo compartment. Quick as lightning Seaman Tewes leapt at the tube and pressed the door shut with his broad chest against it. Scarcely had the new torpedoes nestled in the tubes than a new run started. To keep the boat ready for instant diving, trim and weight had to be adjusted constantly.

The next attack was on *Royal Oak*. Prien manœuvred his boat into its firing position. Endrass stood ready at the firing mechanism. Once again the torpedoes coughed out of the tubes. . . . More explosions, this time more violent than before. A terrific crash, and the air was filled with the noise of bursting and rending.

27

Royal Oak had burst asunder. The great battleship had literally been blown to bits.

U.47 made off out of the loch at her best speed. She had fired all her torpedoes. At the narrowest point, where the booms were and where there was only that thin runnel of a passage, the U-boat found a particularly strong current running against her. Both diesels were really put to the test. Inch by inch *U.47* forged ahead.

Behind them Scapa Flow had leapt into life, for all the world like an antheap which someone has poked with a stick. More and yet more searchlights thrust their gleaming fingers across the sky and over the startled bay. Small patrol vessels, agile as terriers, searched the black waters of the night.

But *U.47*, still travelling on the surface, reached the open sea; and now the great object was to make use of the high speed of the diesels to get well clear of the coast as quickly as possible.

Then came a setback. A report reached Wessels that the starboard propeller was losing revolutions. He hurried into the engine-room. His expert eye at once diagnosed the trouble. The coupling joining the diesel to the propellor shaft was on the point of disintegrating.

"God! What a bloody mess!" He dashed off to report to Prien. Somehow or other the damage just had to be repaired with such means as they had aboard.

Though they were still close in to the British coast, Prien took his boat to the bottom. Wessels and his two faithful chief artificers, Strunk and Roemer, crept into the corner. The motors were stopped. And now Wessels and his team set about proving that man is the master and not the slave of the monsters to which his ingenuity has given birth. Every single one of the screws on the dome of the main coupling had gone. Laboriously, pouring with sweat and forced to contort their bodies in the confined space, the men had to bore out the screws, one by one. Then, of course, it was found that the spare screws on board were all too thick. So there was nothing for it but to bore out the holes. Then new threads had to be cut, and the screws themselves made "to fit".

Hours later Wessels, filthy and smeared all over with oil, stood once more before Prien. "All clear again!"

Prien laughed. "Splendid! Well done, Chief!"

28

And thus ended a fantastic underwater exploit, to which were devoted in the war-log no more than three terse lines.

U.47, however, was by no means out of the wood. To rise to the surface was out of the question, for it now broad daylight. The crew were forced to make use of their oxygen supplies to enable them to breathe.

Twilight was already approaching when Prien at last gave the order to stand by to surface. When he thrust open the hatch of the conning-tower, it was already dark. The precious, cool night air swept through the boat. Its effect was that of fresh fuel added to a dying, flickering flame.

In no time they reached the edge of the German minefield strung like a cordon around the home coast. Before them there remained but one important problem—to find their way through the swept channel. What about course, position? Were they correct?

Alerted by some sixth sense, Wessels pulled up short as he was about to enter the control-room. He heard strange noises.

But Gustav Boehm, the mechanic, had heard nothing, and old Guss was a bureaucratically cautious fellow, an old fox with a sure eye and good ears. Boehm shook his head. Even so, Wessels was not satisfied. He grabbed a sound detector and started on a methodical search of the control-room. Something in the vicinity of the master gyro-compass attracted his concentrated attention. Suddenly he stood upright again.

"Chief engineer to bridge! Stop engines!" There was something wrong with the gyro-compass.

Once again *U.47* went down to the bottom. This time close in to the German coast, and, for good measure, on the edge of one of their own minefields. The compass had been giving a false bearing and there seemed to be every good reason to doubt whether they had even found the narrow cleared channel or whether they were not bang in the middle of their own mines!

With the help of his men Wessels took the complicated master compass to pieces. He traced the fault which had resulted in a 15° deviation. Had she gone on, *U.47* would have landed in her own minefield.

*   *   *

In the broad expanse of the Atlantic the first phase of the convoy battles was beginning to take shape.

After the withdrawal of the training-boats and the smaller types there remained about twenty large submarines to carry on the fight. Of these twenty, a third was always on the way out, and a third on the way home or in dock for refit and overhaul. Only one third, therefore, was actively engaged at a time. Towards the turn of the year only one or two boats were operating in all the sea areas of the U-boat front.

But if they went by the communiqués issued by Supreme Headquarters, the German people must have thought that U-boats in shoals had gained command of the Atlantic.

At about this time Britain's Prime Minister spoke in the House of Commons. He described the battle of the Atlantic as a groping, exacting war of ruse and strategy, of science and seamanship.

*   *   *

At about this time, too, the German U-boats began to feel the effects of the air reconnaissance which had been concentrated in the areas round the English coast, although, as a matter of fact, this latter was still very much in the early phases of its development.

In September 97 per cent of all U-boat attacks could be delivered as surface attacks. By November only half the sinkings were achieved in this way. The U-boats by then were compelled to deliver their surface attacks by night in order to avoid the ever-increasing number of reconnaissance aircraft and destroyers.

The night still offered protection.

There was no radar—yet.

The war at sea became more and more bitter each day.

The mercilessness of total war was already beginning to cast its shadow over the battle of the Atlantic.

Britain demanded that armed merchantmen should be recognised as merchantmen when en route for neutral ports and when sailing through neutral territorial waters.

On 2 October Germany delivered her answer:

"As it must be assumed that vessels proceeding without lights in the vicinity of the British and French coasts are warships or auxiliary warships, these vessels will at once be engaged with all available weapons when encountered in an area between 45° north and 62° north and between 7° west and 3° east."

The area immediately off the coast was primarily the field of activity of patrol vessels and minelayers or sweepers, which show no lights. But as enemy freighters were employing the same methods as camouflage, no distinction was possible. For a long while U-boats were forbidden to attack any merchantman without warning. As a result, on account of the danger of wrong identification, many opportunities of attacking warships were lost.

"From the operational point of view this state of affairs is intolerable!" thundered Doenitz. Raeder gave the orders which the operational situation of the moment demanded.

Some little while previously, the British Admiralty had issued instructions to its merchantmen to ram German U-boats. This, of course, rendered illusory any questioning, from the point of view of international law, of the new German order.

On 4 October an order was issued to engage with all available means all enemy merchantmen known beyond doubt to be armed. To this was added the following instruction: "Without endangering their own boats U-boat commanders will take all possible steps to rescue survivors. Passenger vessels, as before, are not to be attacked, whether armed or not."

On 17 October a wireless signal to all U-boats said: "In view of the fact that it must in all cases be presumed that attempts to ram will be made or that some similar offensive action will be taken, U-boats are hereby authorised to engage with every means at their disposal all merchantmen, whether armed or not, which have been established as belonging to the enemy."

Then, yet another barrier fell. On 17 October the U-boats received permission to attack all passenger ships, including those sailing alone. A long list of the names of the vessels in question flew through the air.

Nearly another year passed before, under the pressure of the ever-increasing severity, fury and stubbornness on both sides, the very last barriers of all were swept aside.

U-BOAT ACES

Top left: Albrecht Brandi, today an architect in Dortmund

Top right: Reinhardt Hardegen, today the proprietor of a mineral oil, paint and chemical firm in Bremen

Bottom left: Wolfgang Lueth, killed by his own sentries as the result of a tragic error at the end of the war

Bottom right: Otto Kretschmer, today holds a senior position in the Federal German Navy

OLD NAMES FOR NEW BOATS

The Weddigen Flotilla tied up at the pier at Swinemuende

Part Two

1940

CHAPTER III

MINING EXPLOITS. SILENT HEROISM

Situation Report—Spring.
  During the first months of the year difficult mining operations were in the forefront of U-boat activities. For the most part these operations represented masterpieces of navigation and silent heroism, unrewarded by any direct and visible proof of their success. But every mine laid meant that the seaborne supply system was disrupted and sometimes even brought to a complete standstill for days on end. And every day thus lost meant the loss of tons of valuable supplies.

*   *   *

Pack-ice on the Elbe and in the North Sea did not make things any easier for Vaddi Schultze, still in command of *U.48*, as he sailed to perform his allotted task of laying a minefield immediately off the British port of Portland. On this unfriendly February day Vaddi had clothed himself 'for the North Pole'. On his head he had a gigantic fur cap, which only enhanced the fatherly benignity of his appearance. Standing there, he bore little resemblance to the hard-bitten U-boat commander so familiar to the public in the official newsreels at home, the granite-faced man of the illustrated papers and the commercially-minded film studios. Rather, he reminded one of a Pomeranian landowner, satiated with the blessings of modest affluence, a little bored, with enough money to treat himself to the dangerous luxury of a trip in a U-boat.

It was not for nothing that he was known as "Vaddi"—"Pop"— on board. He could hardly be regarded as a stickler for regulations. He had bound his crew to him by the force of his personality. Schultze was a teetotaller and the fact that quite recently he had allowed himself a lot of schnapps on the bridge of *U.48* in the company of the sad and utterly shattered captain of a sunken freighter had been the subject of full and voluble comment throughout the boat for the rest of the evening.

Like all regular seafaring men he was as fanatically super-stitious as any medicine man in darkest Africa. Thus, for example, it had come to be an unwritten law on board that any course steered in the open sea had at all costs to be divisible by the lucky number seven. The helmsmen had strict instructions on receipt of a new course from the bridge to work out whether it was divisible by seven and then on their own to acknowledge and to steer the nearest appropriate multiple of seven.

This whim about the lucky seven had anyway become an established fact on board *U.48*. Later, when Vaddi Schultze left the ship and the broad-shouldered Lieut.-Commander Bleichrodt took over, it was very nearly the cause of a court martial.

"Course 227!" Bleichrodt had ordered from the bridge.

"224 it is," answered the helmsman.

"Pay attention below there! 227 I said."

"Aye, aye, Sir. 224 it is."

Bleichrodt, an officer of the mercantile marine and as such a man accustomed to regard as sacrosanct any course given from the bridge, felt the blood run cold in his veins. With a great effort he controlled himself. "My worthy and estimable helmsman I said 227. And when I say 227 I bloody-well mean 227. Got it?"

The C.P.O. butted in to explain that in the open sea *U.48* had from time immemorial always steered a course divisible by seven. And Bleichrodt was a good enough seaman to realise that, that being so, there was nothing he dared do about it. . . .

So much then for the whims and fancies of Vaddi Schultze, now proceeding on his way to lay mines off Portland harbour.

The course led "over the top", between Iceland and the Faroes and then into the Channel from the west.

Shortly before he reached his destination Schultze put *U.48* down on the bottom, in order to have a chance during the coming night of having a look at the British minefield and to take sound-ings. He was lucky. The night was black as pitch. The Naval Intelligence had, in any case, told him nearly all about the British minefield, and his job now was to find an entry and an exit through it. That took several hours, a monotonous repetitive

33

routine of chart scrutiny, taking soundings and checking with the chart again. Everyone in the boat felt as if they were sitting on a barrel of gunpowder. They were all familiar with the innocent leaden horns of the detonator which made a mine look like some horned devil. Just one little touch from the boat, and your first class (single) to Heaven was assured. Everything, however, went according to plan. In his war-log Schultze made the laconic entry: "Mission completed. 03.38 commenced dropping. 04.45 dropping completed." After that *U.48* was free to hunt with her torpedoes.

The first victim was the Dutchman, *Burgerdijk*, 6,853 tons, coming from New York. The Dutch captain was taken aboard *U.48* and it was not long before he admitted that on the instructions of her owners he had been making for a British control port. At Vaddi Schultze's request, before she was sunk a signal was made from the *Burgerdijk* to say that she was sinking as the result of a collision to the south of Bishop Rock. Mackay Radio confirmed the news and regretted that it could give no further details. Naturally —for these were nestling in Schultze's diary.

Five days later the British cold-storage ship, *Sultan Star*, 12,306 tons, the biggest ship of the Blue Star Line, was sent to the bottom. She had a cargo of meat and butter aboard which would have sufficed for three days' rations. These cold-storage vessels are very special ships. They take longer to build than an ordinary freighter, and they are of vital importance to the British Isles. The loss of *Sultan Star* left a painful gap in Britain's supply system. "She sank like a lady," was the typically British comment on the loss by the BBC.

The next day the Dutch tanker, *Den Haag*, 8,971 tons, joined *Sultan Star* at the bottom of the sea. Two days later Schultze sank an unidentified freighter, 114,510 tons—those are *U.48*'s figures for four short forays against the enemy. Ships sunk by the mines she laid are not included in this total.

*   *   *

To all questions on their assignment, Lieut.-Commander Rollmann replied with a quiet smile. He had just returned from U-boat Headquarters, clambering swiftly up the gangway to *U.34*, recently overhauled, refitted and looking very spruce against the dirty, oily water of the harbour.

In the afternoon there were long faces among the crew when one of the usual lighters came alongside laden, not with gleaming tin-fish, but drab, grey-painted U-boat mines.

"He's been sold a pup," growled the disappointed crew. "That explains why the Old Man's keeping his trap closed."

Mine-laying was not a favourite pastime among submariners.

"You can't get anything out of it," they grumbled, meaning tonnage which could be booked to the credit of *U.34*. The first Knight's Crosses had already been awarded and it was only natural that the men should take a pride in doing what they could to help their "Old Man" to get a "gong". And after all, a decoration for the commander shed its reflected glory on all the ship's company.

"It's more important to do the job properly, my lads, and, above all, to get home safe and sound again. Your confidence in me is far more precious to me than a whole row of medals."

As soon as *U.34* was free of the ice girdle off Heligoland, Rollmann turned north-west in the direction of the Shetland Isles.

In the open sea the wind was blowing great guns. Shimmering cascades of poisonous-looking green water came foaming over the ship's bows as she rose to the heavy seas. Seconds later the bridge look-out disappeared beneath a torrent of salty, ice-cold water.

"Making for the western exit from the channel. We'll get there quicker that way," said Rollmann, as inarticulate as ever, but with his usual friendliness.

What he meant was that with a sea running like this he could risk passing through the closely guarded narrows between the Orkneys and Shetlands on the surface, whereas if he submerged the swift-running prevalent current there would make his passage a slow and laborious process.

In the vicinity of the North Channel, a big ship steamed across *U.34*'s bows. She must have been a 15,000-tonner and looked to be half freighter, half passenger ship.

U.34 dived and turned in the giant's direction.

"She's flying her ensign!" called Rollmann, who had been watching the great ship closely through the periscope. "Bow tube clear for action!"

Quickly range, bearing—all the data the torpedo requires—came through.

"Tubes One and Two ready" . . .

"Tubes One and Two—fire!"

The ship gave a sharp jolt. Eardrums thumped a bit, for the compressed air released by the discharge had to stay somewhere. If it were allowed to escape out of the ship it would betray her.

The large second hand on the clock crept jerkily forward. Nothing happened.

"Down periscope," ordered Rollmann. The periscope disappeared and the commander strode into the control-room. As the torpedoes sped on their way, the British auxiliary cruiser changed course. Disappointment gripped everybody aboard, because, with all those mines, they only had a few torpedoes to play with.

"The first plums are always mouldy, Sir," ventured someone.

"Bad beginnings lead to happy endings; that's the way it goes, and it's better than the other way about."

The remark gave some measure of comfort.

Submerged, *U.34* rounded the western tip of the British Isles and turned into Plymouth Sound. "This is going to be a very neat little job," said Ruhland, the chief engineer, as he stood looking at the chart table where the chief quartermaster busied himself with his job. He pointed to the course ahead plotted on the chart.

"15 metres here . . . 18 there . . . and 15 there. The place is like a bloody kids' swimming pool, Sir."

Spirits aboard were low. There was an uneasy air of uncertainty abroad, and the men either lounged about in silence or grimly went about their ordinary duties.

Where are the enemy mines? Where has he put his anti-submarine nets? Was the dope dished out by the Intelligence people accurate? And where the hell had they got all that information from anyway?

The shadows of night began to enshroud the nearby coast. A little later Rollmann sighted a light straight ahead. Having succeeded in identifying it, he took a bearing.

"Correct, we're exactly where we should be," he remarked over his shoulder to the quartermaster, and gave the order for the crew to gather in the bow compartment. Silently the men slid forward.

When his crew had gathered round, their faces pale and grey in the dim light, Rollmann addressed them:

"Men," he began, "we've been given the job of laying a mine-field to block Falmouth harbour. According to our orders we must do our best to lay the mines inside the moles: that is, inside the harbour itself, where there's 15 metres of water. The harbour is guarded by sentries and patrols. Watchkeeper, see to it that all the secret stuff is divided up among the men. The cipher machine is to be taken to pieces. Each one of you will be given a bit of it. And if anyone takes his bit into captivity with him, I'll have his guts for a necktie, even if I have to wait till we get to Heaven for it. . . . Of course, you may finish up in the seaweed, but—not, repeat not, with a bit of the machine in your trousers' pocket. Is that clear? We'll observe strict underwater discipline, of course. Well, now you know all about it. We're risking getting a kick in the pants, but there you are . . . ."

A ghostly, silent activity began all over the boat. *U.34* slid forward. The crew stood motionless at their action stations. Wherever he looked Rollmann met the gaze of feverishly glittering eyes, fixed, wide open with excitement and attention, on him, the man in whom they must and did place their trust.

Calmness personified was Fiete Pfitzner, the chief quartermaster, as with an air almost of boredom he plotted the course on the chart, for all the world as though he were on a picnic at the seaside. With her periscope up *U.34* edged her way towards the harbour entrance. Rollmann suddenly made out a dark shadow directly ahead. As he thought—a patrol vessel! He did not dare to lower his periscope for fear that the noise would give the show away. He knew how very good the British hydrophones were. Still, damn it all, he thought, those chaps over there are only human. They, too, can make mistakes.

The whole ship was as silent as the grave.

The commander whispered something very softly. Only those standing close beside him heard what he said:

"We're now passing the patrol boat on its starboard side."

The chief engineer kept the ship exactly trimmed with precise, mathematical accuracy. There was even a smile on his face—a smile of happiness that the ship handled so sweetly. No one on the vessel could see the excitement that gripped him, leaving him with an ice-cold feeling in his stomach.

U.34 passed through the harbour entrance. To left and right of

37

her towered the mole-heads, and in a moment she was in the middle of the harbour itself, proceeding round it in a wide arc.

"Mines clear."

"Mines clear for dropping," came the report from the torpedo-room.

"Slow ahead both."

The whine of the dynamos rose a little.

"First mine—away!"

With a creaking and scraping the first mine fell clear.

The whole ship's company froze to immobility, held its breath and listened. Would the Britishers hear the noise, and if they did, would they realise what it was? One joker closed his eyes and pointed upwards, as if to say: they're all asleep up there.

And, indeed, why shouldn't they be. A harbour is a haven, a harbour spells security against those damn German submarines.

The men began to move about aimlessly. They seemed to have relaxed their rigid self-control. Mine 3. . . . Mine 4. . . . Mine 5. . . .

U.34 proceeded through the enemy harbour in a broad sweep. The depth of the water was 13·8 metres, which left her with a bare three feet of water under her keel. As she turned it would have been quite possible for her to bump into one of the mines she had herself just laid. Between them and the boat's side there were only very few inches to spare.

As a matter of fact it would not have mattered if she had. These were magnetic mines which would only begin to operate later. They were, in fact, very cunning super-eggs on which the German High Command had built such high hopes.

Thanks to the continuous flow of compressed air back into the boat, the pressure was fast becoming intolerable. The air was foul, sweat poured off the men, even off those who stood motionless. "No. 8 mine . . . away!" With a rumpling groan it tumbled out of the tube.

U.34 now turned toward the harbour mouth. The motors were still at slow ahead. Slowly she crept out between the pierheads, then on past the patrol vessel, still stubbornly at her post, put there for the specific purpose of giving the *coup de grâce* to any too-venturesome U-boat.

Inside the U-boat itself every man was frozen, motionless.

Gradually the water got deeper.

God! What was that! . . . A loud noise, a hateful grating noise that jarred strained nerves almost to breaking-point, yet a noise that normally passed quite unnoticed—the commander had merely lowered the periscope.

"Depth 50 metres," called the quartermaster.

Wearily Rollmann bent over the chart table, placing his hand on the quartermaster's shoulder as he did so, not loosely, but with a firm yet gentle pressure as though he were shaking hands. Fiete Pfitzner looked up and smiled. But he all but gasped as he looked up into the commander's face. Never had he seen him so exhausted, so weary, so thoroughly all-in.

Rollmann nodded and turned into his quarters, two whole square yards of space that constituted his hearth and home afloat. He drew the curtain. The wire mattress creaked once, and then there was silence.

Among the crew, too, the excitement began to relax. One or two men started to speak, and from the engine-room came a song, a softly hummed melody in which one by one the others joined.

The singing woke Rollmann, and Fiete seized his chance.

"Can I have the course, Sir?" he asked.

"385 degrees," replied a weary voice.

Fiete looked first at the chief engineer and then at the officer on watch. "But there's only 360 degrees on the bloody compass," he muttered.

The officer on watch nodded.

"That's all right," he said. "Head straight for the middle of the Channel, and we'll leave the Old Man in peace for a couple of hours."

Two hours later Rollmann emerged, rested and alert.

"Prepare to surface!"

U.34 broke surface. Fresh, sweet air streamed into the ship and through the opened hatch of the conning tower the men below could see the stars.

"Permission to smoke?"

"OK. On the bridge—three men at a time."

CHAPTER IV

OPERATION WESERUEBUNG

Situation Report—April 1940.
Operation Weseruebung was the code-name for the German occupation
of Norway, initiated as soon as it had become known that Britain
was preparing a like operation with great intensity. Since this had to be
undertaken against an enemy vastly superior in numbers and fighting
strength, the German operations broke all the rules of sea strategy.
"Nevertheless, I believe that the effect of surprise will be so great, that
we shall be able to transport our troops safely to Norway. History has
shown that operations carried out contrary to all the principles of war
can indeed succeed thanks to the element of surprise. We are, I think,
entitled to presume that this will hold good for us in the present case."
Thus spoke Raeder at Supreme Headquarters, Raeder the psy-
chologist rather than Raeder the naval Commander-in-Chief. The
main task allotted to the U-boats was to secure Narvik, the focal point
for the transhipment of iron ore from Sweden. Of a yearly total of 11·5
million tons required by Germany's industrial war plan, no less than
one third was shipped from the ice-free port of Narvik. The operation
succeeded. It was the boldest and most difficult, and at the same time
most successful operation in the whole history of German maritime
warfare.

*   *   *

On 1 April, 1940 Headquarters issued the final order.
"Commence Operation Weseruebung at 05.15 hours, 9 April."
For weeks U-boats, large and small, had been strung out within
sight of the bare cliffs of the islands off the Norwegian coast. When
they surfaced they were pitched wildly hither and thither by the
giant rollers of the long swell. Icy seawater swept continuously over
the conning tower. Within a minute the watch on the bridge was
soaked to the skin. The men shivered, not only because the cold
gnawed their bones but also at the thought that one of these days
they would be called upon to break into these fjords, these dark,
sinister shafts that seemed to beckon to them like the gates of a

dead world. One crumb of comfort was the reality of the scudding clouds and the big, brown Norwegian gulls, which accompanied the German U-boats, crying shrilly.

U.47 with Prien in command sighted three battleships. Sailing north at high speed they disappeared over the horizon. *U.47* could not cut them off. She had not the speed for a job like that. But what about the new U-boats? There had been some odd bits of news going round . . . about a certain Herr Walter and his secret activities in a red brick house in Kiel. Among the officers heads were being scratched about some new form of propulsion which, it was claimed, would give the U-boats a maximum speed of 26 knots. No one knew anything for certain, not even the flotilla commanders. And that was just as well.

Prien, too, had his tubes loaded with a new type of torpedo. It left no tell-tale track of bubbles and it had a new kind of magnetic detonator. These had already proved their worth months ago. They were quite simple. The torpedo is set for a precise depth. It passes below the ship. The magnetic pistol in the nose fuse, actuated by the ship's magnetic field, released the initial firing as the torpedo passes underneath the hostile ship and sets off the explosive charge. The explosive effect of these torpedoes is terrific.

It was to these magnetic torpedoes that the Germans—Raeder, Doenitz, the commanders, the torpedo experts and the constructors—pinned their hopes.

They were not to know that their hopes were destined to evaporate into thin air.

*   *   *

On one of the U-boats as lieutenant and watchkeeping officer was Erich Topp, later to become a lieutenant-commander and recipient of the Knight's Cross with Swords. Topp had his own ideas about the way in which U-boats had been employed in Norwegian waters. Nor did he make any secret of them in front of his commanding officer. In his diary he wrote:

"U-boats are not suitable for this purpose. The U-boat has been designed as a destroyer of commerce, and in order to be effective it requires the wide spaces of the open sea. It can, admittedly, sometimes be employed as a surprise attacker in the role of solitary raider in coastal waters. But it is contrary to the nature of the vessel to operate in a narrow fjord. According to the season of the year in these latitudes it has to cope with very short nights and, indeed, with no night at all when the midnight sun shines. In these conditions the U-boat has not at its disposal the time required to charge its batteries. The fjords offer acoustic conditions which are most unpleasantly favourable to the enemy. From the navigation point of view they are a problem and the data given in the hydrographic surveys is inadequate. By and large the charts only show precise depths for those channels which are normally used by merchant ships, and remain blank as regards the periphery and the small subsidiary fjords which are just the places which a U-boat must needs seek for safety."

Topp continues:

"We've been lying up here for days, in some Norwegian fjord, some small, unknown fjord in this labyrinth of Norwegian rock and cliff. But rarely is a lighthouse to be found on any protruding cliff. Only every now and then is some diminutive house to be seen tucked away from the wind as if seeking shelter in this chaotic landscape, in which there is no mercy, no comfort, no redeeming feature.

"For the moment our orders are merely to observe and report on the enemy movements. Only British warships may be attacked. But so far we have seen none. On the other hand we are blessed with the beauty of the majestic landscape and some of the more majestic peaks begin to assert their own individual entity, their precipices forbiddingly black, their slopes a bluey-grey; and on them lies the eternal ice.

"The alarm always sounds at about the same time, for we have to remain submerged and unnoticed all day.

"Sometimes, as on Easter morning, the early hours bring us a flurry of hail and snow. And when that happened we stayed on the surface, and sometimes the shores of the fjord were shrouded in early morning mist or covered with snow clouds; then, too, we enjoyed the hours of precious freedom. But this happened but rarely; the cold, blue northern sky with its days of clear, translucent light predominated.

"We could only gaze through the periscope at the superb beauty of the fjord by day.

"Everyone taking his turn at the periscope remained silent. The control-room was as silent as the grave. We felt overawed by our surroundings. Storms could rage, water could come pouring down the cliffs into the valleys below, mountains could chisel a new ice age under the pressure of newly forming glaciers, and yet these ranges would neither flinch nor stir.

"Every day one had to remind oneself that there was a war on, and that, in the sublime peace of our majestic surroundings, was hard to realise.

"With the last rays of the sun we rose to the surface and once again found ourselves bound in fascination by the endless variety that this one, single landscape afforded us. All of us—the commander, the chief engineer, the stoker and seamen—we were all under its spell.

"The air was cold and crystal clear and the sky illuminated with brightly sparkling stars. Only the mountain ranges, covered with a wreath of fleecy cloud, remained hidden. The last light of day had not quite faded.

"Then behind the mountains a shimmering shaft of light shot up, glowing and then growing dim, then another, at first tender and faint, and another, until the whole horizon was ablaze with a cascade of light, shining upwards to the light ring in the zenith. The Northern Lights.

"For fifteen hours a day for six weeks we remained underwater in a foul and vitiated atmosphere. We dared not consume each day more than the day's ration of the six week's supply of oxygen aboard. The number of potash cartridges which absorb the harmful carbon dioxide was also limited.

"But we had to remain alert, for there was just a chance that the enemy might appear.

"We waited and waited and waited. . . ."
6 April.
"We received the code word 'Hartmut'. The Narvik expedition began. Everybody was tremendously excited, as the commander explained the object of the operation."
8 April.
"In the morning we were forced to submerge by an approaching destroyer which appeared suddenly out of the mist. Identification was not possible, but it was assumed that she was a German destroyer on patrol.

43

"Would our destroyers do the trick?

"Would they break through into Narvik?

"During the night 8/9 April we look up our intermediate station. 9 April, 04.00 hours.

"When we surfaced we received with great relief the wireless signal: 'U-boats to proceed to Narvik. Narvik is in German hands.'

"A straggler passed us. A few hours later the destroyer *Giese* signalled: 'Baröy passed.'

" 'Action stations!' The signal from U-boat Command came flashing over the wireless. We went full speed ahead. The weather was still foggy. A sudden alarm. Ahead of us was the silhouette of a submarine; as we approached she disappeared.

" 'Quiet! Absolute quiet!' ordered the commander, raising a beseeching hand, like a conductor coaxing his orchestra to soft melody.

"Through the periscope there was nothing to be seen. But from the group hydrophones a soft noise can be heard, a noise typical of electric motors.

" 'Damnation!' came involuntarily from the commander's lips. 'Damn it, we must get through before that fellow forestalls us!'

"We surfaced and proceeded at our maximum speed. The dancing snowflakes were so thick that we could not even see our own bows. None of the officers was familiar with these waters.

"Shortly before we reached Tranöy the weather cleared. We had got round and ahead of the other U-boat.

"But straight ahead there was a ship, a steamer making for the harbour. We followed close in her wake. Soon we read her name on the stern—the Swedish tanker, *Strassa*. Panic siezed the crew when they saw us. They started rushing about the upper deck, struggling into their life jackets. Then they started lowering the boats. Some waved their arms, seemingly at a loss as to what they ought to do. The fjord was narrow. Very narrow indeed. On each side iron-grey walls rose sheer out of the sea, their crests covered with ice. The rearguard of the ice season, and over their crests the wind blows sharp and cold.

"We overtook the tanker, but no one took any notice of her. No one had even a glance to spare for the beauty of the fjord. What we were seeking was the enemy.

" 'Alarm!' Through the mist emerged the outline of a destroyer, bearing straight down on us. We fired recognition signals. They were answered from the destroyer. A German destroyer. Packed tight against her guard rail was a solid mass of mountain troops. They shouted and cheered and waved to us.

"As the weather cleared, we saw the destroyer preventing the Swedish tanker from slipping away northwards through the Tjeldsundet Sound. We passed Baröy. Sunshine and flurries of snow succeeded each other in swift succession. April, the April of the Far North.

"Off Ramsund two more destroyers. They could only be German. We approached within hailing distance. A quick exchange of hand signals. . . .

"Germans they were. They were seeking the batteries marked on the German maps, but they could not find them. There weren't any, that's why.

"We steamed on until we reached our position, a place called Ofoten-Fjord. On both sides snow-clad mountains rose steeply. A few houses could be seen, dotted about here and there. And we could see ski-ers on the slopes—on both sides, for the fjord was very narrow.

" 'Right!' said the commander, 'and here's where we'll pitch our tents!' and he tried a smile at the thought of the task imposed upon us; for we were to have the doubtful pleasure of holding up the pursuing enemy.

"Things, however, were destined to turn out differently. . . .

"On 10 April, throughout the middle of the day a wild snow storm raged.

" 'A knocking noise, at intervals, on the ship's side!' reported the quartermaster from the control below.

" 'What sort of a noise? What is it?'

" 'Can't say, Sir, exactly!'

"At exactly 06.30 I, too, heard the noise from the bridge. It was an unceasing hammering, or rather, it was really more like a droning hum. It was coming from the direction of Narvik. There was no doubt about it—gunfire. Could the Norwegians be showing resistance?

"The thunder of the guns grew louder. The port look-out swung round, lowered his glasses and pointed at the coast:

45

" 'A motor torpedo boat or a motor launch—certainly a naval vessel!'

" 'A Norwegian—making a bolt for it. What else could it be?' said the commander.

" 'And suppose it isn't?'

" 'Of course it is. Narvik has fallen—obviously. And the Norwegians are bolting. But let off a recognition signal, if you like.'

"We fired a recognition signal. As the stars sank down, the motor boat stopped. But it did not come any nearer. We gave her five shells from the 2·2 cm.—aimed over their heads. After all, there was no need to kill them without further ado. The occupants of the boat came to their senses slowly, hesitantly; the boat got under way and came towards us.

" 'D'you notice anything?' grinned the chief quartermaster. He had lowered his glasses and was gleefully rubbing his hands. The faces of the men on the bridge broke into broad grins. And then we all laughed.

"The boat was full of German mountain troops, from Innsbruck, from the Oetztal or perhaps from the Stubai Alps. They hailed us, but twice we had to ask for a repeat. In their joy they had reverted to broad dialect, for which we had no dictionary aboard.

"Slowly they came alongside and bit by bit we pieced together what was happening. Their orders, they told us, were to occupy a depot in Ramsund.

"They knew no more about events in Narvik than we did. Scarcely had the boat cast off than I caught sight of three silhouettes emerging from the mist. Three white waves foamed at their bows, like white V's painted on a grey sky.

"Alarm!

"Like lightning we disappeared down the conning tower, the commander bringing up the rear. There was no chance of staging an attack. The destroyers were over us and away in no time. Everything remained quiet and peaceful.

"Yet another destroyer. At close range, inclination—zero, direction—mouth of the fjord. Just as I took a quick look through the periscope I saw a high column of smoke exactly above the exit to the fjord. Minutes later our U-boat shuddered under a violent impact. In the periscope there appeared a high column of fire, surmounted by a gigantic cloud of smoke. A burning ship was

46

being reduced to fragments. The destroyer had disappeared.

" 'Will someone tell me what's happening here! Everything's topsy turvy. Who is a friend, who an enemy? Has a British submarine been firing at a German ship, or has a German U-boat been shooting at a British destroyer?'

"It was only later that I found out what it was all about.

"The destroyer we had seen coming in had snapped up the German supply ship, *Kattegat.*

"The cat was out of the bag. Swiftly the British prepared for a counterstroke. They put in everything they had—battleships, cruisers and destroyers. In all their vast naval superiority they swept across to Norway. It was no longer merely Norway that was at stake, it was the reputation of the Róyal Navy. Its very weight must and will win the day.

"On our ship we were all in a state.

"Every little noise was reported by the hydrophone operators as a submarine. Actually, of course, we had no idea at all what caused the ship to shudder. Explosives and detonations were going on all round us, re-echoed and repeated many times by the narrow walls of the fjords. Imagination ran riot.

"At long last twilight descended. A fruitless day, a day without recompense. At long last we could surface to recharge our batteries.

"We were all exhausted, we—and the batteries.

"I turned in for a bit of a rest.

" 'Alarm! Diving stations!' In a flash I was wide awake.

"The commander hastened with long strides into the control-room. He cancelled the order to dive. The chief quartermaster was all of a dither. With nerves on edge he murmured something about 'destroyers rushing at us at full speed'.

" 'It's quite impossible for them to spot us here'—thought the Old Man—'and quite impossible for them to guess that we're here, close in to the shore.'

"But the quartermaster was right, destroyers were approaching. But they were coming from the direction of Narvik. Again the nerve-racking question. Friend or foe? The torpedo tubes had been reported clear for action.

"But the destroyers were German. At high speed, with beards gleaming with phosphorus at their bows, they steamed by. A good hour later back they came again.

"From his little cubby hole the radio operator handed out a signal from U-boat Command to the commander: 'Proceed to Narvik for a conference with Commander, 4 Destroyer Flotilla.'

"This order was as good as a strong cup of coffee for every man aboard. After the inaction of the last few days, it put fresh hope into us that this trip might after all prove worthwhile.

"From a long way away Narvik could be seen. The snow was covered with a sheen of blood-red light. The red glow of fires was reflected in such windows of the few wooden houses as had survived. The lights at the harbour entrance had been extinguished. Slowly and most carefully we approached the entrance, and the nearer we got, the more silent we became. The face of war became starkly visible.

"Wrecks—wrecks—wrecks!

"One wrecked ship after another.

"Masts!—masts!—masts!

"Heavens above! All hell must have been let loose here. And this was only the entrance, the prelude.

"A pinnace came alongside. A navigator clattered aboard and reported to the bridge. He had been ordered to pilot us through the wrecks. And as he did so he told us what had happened:

"The destroyers had put in to Narvik according to plan. On board each ship were two hundred fully-armed mountain troops. The Norwegian coast defence ship was seen to be preparing to resist. From the destroyer *Heidkamp* Captain Gerlach, staff officer to the commander of the destroyer flotilla, was sent over in a pinnace. To the Norwegian captain he posed the fateful question:

" 'Do you propose to resist or not?'

" 'We do and we shall.'

"The German officer saluted and returned to *Heidkamp*. A red star hissed up into the sky, red as blood. A salvo of three torpedoes leapt from the tubes. The Norwegian coast defence ship disappeared in a huge column of water. The destroyer, *Berndt von Arnim*, led the way in and was greeted at a range of a few hundred yards by the fire of a second coast defence ship. The first salvo fell short. The second went over and into the cliff. There was no time for a third. The torpedoes from the destroyer had found their target. Of seven torpedoes fired, two hit.

"The preliminaries had resembled the medieval negotiations undertaken by heralds.

"Both sides had waited. The Norwegians displayed a chivalry worthy of their high traditions. With guns loaded they had waited till the German officer had returned to his ship.

"That the Germans proved to be the swifter was bad luck on the Norwegians. Raeder's psychological prognostications had been translated into bitter truth for the crew of the coast defence ship. The Norwegians were too slow. They reacted too late.

"The disembarkation of the troops had then proceeded according to plan. One by one the destroyers went alongside the German supply-ship, *Jan Wellem*, to take on oil. Four other destroyers, under Captain Bey, were detached and sent to two other fjords. In the meanwhile, under cover of the poor visibility, five British destroyers dashed in to the attack. At the entrance to the fjord they turned away and fired their torpedoes. *Heidkamp* and *Schmidt* were sunk, and with them eight merchantmen. *Dieter von Roeder* was badly hit in two places. Bey's division joined in the battle. Two British destoyers met their end. *Hunter* was rammed and sank, and another was beached in flames. The remaining three disappeared at high speed.

"After a conference with the commander of the Fourth Destroyer Flotilla we proceeded to Narvik.

"At night we remained on patrol off Farnes. Towards morning we put out to sea, but returned very soon and tied up alongside the destroyer, *Thiele*. Ten dead were taken ashore, among them the whole of one gun's crew. On the inside berth lay *Berndt von Arnim*. Both vessels were slightly damaged.

"In the evening we went out again. The patrol ended without incident."

12 April.

"It was decided that we should take on stores and fuel. We were now alongside the destroyer *Luedemann*. Here a pleasant surprise was in store for me. On board the *Luedemann* I met my old shipmate, Perl.

"That afternoon *U.64* arrived. Her commander reported: 'Strong enemy destroyer patrols are cruising off the entrance to the fjord. Narvik threatens to become a trap.'

49

"*U.49* reported hostile aircraft flying eastwards. Shortly afterwards the air alarm went. All personnel, other than those required aboard, were sent ashore. I remained aboard with the M.G. crew. The aircraft flew in, over us and the destroyers and away. We fired like madmen. But nothing came down. Bombs, yes. One fell into the water fifty yards away. My lads were astounded. So was I. Here we were with all the weapons necessary to knock hell out of them and all perfectly handled according to the drill book and—not a sausage! Well there was one consolation—the fellows up there must have been just as disagreeably surprised to see all their bombs scoring misses. But that was war all over. Anyway the attacking aircraft did get one hit, a shed which had been set on fire. Beside it lay some bodies.

"Well—that's how things looked in Narvik. And Raeder submitted the following report to Supreme Headquarters:

" 'Every available ship in the German fleet has been committed. All available U-boats are in action. Three U-boats are in Vaags-Fjord, five in West-Fjord, three are proceeding to Narvik with ammunition and stores. One is on its way to Nansen-Fjord. Two further U-boats are preparing to proceed to Nansen-Fjord and Folden-Fjord. Three are off Drontheim. One has been ordered to proceed to Romsdals-Fjord, five are operating off Bergen and two off Stavanger.' "

*　　　*　　　*

U.48 was also there.

Vaddi Schultze was still in command, with Teddi Suhren as his watch-keeping officer. Seaman Horst Hofmann was aboard, too, this time as a member of the crew. *U.48* had received orders to support the Narvik group and to proceed to Narvik. As the U-boat entered the inner fjord, Sohler was just coming out to take up a new position. Schultze told Sohler of his new orders. Over the wireless there was no further news. Horst Hofmann now takes up the tale:

"We went straight ahead, Sohler following us. From Sohler we heard that things have gone pretty badly with the German destroyer group and that it had probably been destroyed.

"Nevertheless, this morning of 13 April we proceeded straight into the main Narvik fjord. Again and again aircraft appeared

50

suddenly, and again and again we were forced to dive. I've lost count of the times we had to submerge.

"Suddenly a destroyer appeared ahead of us. Schultze held her fast in the illuminated crossed wires. It was misty, and Schultze remained glued to the periscope. Suddenly his head jerked round.

" 'Suhren! Suhren!' he shouted. 'Come here and take a look! That fellow's signalling Ack Ack!'

"Suhren peered through the periscope. It was true. The strange destroyer was flashing a ceaseless stream of A's.

"On board *U.48* no one knew whether it was a British or a German destroyer. Schultze made the underwater recognition signal— four, five, six times. No answer.

"There was nothing for it. We had to surface and give confirmation of the signal.

"A tricky situation. None of our own destroyers, surely, could be sculling about here?

"Schultze clambered on to the bridge, followed by Suhren and the bridge watch. Suhren made the recognition signal on the morse lamp. Meanwhile the destroyer had approached closer, moving slowly. But after the second recognition signal from *U.48* she increased speed. Her bow wave grew higher and steeper. That was our answer.

"Alarm! Crash dive!

"Those on the bridge hurtled as best they could through the hatch, and down dived *U.48*, down as deep as the waters of the fjord would allow. Then the fun started. Depth charges exploded shatteringly over our heads and all round us.

"That, however, was all. And quite enough, too.

"The date was 13 April. And we had exactly thirteen depth charges pitched at us, no more and no less. Schultze grinned in silent satisfaction. There was no doubt about it, seven and thirteen were the lucky numbers.

"These thirteen depth charges, however, proved to be only the overture. The days that followed were days of unmitigated hell. Every day and every hour of every day we were attacking destroyers or finding ourselves trapped in the destroyers' clutches. Day in, day out, night after night. And the nights were short, far too short to allow us to charge our batteries and to maintain the boat ready for action. Sleep was out of the question—we hardly found time to get something to eat. One after the other we fired all our magnetic torpedoes. Not one of them exploded.

"What the devil was wrong with those bloody torpedoes?

"Exactly the same thing happened a few days before off Bergen when Schultze attacked a British heavy cruiser and fired a salvo of three at her. Not one of those damned tin fish found its mark. Frantically, meticulously, the torpedo-gunner's mate inspected the huge, steel cigars, but nothing could he find which might have accounted for their failure. The only redeeming feature had been that Vaddi Schultze had remained benignly calm.

"And now up here, the same damn show all over again. Here, too, the magnetic torpedoes refused to explode. Try as we would all our efforts remained completely fruitless.

"The hell of Narvik became our particular hell, too. For four solid days we scurried up and down and round and round the fjord, submerged. We used up the air in our oxygen flasks to the very last drop. And we fired off every torpedo we had. Not one gave a good account of itself. What had gone wrong? Had the gyro failed to function? Had something happened to the magnetic fuse? Or was the German secret no longer a secret to the British?"

*   *   *

The ship in which Topp was serving as first officer had an equally arduous experience. Let us take another look at his diary:

"On 13 April we moved to a new position. 'You are our last hope,' shouted the crews of the destroyers to us. Two heavy German aircraft were cruising round exactly over Narvik, dropping food and ammunition; and a sigh of relief went up from those still trapped in a harbour lost and cut off from all reinforcement.

"On 14 April British aircraft flew over the positions. They were escort aircraft, sent to reconnoitre the fjord. Suddenly through the periscope a number of destroyers came into view, steaming in three columns towards us; and behind them the grey shadow of a battleship.

"It was the *Warspite*, a giant among giants, steaming inevitably straight into our sights.

"The atmosphere on board was electric. It was as though the U-boat had clenched its teeth in its excitement. One or two men

52

glanced nervously at the hydrophones as we turned to pass beneath the column of destroyers. No reaction from the enemy. We ourselves could hear his Asdic operating as it groped to find us. But he failed to locate our position. . . . We waited . . . still no depth charges. . . . still no depth charges. They probably took the Asdic echo to denote submerged rocks.

"Tubes one and four had long been cleared for action. On these two torpedoes depended the fate of the whole expedition. If *Warspite* sank, Narvik was saved. And not only that; if we could sink the *Warspite*, with her would sink, too, the morale of the British troops landed at Andalsnes—five thousand of them! If we could destroy the *Warspite*, Allied resistance would collapse and with it the belief in the invincibility of the British Navy.

"We went slow ahead, very slow. But we had to keep moving in order to maintain periscope depth. We waited. Forty-eight hearts beat so furiously that we could almost hear them.

"Then this nervous tension was shattered by a jolt that caused the whole vessel to shudder. From beneath the keel we heard a dull thudding and scraping. At the same instant we began to rise and the boat was down by the stern. The Commander acted like lightning.

" 'After hydroplanes hard down! Flood ballast tanks!'

"In the periscope there appeared just the net cutter, and then the bows of the ship, foaming through the water. A moment later the upper edge of the turret and the loop aerial of the direction-finding gear mounted on it became visible.

"Further out British destroyers were approaching at speed. Some six hundred yards on the beam was *Warspite* firing on Narvik. As filthy bad luck would have it, she came straight into our line of fire. But we were no longer capable of firing, and a great, a unique, chance is lost for ever. An impish submerged rock had been the cause of all the trouble. We had run straight into it and had been thrust upwards by it.

"Both motors were put to full astern to pull us off. The destroyers took not the slightest notice of us. Could it be that they had not seen us? In all the welter of misfortune that had overtaken us this was our one piece of good luck.

"The massacre of Narvik took its course. Everything lying in the harbour—neutral ships, German freighters, harbour craft and the

53

German destroyers—all came under the death-dealing fire of the British battleships and destroyers. The German destroyers went to their death, attacking and firing to the last round.

"But they had accomplished their task. Two thousand troops had been disembarked.

"There remained now for the U-boats but the one task of interfering with the enemy's supplies and reinforcements. On the same afternoon the battleship and eight destroyers emerged. But we were in a hopeless position, driven below the surface. It is only at 22.00 that we were able to surface. About midnight, another alarm, and once more we were driven into the depths by British destroyers."

15 April.

"We surfaced once more to charge our exhausted batteries. The nights were becoming shorter and shorter. By three o'clock it was already so light that we could see the British destroyers patrolling to and fro off Narvik. There was nothing for it, we had to submerge again. The batteries had been but meagrely charged. They were still all but exhausted. The commander did not dare to use their last reserve of power to proceed under water. At a depth of about 60 feet we lay on the bottom, hoping that we might get a chance to attack any enemy ship which passed our way. But the current was too strong. The tidal stream from the Atlantic ran into the open fjord with such force that we were pushed along the bed of the sea. The radio operator handed the duty officer a signal received by long-wave wireless. An order from the Fuehrer: 'Narvik will be held at all costs!'

"That, of course, applied to us, too. That meant—once more into the dog-fight. The chances of attack were meagre; the chances of survival more meagre still. When the commander ordered the destruction of all secret material on board, every man in the crew realised what that meant. It meant that the commander regarded the destruction of his U-boat as certain.

"On the way to our new position at Point Nero 3 we met *U.48* and told Herbert Schultze what the position was in Narvik. But all he knew was Doenitz's first order: 'All U-boats proceed to Narvik.' And to Narvik he proposed to proceed. To his query regarding the whereabouts of the German destroyers, he received the laconic answer: 'Wiped out.'

" 'Even so, I'll have a crack at it,' Schultze answered and turned away.

"More destroyers passed and we were driven down again. They attacked us with depth charges. The crash of the explosions was truly terrifying in these narrow waters. In the afternoon we made another attempt to recharge our batteries, but aircraft once more forced us to submerge. In the evening we surfaced again. This was the moment when the beauties of the fjords unfolded for those with eyes to see. But no one noticed them. We were fighting for our lives.

"The batteries had not enough strength to enable us to launch even one more attack.

"At low tide the water level dropped considerably and a dark sliver of rock, free of snow, was exposed. Under the protection afforded by this dark background we tried to re-charge. We who ought to be hunters were now the hunted. A destroyer steamed by. It failed to see us. A second destroyer approached. This time we'd been seen sure enough, and the destroyer swung its bows in our direction. We crash dived to the bottom. Thirty-five feet of water—just enough to cover us. The destroyer tried to reach us with depth charges pitched at a distance. Some of them exploded uncomfortably close; but they did us no damage. The enemy got under way, but then stopped again in order to operate his locating gear. For a while all was quiet again. We did not move, but get away, somehow, we must. We could not stay where we were. In an hour's time it would be low tide and the water would be eight or ten feet shallower and more. And when that happened, they'd have had us. We should be sitting like a target at artillery practice.

"It was a slice of luck that, notwithstanding the still comparatively high state of the tide, the destroyer commanders seemed to be wary of the shallows."

16 April.

"At 4 a.m. we slid slowly down to the bottom into a hundred and fifty feet of water. The stern of the boat was tilted a good few degrees lower than her bows. Once more we finished up with our bows on a rock. One of the destroyers had noticed our change of position. Back and fro it steamed several times over us, deluging us with depth charges as it passed. The detonations were heavy and the damage worrying. We had to stay where we were all

55

through the long day, for our batteries were completely exhausted. At 20.00 we rose gingerly to periscope depth in the hope of reaching deeper water. The batteries had recovered just a little, and we were able to go ahead submerged, but only very slowly. It was enough to make one weep. At sixty feet the keel touched the bottom again, with a sharp, high-pitched scraping noise that was audible all over the ship. Another rock—not shown on our chart. Why should it be, anyway? No merchantman has ever any business in this fjord. At 20.30 we surfaced. The diesels leapt into life. Very, very carefully we drew away, at half speed ahead, out, out of this witches' cauldron.

17 April.

"It was 03.00 in the morning. We were off Flatöy and were forced to dive at the approach of some craft steaming without lights. It was too light to deliver a surface attack, and our position was unsuitable for an attack submerged. At 04.00 we sighted a submarine, straight ahead of us. We carried on towards it. The stranger submerged. We did the same. One of us? Or a Britisher?

"There was so much that remained uncertain, unsolved in this struggle waged in flurries of snow, in mist and fog among the dark, forbidding caverns of the Norwegian fjords.

"At 16.00 fresh orders reached us. Return to port. And not a moment too soon either. The crew were all in. Everybody breathed a sight of relief.

"17.30 enemy cruiser in sight.

"We headed straight for her, submerged. The cruiser started to zigzag. We tried to get ahead—in vain. The cruiser turned and disappeared between the Lofoten Islands."

18 April.

"We were still in the operation area. Shortly after midnight we sighted a battleship with destroyer escort. To hell with orders to return to port. Of course we should attack. Or, anyway, we'd have a damn good try. Proceeding on the surface we turned towards the enemy formation, moving in an arc. A submarine must, of course, get ahead of its target in order to be in a position to fire. A torpedo is not a shell. A torpedo is a powered entity.

"The bright Northern Lights betrayed us; just at that very moment a glittering display of lights spread over the whole northern sky, like multi-coloured veils billowing and waving their way across the illuminated heavens. Now one of the destroyers turned towards us.

"Crash dive. Down into the depths. The hydrophone operator reported destroyer propellers heading straight for us. We reached a depth of three hundred feet as the first depth charges began to explode. Three hours later we surfaced again.

"At 07.00 we sighted three escorted transports steaming across the horizon. There was no chance of delivering an attack. We reported the ships' position and course and for a while maintained contact with them. Then, however, the merchantmen faded out of sight. In the afternoon air alarm and bombs. In the evening we surfaced again. Before us lay the open sea, the broad Atlantic, the way home."

*　　　*　　　*

With the exception of Wolfgang Lueth, *U.39*, not one German U-boat had a single success to mark up throughout the whole of the Norwegian operations. Prien, Kretschmer, Schultze and all the others—not a single one between the lot of them. It was not the fault of the commanders or the crews or the boats themselves. The new magnetic torpedoes had proved a failure.

"The torpedo crisis is a national disaster," declared a disillusioned and horrified Admiral Raeder. There were Courts of Enquiry and Courts Martial. Senior engineer officers and constructors were brought to book. All this, however, did not alter the fact that Britain was ready and in time with her counter-measures against the German magnetic torpedoes.

The U-boats stationed in Norwegian waters were recalled and re-fitted for action in the Atlantic. Only a few transport U-boats remained in the vicinity of Norway.

CHAPTER V

THE U-BOAT AND ITS UNWRITTEN LAWS

Situation Report.

After the Norwegian operations there followed the occupation of Holland, Belgium and France. The gates of the Atlantic were now thrown open to the U-boat Command. For the first time Doenitz found himself in a position to apply the pack-tactics, which he had successfully tried out before the war. Had the German Navy had more U-boats at its disposal these tactics might well have proved fatal to Britain. But this lack of U-boats was one of the symptomatic failures of the dictatorship system and the result of the naval inefficiency of the authorities primarily responsible.

*   *   *

A great deal has already been written about life aboard a U-boat. But little or nothing has yet been said about the U-boat itself, its anatomy and the laws governing its existence. Three-quarters of this cylinder, wrought of the finest welded steel, which in the large types measures some twelve feet in height at its point of greatest diameter and which the old submariners call "the tube", is crammed with technical appliances. First and foremost among these are the diesel engines which take up so much space, and the electrical machinery. Gigantic batteries, pumps of every description, valves by the score, compressed air and oxygen containers, reserve torpedoes, tubes and pipe-lines, armatures and hand wheels, overhead tanks and manometers fill up the tube-like interior of a U-boat so completely that there is precious little space left for the crew. In the pressure hull itself there are, in addition to the batteries under the floor-plates, the compensating tanks and flooding tanks which are used to regulate the balance of the boat when submerged, the foundations for the diesel engines and the electric motors.

It is easy to realise that life in a steel tube thus crammed with technical gadgets of all kinds must follow a peculiar pattern of its

58

own and that it embraces habits and customs which are unknown to any other type of vessel, be it warship or merchantman.

The only entry into a U-boat is through one of the hatches cut in the welded pressure hull. These are not much taller or broader than an average man. During operations the conning-tower hatch is the only one used. The iron ladders which lead up from the control-room, situated amidships under the conning-tower, can be used by only one man at a time. Anyone wishing to descend from the conning-tower to the control-room, or vice versa, must first give warning. He who shouts first has right of way.

When the U-boat has to do an emergency dive, there's no question of any orderly descent. The men on watch on the deck shoot down into the control-room like greased lightning. These conning-tower gymnastics, upwards and downwards, are a chapter to themselves in life in a U-boat. Each individual has to learn agility in exactly the same way as a child learns to stand and walk. A very great deal depends on this for no commander would leave anyone on deck, if he could help it, when the ship is in danger. It is also customary for the captain or the officer acting for him to be the last to descend and to close the hatch with a deft turn of the hand.

When the boat is proceeding submerged no one is allowed to move around as he pleases or, indeed, even as he is required to do by his duties. Bearing in mind that a U-boat when submerged is in a state of near perfect balance, which the chief engineer has brought about through the most minute adjustments to the various tanks, it is quite understandable that any transfer of weight would upset that balance. When it is necessary for someone to pass through the control-room—the centre of the U-boat and the point of balance—it is therefore essential and compulsory for that man to notify the officer of the watch there. He asks for permission to go forward, or aft. Only when he has received such permission may the man make a move.

Smoking within the vessel is strictly prohibited owing to the presence of explosive gases given off during the charging of the wet batteries for the electric motors. In some of the large types of U-boats the commander will permit those actually in the conning-tower to smoke a cigarette when the boat is on the surface and

59

the conning-tower hatch is open. But the conning-tower can only accommodate two or three men at a time.

When the submarine is proceeding on the surface, anyone who wants to smoke must ask permission to go on to the bridge. But as no unnecessary personnel is allowed to hang about on the bridge, here again permission can only be granted to one or two men at a time. The occasions when submariners can enjoy a puff of a cigarette on active service can, as may be imagined, be counted on the fingers of one hand; those on watch on the bridge are often an exception. But only some commanders are prepared to permit smoking while on watch; even this, however, is subject to certain restrictions, for at night, in the clear sea air, even a dimly glowing cigarette end can be seen from quite a long way off. Thus to the ordinary hardships are added a number of purely personal restrictions such as are encountered by no other men in the navy or indeed in any of the services. Even when things are really sticky, the infantryman can soothe his nerves with a quick puff or two, but in a submarine it is just when things are at their stickiest and the situation is critical that this consolation is denied.

In the cramped space available it is, of course, not possible to provide sufficient sleeping quarters. Only the more senior ranks are allotted cabins, but these they, too, have to share with each other, turn and turn about. The remainder of the crew has to be content with hammocks or mattresses on the floor plates.

Food is of prime importance in a submarine. The submariner will put up with hardships, dangers and deprivations without a murmur, but poor messing he will not tolerate. It doesn't worry him to have to eat half his meals standing on his feet or crouching uncomfortably on the deck, but if the cook spoils the stew or the petty officer responsible for the stowing of the provisions has been stupid, then they both hear all about it.

On the large types of U-boats fifteen or sixteen tons of provisions have to be stowed away. A great deal depends on how they are packed into the narrow spaces available, for obviously there must be a common-sense plan which will ensure that a varied diet is readily available. Behind the lockers, on top of the lockers, between the stanchions in the control-room, in the bows, in short, everywhere where some little hole or corner can be found, the tins of provisions are tucked away.

Cases have been known in some vessels where the crew got nothing but red sausage as their main dish for days on end because the other tins had been so unskilfully stacked. And woe betide the unfortunate man responsible if some important seasoning is lacking which is essential if the food is to be made really tempting; for in the bad air and with such little exercise the men quickly lose their appetites.

The galley deserves a chapter to itself. It is only about four square yards. In the smaller types of U-boat it is even tinier. In this minute kitchen, whose space is further cluttered with an electric range and all its pots and pans, the cook has to prepare food for forty or fifty or, in the larger vessels, even sixty men. The performance of a U-boat cook borders on the miraculous. Not content with ensuring that the crew get a succulent and nourishing dinner each day, he will often serve up a meal with two, three and, on holidays at sea, even four courses.

Then there's another thing.

The use of lavatories is regulated in a U-boat by a red traffic light. The larger U-boats possess two such apartments, but while one is used for its legitimate purpose, the other is normally stacked high with tins of provisions and all the preserves required to provide a varied and tasty diet.

It is around these illustrious localities that thoughts are centred during the long weeks of a commission at sea.

This is what Dieter Heilmann, former first watchkeeping officer and now a lawyer and an epicure in Minden, has to say on the subject:

"There were more than forty of us and whenever anyone entered, on went the red light—a most impertinent red, too, was the red of that red light. It shone in the bows, in the petty officers' mess, in the wardroom, in the wireless office, in the hydrophone room and in the control-room. It was reflected by the wood of the lockers, by the leads and by the pin-up pictures. And it shone and shone, unwaveringly and for ever, and never so unwaveringly and eternally as when one was longing for the damn thing to go out!"

For the petty officer in the control-room it was a hard life. From his post he could not see the little red light. Ten or fifteen times a day he would thrust his head round the bulkhead and ask

61

with a troubled monotonous voice: "How's the red light?" Long after I have forgotten everything else, long after I find myself able to go about my lawful occasion when and how I please, I shall always remember that yearning question trembling on the lips of forty odd men—"How's the red light?"

Of Wolfgang Lueth, one of the two naval holders of the Knight's Cross with Diamonds, it is said that he used to pin up in this quiet little cubby hole the ship's news bulletin and sometimes, too, the ship's orders and the minor punishments he had to mete out. Lueth, a commander and a man whose sense of humour was as keen as his psychological understanding was profound, said with a malicious twinkle: "There my men have the time and the opportunity to read and think over in blessed peace the various orders and notifications a commander has to give."

*　　*　　*

The occupation of Norway and the defeat of France, the Netherlands and Belgium that swiftly followed it, had the gravest repercussions on Britain's anti-submarine warfare. In their efforts to transport their forces from Dunkirk back to England, the British lost a large number of their small anti-submarine craft. As a result, convoys could only be given much weaker escorts for some considerable time.

But for the U-boat command the gates to the Atlantic now stood open, both in the north and in the south. Germany now commanded the whole of the European seaboard from the North Cape down to the Bay of Biscay. The Norwegian harbours, Bergen, Drontheim, Christiansund and Narvik, and the French ports, Brest, Lorient, Bordeaux, La Rochelle and St. Nazaire, were earmarked as U-boat bases. Secret negotiations were being conducted with the Italians with the object of obtaining bases in the Mediterranean. Japan, too, agreed, albeit hesitatingly and rather unwillingly, to allow German U-boats to enter, to dock and to take on ammunition in Japanese harbours.

The British authorities admitted that the situation was "very grave", and foreign observers were predicting the fall of Britain, the last bastion in western and southern Europe confronting the Axis Powers.

Doenitz certainly now had an impressive array of bases which shortened the distance for his forays into the Atlantic. But there were still not enough U-boats to allow him to make use of these bases to the extent he would like.

Those U-boats out on operation now surprised the enemy with new tactics. The meagre number of ships achieved such success that it seemed as though whole packs of these grey wolves were ranging over the vital areas of the Atlantic shipping lanes. Convoys were no longer being attacked by day. The U-boats maintained contact with the convoys until evening set in, called other U-boats to the scene by radio and then delivered concerted attacks during the night.

"Their boldness is astonishing, their navigation masterly and their seamanship admirable," was the frank admission of the British authorities, worried to the verge of despair over the apparently hopeless situation in which they found themselves. On 17 August, 1940, the whole area round the British Isles up to 60° north and 20° west was declared to be an area of unrestricted submarine warfare.

Of the fifty-nine vessels sunk in September 1940, no less than forty were merchantmen sailing in convoy.

*　　　*　　　*

When the newly constructed U-boats at long last became operational Britain's position became perilous in the extreme. Month by month the list of sinkings grew longer. In October 63 ships with a total tonnage of 352,000 tons were sunk. During the full moon period two convoys, in the words of the English report, were "literally hacked to pieces". The wolf packs, as the islanders had begun to call the U-boat flotillas, fastened their fangs with amazing tenacity into the cumbersome herd of ships of all classes and sizes, slowly pursuing its ungainly way across the ocean. Some commanders abandoned the tactics learned in training of remaining outside the escort screen and firing fans of torpedoes at the convoys. Lieutenant Krelschmer—Otto the Silent—had evolved his own methods. During the night he would surface, break through the ring of escorting vessels under cover of the darkness and slip like a wolf into the middle of the herd. "One ship one torpedo" was the motto which brought him such swift and stupendous success. While his brother commanders

63

were mixing it with the destroyers outside the ring of escort vessels, he would station himself midway between the two columns of freighters and slaughter steamer after steamer. It was only later, when it was much too late, that these tactics were adopted by all commanders and practised as a tactical exercise.

In response to urgent and despairing requests from Britain America exchanged fifty destroyers for the lease of bases in the West Indies.

The time seemed ripe for the throttling of the British Isles by cutting off all essential supplies of food and war material. The threat that Britain had hurled at Germany on the declaration of war was acting as a boomerang. It was not Germany, but Britain who had to tighten her belt.

Since the beginning of the war 1,026 British, Allied and neutral ships, with a total tonnage of nearly four million tons, had been sunk. Of these, 568 flew the British flag. Not all of them, of course, fell victims to the U-boats. The German surface ships and the Air Force each had a share, which, though very much smaller, was still very considerable.

There was just one item that Britain could enter on the credit side. With the acquiescence of the Danish Government in exile, the British organised air bases on Iceland. This closed the gap in the supervision of the northern portion of the Atlantic. In this way Britain at least obtained a position on the flank from which to guard the approach lines or, as they were called, "the Western Approaches". Attempts to persuade Eire to grant bases failed. The Irish Republic continued to insist on the maintenance of its neutrality. And this attitude was respected by the British War Cabinet.

*   *   *

The appearance of German submarines off West Africa came as a surprise. Four merchantmen were quickly destroyed. In November another convoy was attacked and six of its ships sunk. In that same November, too, the heavy cruiser *Scheer* attacked a convoy consisting of thirty-seven ships coming from Halifax under the escort of the British Auxiliary cruiser *Jervis Bay*. The approach of this convoy had been notified by the German Radio Interception Service, and when the attack was delivered the convoy was still beyond the range of air cover and the escort vessels coming from the south to take over had not yet reached it.

So, for Germany, 1940 ended on a note of cheerful optimism.

*   *   *

It is true that 1940 did not fulfil all the expectations of the German U-boat Command. Lack of U-boats was one of the reasons for this. For the British it had been a year of deep and bitter disappointment.

But this dismayed them not a whit; on the contrary it evoked all the obstinate courage that is the foundation of the Anglo-Saxon character.

But in Germany the Special Communiqués of the German High Command gave the people a sense of security and the feeling: "Nothing can happen to us now."

Although no official figures of U-boat losses had been published, some details did leak out, and these showed that, when the successes achieved and the increased number of U-boats engaged had been taken into consideration, the losses sustained had been most gratifyingly small. The casualty list in 1940 contained the names of nineteen U-boats.

Since the beginning of the war twenty-seven U-boats in all had been destroyed, an average of one and a half ships per month— a comparatively modest percentage.

Part Three

1941

———————

CHAPTER VI

OTTO KRETSCHMER AND GÜENTHER PRIEN

Situation Report.

> *The beginning of the great U-boat offensive. The groups detailed to attack Atlantic convoys were strengthened. The grey wolves now popped up in the Mediterranean as well, thrusting their way in groups through the Straits of Gibraltar into their operation area. Co-operation with the Air Force showed gratifying improvement. Goering provided long-range bombers of the Condor type for reconnaissance purposes as the need arose. But an air arm of their own was still not granted to the Navy. Doenitz was still dependent upon the goodwill of Air Force Headquarters. Very frequently the U-boats operating in the wide spaces of the Atlantic were still compelled to rely on their own efforts alone in finding the enemy convoys. This eternal searching took up a great deal of valuable time. Many a U-boat returned to base, its torpedo tubes still full, forced to break off operations by its waning stock of fuel.*
>
> *The Royal Air Force, equipped with new depth charges, scored its first success. On 6 January 1941, a Sunderland piloted by Flight Lieutenant E. F. Baker succeeded in sinking an Italian submarine to the west of Cape Wrath. The Italian tried to dive when the aircraft appeared, but was caught by two of the new 250-lb. depth charges. An hour later the surface of the sea was covered with a thick layer of oil.*
>
> *In March the German U-boat arm suffered its most severe losses since the initiation of the pack-tactics. Six U-boats were lost, and among their commanders were Prien (U.47), Schepke (U.100) and Kretschmer (U.99). Contrary to all rumours Prien had remained at sea. Here is the report of Otto Kretschmer who, with 350,000 tons to his credit, was the tonnage king of the Second World War and who is now a commander in the Federal German Navy.*

*　　*　　　*　　　*

"Get a convoy lined up for me, Guenther!" These were the last

66

words that I exchanged with Guenther Prien, as, on 20 February he set out from the Lorient base in *U.47* while I remained in port, still busy taking on stores and ammunition. There had been the usual show—a band, much waving of hands and many shouts of good luck and happy return.

Prien stood in the conning-tower in his new leather jacket, happy and still with that air of ingenuous youthfulness. Yet in his heart he was grave and concerned over the fate of the men entrusted to his care. The 'good old days' of the first months of the war were now no more than hazy memories.

Two days later I followed Prien out into the Bay of Biscay and very soon I heard that he had kept his promise to me about a convoy. He had fallen in with a convoy sailing on a south-westerly course from England to America. Prien had maintained contact, and thanks to his reports which were passed on by radio at regular intervals by shore control "to all concerned", we were able to steer a course directly on to the convoy.

A wild sea was running. Huge breakers rolled over the U-boat. Soaked to the skin, our eyes smarting painfully from the sea-water we stood on the bridge. Whenever the sun appeared or, at night, a star showed up, we took a sight. But these occasions were rare. When they did occur, then we had to look pretty slippy. Petersen was first-class at the job. He was my navigator and it was quite astonishing to see how he used to measure the angle of altitude with his sextant, even in weather like this, to "shoot the sun", as the sailors call it.

Later the sea calmed down, and only a long, high and heavy swell remained. Every now and then mist enveloped us.

According to our reckoning we should now have been in the vicinity of the convoy Prien had reported, which had been sailing to the south-west. I decided to dive and listen with the hydrophones.

Sure enough the apparatus gave us a bearing. Judging by the strength of the echo, the convoy could not be far away. It must have been just about at this moment that I caught sight of the black conning-tower of a U-boat, straight ahead of us, and beyond it the outlines of merchantmen and two destroyers in the act of turning directly towards the U-boat.

It was a rare thing to meet a friend at sea in circumstances such as these. The U-boat ahead was Prien's. The destroyers forced us to dive. But we still maintained contact.

67

Prien was soon busy notching successes.

One of my attacks, too, got home, and then we were driven off by a really heavy depth-charge attack. I had the luck, and Prien got the bombs.

Later when we cruised over the scene of the attack, we found a number of burning ships. The German Air Force, informed of Prien's report by the U-boat Command, had gone in to the attack and had treated the convoy very roughly. This was one of the few occasions when co-operation between U-boats and the German Air Force functioned perfectly and when the airmen were able to complete the task which had been begun by U-boats but obstructed by the onslaughts of destroyers.

By this time I had lost touch with Prien and I accordingly set course for the operation area allotted to me. U-boat headquarters used occasionally to give us each a specific area, with the object of extending reconnaissance over the widest possible area; then, if a convoy were sighted, the U-boats would concentrate and put their pack-tactics into practice.

Since in this war signals could be sent to U-boats even when they were submerged and contact with U-boat Headquarters was never broken, the operations of all the U-boats at sea could be directed and controlled by one senior authority. The so-called ultra-long waves—between 12,000 and 20,000 metres—are the only frequencies which will penetrate to a considerable depth under water. For normal signal traffic we used short waves, anything between 12 and 80 metres.

While proceeding to my operation area, between Iceland and Ireland, I received a W/T signal instructing me to carry out a reconnaissance sweep in conjunction with some other U-boats. This meant crossing the area indicated on a course parallel to that of the other vessels. It was when this reconnaissance had been completed that I again met Prien. The weather had once again deteriorated in the meantime and it was impossible to get within hailing distance.

We exchanged a few friendly words by morse and then parted and set course for the areas allotted to us.

Shortly afterwards Prien sent a signal to say that a convoy was emerging from the North Channel between England and Ireland and was steaming on a general north-westerly course. It was already beginning to get dark when I altered course to

68

bring me on to this new convoy, and it was nearly midnight when I came up to it. Prien in the meanwhile had attacked and scored a few hits. In his signal he estimated his successes at 26,000 tons. His attacks, of course, had alerted the British escort vessels, and any surprise attack was out of the question. Even so, under cover of darkness and from a position ahead, I succeeded in breaking through the destroyer screen on the surface and in following my usual tactics of slipping into the middle of the convoy.

Here one was pretty safe. None of the enemy destroyer commanders would for a moment have believed it possible that a German U-boat would dare to take station between the columns of steaming merchantmen. I chopped a couple of freighters and one or two tankers out of that convoy.

Then Prien attacked again, followed by Matz, *U.70*, and Eckermann, *U.A*, who in the meanwhile had caught up with the convoy.

Ships afire, ships sinking, the sea covered with burning oil—it was a grim scene that the surviving remnants of the convoy left behind.

At 04·24 on 7 March Prien once again signalled the position, speed and course of a convoy.

After that we heard no more. Then the escorting destroyers forced me to dive. Even when, later, we had still heard no more from Prien, we were not particularly worried. He had probably submerged really deep, to avoid the depth-charges. Or perhaps his W/T had broken down. Both Matz and I were being kept very busy by the destroyers, which were hard on our heels. Matz, as a matter of fact, was having a more strenuous time than I was. After two hours of it I surfaced again.

At 06·50 Matz reported damage to his conning tower. Then we were both forced by the destroyers to dive again. This time, too, I managed to keep clear of the depth charges. They came down on Matz, who was close beside me. His boat suffered severe damage and was eventually sunk. Matz himself and most of his crew were taken prisoner.

For nine whole hours the fury of depth charge explosions continued! It was nearly 17·00 before they ceased, and I ventured cautiously to the surface.

By radio I was ordered by Doenitz to try and finish off a ship which I had torpedoed around midnight, but had not succeeded in sinking. Our radio interception service had meanwhile deciphered the ship's signals. She was the Norwegian whaling factory ship *Terge Viken*. She was asking for help, reporting that she had been hit amidships and was making a great deal of water. Well, that suited my book all right. In any case, I had wanted to have another look round the scene of the action.

Meanwhile U-boat Headquarters had been calling up Prien. Again and again his call sign came over the air. But from Prien himself there was no answer.

When I got to the spot, there was no sign of the Norwegian whaler. I presumed she must have sunk in the meanwhile. But in her place a destroyer was cruising round, probably the one that had taken off her crew. I was spotted and escaped into the depths by the skin of my teeth.

During the night we reloaded the tubes, a long and laborious business. While this was going on we picked up a signal informing us that Lemp, *U.110*, had sighted a convoy bound for Canada in the vicinity of Iceland, course south-west.

We succeeded once more in intercepting the convoy. Again I got through the escort screen into my favourite position between the columns. I fired every torpedo I had and succeeded in hitting the tankers *Ferm*, *Bedouin*, and *Franche Comté*, and the merchantmen *Venetia*, *J. B. White* and *Korsham*. Then I turned for home. As I proceeded I passed over the Lousy Bank—a literal translation of the name given to the shallows to the south of Iceland. And for us they certainly turned out to be very lousy banks indeed, for here I ran slap into the arms of a destroyer group. My boat was badly damaged by depth charges. My fuel tanks started to leak. My propellers fouled, and I was compelled to surface—or sink for good. When I came to the surface one of the destroyers was in a perfect position for a shot. But even if we'd had one, we could not have fired a torpedo; we had used up every ounce of compressed air. The two destroyers opened fire. There was nothing for it. We abandoned ship. My chief engineer, who once more went below to accelerate the process of scuttling, was lost in the execution of his duty.

The destroyer *Walker* took the survivors of my crew and myself aboard. Here I learned that the other destroyer of the group, H.M.S. *Vanoc*, had only a few minutes before and at the selfsame spot rammed and sunk *U.100* (Schepke). Schepke himself met a tragic end. His ship was on the surface and out of control when the attacking destroyer rammed and destroyed her. Schepke had remained jammed between the bridge and periscope.

On board H.M.S. *Walker* we were admirably treated. To my astonishment I was allotted the captain's cabin. In the evening I had another surprise when into the captain's day cabin marched the captains of the vessels we had sunk. And these old salts, grand sailors and grand men, had been ordered to sleep there, while I, a German and the enemy, had been given a cabin.

The British captains behaved splendidly towards us. To them we, like themselves, were ship-wrecked sailors. In the Christian seafaring spirit in which they had grown up and become old and grey, they shared their tobacco and cigarettes with us, and in truly friendly fashion they saw to it that I lacked for nothing. In the evening, to pass the time and to avoid having to say things which, between men, needed no saying, we played rubber after rubber of bridge. The destroyer's doctor, too, sometimes joined us and played a hand or two.

We were put ashore at Liverpool and were then taken to a delightful country house not far from London. This little paradise on earth had not, however, been organised simply for our benefit. It turned out, in fact, to be one of the usual preliminary interrogation camps. In every room in which we thought we were alone and among our own kind microphones had been installed, and every single word that was spoken was recorded on a tape machine and carefully studied.

One day a British officer arrived and asked me to accompany him to the director of anti-submarine warfare.

There was some difficulty in procuring me a suit of civilian clothes in which to visit Captain Creasy (as he then was). But eventually everything necessary was obtained from the officers' clothing store except a pair of shoes to fit me. But this problem, too, was solved by one of the interrogating officers, a naval lieutenant. He jumped up, stood beside me and measured his foot against mine. Seeing that they were about the same size, he whipped off his own shoes and presented them to me. They fitted beautifully.

On the way to St. James's the lieutenant who was escorting me told me that Captain Creasy had originally intended to receive me officially at the Admiralty. Later, however, he changed this into a private "invitation" to his quarters in St. James's, where he occupied a whole floor. On the way there we started talking about Prien.

The lieutenant, obviously, had had a previous word with the officers of the destroyer *Wolverine*—or had at least read the report on the action. According to it, a U-boat had been located near the convoy in question and had been engaged with depth charges. Even after the explosion of the second series, however, there had been no signs to show that a hit had been scored. But shortly afterwards the surface had been disturbed by a terrific explosion, accompanied by orange-coloured flames. Nothing had been found, not a board, not a bit of deck-grating, no oil—nothing. But the Asdic gave no further impulses.

While telling me this, my escort watched me out of the corner of his eye, to see how I would react.

All I said was that this subsequent explosion seemed to me to be unusual, and the orange-coloured flames even more so.

My reception by the director of anti-submarine warfare can be described as being almost a meeting of old friends; it certainly went far beyond the bounds of formality. . . .

We talked about general topics of an apparently innocuous nature, but as I was told after the war by Admiral Sir George Creasy a number of cunning test questions about Doenitz had been slipped in. Then from his lips I heard a precise account of all my enterprises to date in the Atlantic.

Everything he said was accurate. I felt a shiver run through me, and I was hard put to it to preserve my calm and to reply with a polite smile:

"Really very interesting!"

"Isn't it?"

"You surely don't expect me to offer you any amendments? A lot of it is quite wrong. But to err is human, Captain."

"Of course it is, my dear Kretschmer, of course it is. But I'm not trying to pump you or to get you to give away secrets. All I wanted to do was to make the personal acquaintance of one of the best-known German U-boat commanders. I wanted to have a look at the sort of officers and men we were up against. I can only offer you my congratulations and express my admiration for your exploits, Captain Kretschmer. You know, we just can't understand how you fellows manage to remain on the surface, even in the worst weather . . . " Captain Creasy paused for a long while.

". . . and that you can still attack and sink ships in weather in which any seaman would be fully occupied with ensuring that his ship rode the storm."

What ought I to reply, I wondered? I got out of it by asking a question myself.

"But your own submarine commanders are also first-class seamen, sailors through and through. Do you really find it strange that we should put to sea in bad weather? Your fellows don't submerge, either, when they are following a target. . . ."

"You're wrong. They submerge all right when it blows as it has been during these last few weeks."

Creasy simply could not understand how it was at all possible to take a bearing from the heaving platform of a violently pitching and tossing submarine. His admiration was genuine and sincere.

* * *

And what had happened in the meanwhile to *U.70* after the first heavy attack which, as I have said, had damaged the vessel so badly?

About the last hours of *U.70* her commander, now Dr. Joachim Matz, writes as follows:

"In the meanwhile I got down to it with the chief engineer to work out how long we could stay below. Our conclusions were not very encouraging.

"If all went well we could stick it until the late afternoon. The batteries would not stand more than that; we had already used up too much current in our enforced surfacing. But as usual the technicians had been cautious in their estimates and had kept a small reserve up their sleeves. So it seemed to me that provided nothing else happened we might be able to carry on until evening. To get clear away submerged was out of the question.

"Compressed air, too, was pretty low; here again we had used up too much in our repeated surfacing, and we had had no time to pump in fresh air.

"So at a depth of about 300 feet we waited for the next consignment of depth charges. Experience had taught us that at this depth we were comparatively safe. But we had to have patience, lots of patience and then—still more patience.

"The initiative was now in the hands of the British, who could sit comfortably up there and drop a pattern of depth charges every half-hour or so.

73

"In the U-boat everything was quiet. Those off duty lay peacefully in their bunks, just waiting. At every important spot a man was on duty; in the control-room good old Gerhard Wall, our chief engineer, kept a competent eye on the depth-keeping gear. The boat was steady at 300 feet, and slight movements of the hydroplanes kept her at that depth. The whirr of our propellers was so soft as to be hardly audible, giving us a speed of something between one and two knots. The gyro compass in front of the helmsman scarcely moved, and he had little difficulty in keeping the course. Only the petty officer telegraphist was kept busy and alert on the hydrophones in order to give warning of the next enemy approach.

"Then they came at us again! The grinding noise of propellers became louder. The bearing remained static; and that meant that the destroyer was coming straight at us. Then with our own ears we could clearly hear the rhythmic beat above our heads. . . . Twenty seconds of oppressive, absolute silence and then with a roar and a crash down came a pattern of charges helter-skelter all round us. The ship shuddered from stem to stern, shook herself; lockers sprang open, from here and there came the tinkle of splintered glass, but we suffered no serious damage, thank God. Calm reports flowed into the control-room from various stations. The chief engineer kept a constant, unwavering eye on his gauges. So far everything was in order.

"Everything, that is, except this blasted leak in the shaft of the direction finder, which had now become pretty serious. The technicians tried to caulk it, but try as they might, at this depth it was just not possible, the water pressure was too great.

"Hour after hour passed in silence, broken at intervals by the clatter of each succeeding enemy attack.

"With stoic calm the navigator made a mark on the chart-table for each depth charge dropped and for each salvo a few marks with a bracket above them.

"If it hadn't been for that bloody leak, I'd have gone and taken a nap in my cabin.

"More hours passed, and all too slowly the minute hand crawled its way round the clock. Evening was what we were all waiting for. With that leak, things could not go on like this for ever.

"There was nothing for it—we had to blow all the compensating tanks if we were to keep the boat trim. Pint by pint, gallon by gallon the water continued to seep in. Apart from the D/F shaft there must have been some further, minor leaks somewhere. Nothing else could account for the fact that the ship was getting heavier all the time.

"It was now about half-past eleven, and we had already been submerged for five hours. The faithful navigator had marked more than fifty depth charges on his chart-table.

"The chief engineer was having difficulty in keeping the boat under control. The amount of water we had shipped was now becoming very noticeable. We used our pumps, but only very cautiously, in order not to make too much noise.

"For, notwithstanding the enemy's locating apparatus, I kept on trying to see whether, by numerous alterations of course, I could not after all slip clear of him. But to do that I had, after each fresh attack, to call for a temporary increase in speed. And if we were to stick it till evening we had to save every bit of current we could.

"So we obstinately continued on our way. Every quarter of an hour the chief engineer was forced to give the diving tanks a puff of compressed air to lighten the boat, for all the compensating tanks had been pumped empty long before. But in the bilges the water had begun to lap in a most disturbing manner, and at a depth of 300 feet and more the pumps are not much use. Nor dared we go on pumping all the time. So we continued to crawl along. In spite of this, however, there was an air of confidence throughout the ship.

"The hydrophone operator reported that there was now only one solitary craft on the surface in our vicinity. Had the two others gone? Had they given up the chase? Whose obstinacy was going to win the day? Ours or that of our pursuers?

"Well—if it all depended on obstinacy we ought to be all right. We submariners are used to sticking it out. But at all costs we had to prevent anything further damn silly happening to the boat which had already had about as much as she could take. More than that we could not do.

"12·00. We'd stuck it for half the day; now for the other half; and it would be devilish hard luck if we didn't get through that, too. The ship, admittedly, was in pretty poor shape. The place was littered with broken glass, everything that had not been firmly

75

fixed had been brought down by the shaking the charges had given us. The contents of all the lockers had been spilled out and lay scattered everywhere. All that, however, didn't matter two pins.

"The only thing that did matter was to keep the good ship, which had served us so faithfully, at her correct depth and prevent too great an amount of water from seeping into her.

"12·10. Report from hydrophones: 'Destroyer approaching.'

"At the same time we were able to hear her propellers. Then she was over us and—away, and all we had to do now was to wait for the crash of the explosions.

" 'Cross your fingers, lads! Let's hope we get away with it!'

"Then—down they came. Once again the boat shuddered from end to end. The salvo had been well distributed, as we could feel. Tensely our eyes turned to the instruments. God! What's happened! We had begun to sink rapidly. Inexorably the needle of the depth indicator moved to the right—380 feet—400—420—440—460—it went on with gathering speed. At the same moment came a report from the control-room aft:

" 'Leak!'

" 'Both motors, full ahead! Hydroplanes hard up! Everybody aft!'

"Would we be able to stop her dive—or were we plunging on and on into the depths? There were 10,000 feet of water below us here, and that's too much, even for us.

"Frenziedly the men off duty leapt aft through the bulkheads, to transfer the weight aft and lift the bows. At last with a slight jerk the indicator reached 650 feet, the maximum permissible depth, and quiveringly hesitated. For some seconds each of which seemed as long as an hour, it remained, quivering, hesitatingly while the motors began to thresh wildly.

"Then slowly the indicator started to move again . . . 600 . . . 550 . . . 450. . . .

"With increasing speed the ship began now to shoot upwards. But that wouldn't do either, by God! Up there our friends were waiting for us. Somehow or other she had to be halted and damn quickly, too! Somehow or other we had got to hold her at 300 feet. Surely, this could not be the end. So—all men forward to get the ship on an even keel again. 'Decrease speed. Both motors, slow ahead!'

"We had already risen to 360 feet and the ship was still rising.

76

More weight forward, then. The upward movement had to be stopped. But now we were trying to call the tune without consulting the man who paid the piper. Now the freely moving air in the diving tanks began to take a hand. Scarcely had the ship got on to an even keel than she stood on her nose again and down we went again, willy nilly; in a few seconds the indicator stood once more at 450 feet . . . then 500. So once more the order: 'All hands, aft!'

"The men at the hydroplanes, now operating by hand, worked with a furious energy. The chief engineer was doing his utmost to regain control.

"At last, a little below 600 feet the downward plunge was halted. One more puff now into the diving tanks from our meagre store of compressed air!

"A sigh of relief went up. Once more we had succeeding in getting our U-boat under control. Now, surely, we should have a little respite! Surely we should be able to hold her steady at 300 feet.

"Alas—vain hopes! No sooner was she on an even keel again than down once more went her nose. In went the last of our compressed air, sixty pounds of it, our very last reserve. The main valve remained open. There was not an ounce of air left with which to control the ship. All now depended on the motors.

"With unusual clarity I suddenly realised that our lives hung by a thread. I was face to face with those rare seconds in life when one feels the full, furious burden of responsibility. The rest of the story is quickly told.

"Literally with a last effort the motors stopped the downward plunge somewhere between 550 and 600 feet. Slowly the ship righted herself, the bows began to rise, while the electric motors hummed and the crew stood motionless in the stern. Except for brief essential words of command not a sound was to be heard. Not a man in this fine crew uttered a single, unnecessary word. There was not one among them who did not realise that we were all in the same boat, about to sink or swim together.

"We continued to rise, and now the effect of the use of our last reserves of compressed air began to make themselves felt. Having passed the critical point for the third time, the ship continued upwards, and nothing could stop her.

" 'All hands prepare to abandon ship!'

"We hadn't over much time. In a matter of seconds we broke

surface. The idea then was to open the conning-tower and galley hatches and get every man up on deck as quick as possible.

"In spite of my fears, we all got out safely. As I reached the deck, I saw the destroyer—in reality it turned out to be a corvette—close beside us. She was firing rather wildly. From the bridge a voice shouted in bad German: 'Jump overboard, I'm going to fire!' And fire they did, though as far as I could see no one was hurt in those first few moments.

"I ordered the crew overboard. Led by their officers they safely reached two rafts, to which they were able to cling. They were, of course, also wearing their life-jackets. A few of us remained on board. The chief engineer had been swept overboard while trying to re-open the galley hatch which the sea had closed again. Once again the British opened fire at close range with machine-guns. Why they didn't hit us, I don't know. What they were really trying to do, I think, was to frighten us off the ship which they were hoping to board. They lowered a boat. But we, too, knew a thing or two. Severely damaged though she was, our U-boat was still afloat. But they wouldn't get her! Suppose someone had forgotten to open all the vents! While I still hesitated Paul Kollmann, splendid fellow, disappeared down through the hatch to make sure. Thank God! he was soon on deck again. Then down I went myself to take one last look. The control-room was empty and in a state of chaos. However, this was no time to hang about. After a swift glance at the vents to be sure they were open I climbed quickly up to the bridge again.

"The whole of the U-boat's stern was already under water. We jumped for it. When I was about twenty-five yards from her she reared steeply up. Menacingly the stern pointed upwards at the heavens for a few seconds, and then *U.70* plunged for the last time to the bottom of the North Atlantic.

"Twenty of my good shipmates were lost. Not far from the same spot *U.47*, with Prien and all his crew, was lost. It was only later that I heard that the British claimed first to have rammed her during the night and then to have completed her destruction with depth charges.

"The comradeship of life aboard a submarine and the splendid corporate spirit with which it is imbued remains with me as one of the greatest things in my life."

CHAPTER VII

MUETZELBURG AND LUETH, U-BOAT ACES

Situation report—Spring 1941.

Hitler made an ill-considered declaration early in January 1941: "In the Spring our U-boat campaign will begin, and then those people over there will see that we have not been asleep." Churchill doesn't babble. He acts. After this speech he concentrated all his energy on counteracting Hitler's threat of an intensification of submarine warfare. He coined the phrase "Admiral Time". Britain was ·negotiating with the USA.

In this same January secret conferences between the British and American staffs took place on the organisation of American air and naval bases. In April American warships formally accepted responsibility for all convoys within a 500 mile limit of the American coast. American troops were stationed in Newfoundland and Iceland in support of British anti-submarine bases. An American named Henry Kaiser submitted to the American Government proposals for a revolutionary change in the technique of ship-building. His suggestion was that ships should be mass-produced, to help Britain.

These plans, however, were still purely theoretical. But time worked in their favour. The number of new U-boats being completed still exceeded by far the losses sustained. Seventeen or eighteen U-boats were ready to be commissioned each month, whereas, with the exception of the catastrophic month of March, the average monthly losses amounted to anything between one and four boats. In Britain, on the other hand, the ratio between new ships launched and the ever-increasing losses was one to three.

The battle of the Atlantic was entering its most remorseless phase. Lieut.-Commander Muetzelburg was one of the new aces who were strengthening the stranglehold on Britain's lines of supply. Kretschmer had been taken prisoner, but the tactics which brought him success to a total of 350,000 tons—or roughly the total tonnage of a medium-sized maritime nation—lived on.

*   *   *

79

The German radio interception service has reported a fully laden convoy proceeding from Canada to Britain, and the U-boats were concentrating on it. *U.203* was in mid-Atlantic when early one morning the noise of propellers was picked up by the hydrophones. The sound resembled a dull, subterranean grinding noise.

Muetzelburg, who has already turned in, rose hastily when the information was brought to him. He made a swift inspection through the periscope but saw nothing. The horizon was empty. *U.203* rose to the surface.

"Send the cook up to the bridge," called Muetzelburg.

The cook, a butcher by trade, a fellow with a chest like a barn door and the equitable temperament of a St. Bernard, had been expecting the summons. He had the sharpest eyes on board. Indeed, he could often see better with his naked eye than his colleagues on watch with their excellent Zeiss binoculars.

For seventy minutes *U.203* followed the course indicated by the hydrophones.

Even the cook, however, could see nothing. But Kampe, the hydrophone operator, reported:

"The echo is getting louder."

Another ten minutes passed. Nothing. Not a sight anywhere.

After a further quarter of an hour the cook raised his hand.

"Mast-heads, bearing 088 degrees!"

At once all the binoculars concentrated on the spot indicated.

"Sure you're not wrong, cook?" asked Muetzelburg after he had swept the horizon with his glasses.

The cook blew out his cheeks in indignation, took a deep breath and looked as though he had been swallowing baking powder by the ladleful.

"No, Sir," he said. "I am not wrong. Actually there are now a few more of 'em."

It was at least five minutes later that the bridge watch, armed with binoculars, picked up the mastheads. It was the convoy reported by the radio interception service.

U.203 was exactly on its port beam. In a wide curve Muetzelburg worked his way closer, until he could discern the silhouettes of the individual merchantmen. For a while he proceeded parallel to the convoy, in order to ascertain its general course. The convoy was zigzagging—that is to say, executing a series of pre-arranged alterations of course at stated intervals—in order to avoid U-boats. *U.203* conformed to these alterations of course, while the navigator plotted them. In this way the mean course of the convoy was worked out and this information was signalled back to U-boat headquarters and passed on from there to all other U-boats in the area.

It was only after darkness fell that Muetzelburg increased speed. On the surface and under cover of the night he slipped through the screen of destroyers and, at slow speed, noiselessly took up his position in the middle of the convoy. He proceeded on a course parallel to that of the freighters. On the bridge complete silence reigned, and in the ship itself all was quiet. Only the motors hummed their familiar melody. Lieutenant Heyda, the first watch-keeping officer, has been busy picking out the most worthwhile looking targets in the convoy, while Muetzelburg was working out his general plan of attack.

To port, a bare hundred yards away from *U.203*, was a big 6,000 tonner. It seemed as though they could hear the water cascading from her bows, and they visualised the captain and his officers dimly outlined against the night sky tramping uneasily from one side of the bridge to the other, and stopping every now and then to sweep the horizon with a suspicious scrutiny. This heavily laden ship was in the very middle of the convoy. Her captain must have felt that he was secure and safe. No one aboard gave a thought to glancing at the water just ahead and a little to the side of the ship for any suspicious shadow or for the betraying flash of a bow-wave. For a U-boat to break unobserved through the wary screen of destroyers was regarded as impossible.

Muetzelburg had deliberately manœuvred his ship so close to the merchantman that he was able to operate in the shadow thrown by her. Heyda meanwhile had selected the two biggest ships. He slipped close up to Muetzelburg and silently pointed an outstretched finger at the unsuspecting vessels. Muetzelburg nodded. Softly he asked whether the torpedoes were cleared for action.

"All ready!" came the answer.

Muetzelburg stiffened for a moment, then gave his orders. . . .

A salvo of two leapt from the tubes. Each torpedo hit one of the big freighters steaming one behind the other in the third column to starboard.

81

The night was torn asunder by two huge explosions. Both vessels sank. Then all hell was let loose.

Star shells lit up the sky. Searchlights flashed fingers of light in all directions.

But the escorts were searching for the U-boat outside the convoy.

Depth charges were dropped and exploded without a pause. A mad, fantastic spectacle stormed through the night.

Muetzelburg held course in the middle of the convoy and, unthreatened by any escort vessel, calmly selected his next victim. In order to have his ship fully cleared for action he had ordered that the two tubes just fired be immediately re-loaded. Twenty minutes later the torpedo officer reported these two loaded and ready once more for action.

Thrice more *U.203* fired single torpedoes. Three more hits. Three more ships sunk.

"One torpedo one ship" had once been Otto Kretschmer's motto, when he abandoned the tactics laid down by Doenitz and on his own responsibility tried out his idea of infiltrating into the middle of the convoy—and proved its efficiency with such conspicuous success. In Muetzelburg, Otto the Silent had found his successor.

On Muetzelburg's U-boat there was none so cold-blooded as not to feel a heart pang for those fighting for their lives amidst ships bursting asunder, hissing, groaning and with shrill screams of anguish sinking into the depths.

Save them? To try and save these men would be suicide for the attackers.

Muetzelburg wanted to make one more run, and Heyda was seeking a "worthwhile" target when suddenly a corvette crept round the bows of one of the freighters—a wild and bold man-œuvre. Only by inches did the vessel's bows miss the corvette's stern.

The corvette switched on its searchlights and instantly found the mark. Was it just luck or had the German U-boat been discovered?

Away! In the devil's name, away! But where to?

Muetzelburg called instantly for maximum speed, at the same time the alarm sounded, and in the same instant the bridge watch came hurtling down the conning-tower, with Muetzelburg bringing up the rear. The ship was already being flooded, and a ton of water came thundering down with tremendous force through the not quite closed hatch into the interior of the U-boat. That, however, did not matter, did not matter at all. It only made the U-boat a little heavier. Everything else could well be left to the chief engineer who had already switched over from diesels to the electric motors.

During its brief burst of full speed the diving U-boat had gathered such momentum that it simply shot into the depths. In forty-five brief seconds *U.203* had disappeared completely from the surface. Then the hydroplanes were brought into play. Muetzelburg did not go deep, but put his helm hard over so as to bring his ship under the keel of the merchantman steaming to port of him. The depth charges dropped by the corvette in the U-boat's course, as last seen, missed the target. The corvette dared not drop any too close to the side of the ship under which *U.203* had taken refuge. It was only then that Muetzelburg went down, first to 550 feet and later to 700. On the surface the destroyers were on the hunt. Whenever they moved, Muetzelburg, too, proceeded on his way. When they stopped to sweep around with their Asdic, he, too, stopped. Depth charges were exploding everywhere.

At the hydrophones sat Bartel, the young telegraphist, looking like a conscientious book-keeper. He calmly kept the score with a bit of chalk, four upright strokes and the fifth diagonally across them. The groups of five grew more and more numerous.

In the first six hours, no less than seventy depth charges were dropped.

Some of the crew did not even hear most of them. They had already turned in.

"A tough lot!" smiled Muetzelburg. "Ashore they're a thorn in the flesh of any commander. Afloat they're worth their weight in gold."

The convoy was gone; five freighters, 28,000 tons of tonnage, were missing.

*   *   *

In conjunction with others, *U.203* attacked a Canadian convoy in September 1941.

The battle had been raging for some hours, and the convoy had been cut into a number of small groups each of which was being attacked in turn by the U-boat wolves.

It was broad daylight. *U.203* was at periscope depth and going in to deliver her third attack. Normally, U-boats did not attack by day; but this was an exception. During the night the convoy had been so completely split up as to rob it of the air protection provided by the accompanying auxiliary aircraft carriers, and so the U-boats were able to attack in the "black pit"—the area which was beyond the reach of aircraft from Coastal Command. Only a few destroyers were there rushing furiously from group to group in a desperate endeavour to protect the ships committed to their care.

Muetzelburg had three ships in his cross-wires when the man on duty at the hydrophones picked up the sound of a very different type of propellor, coming from astern. It was a clear, grinding sort of whine, which seemed to penetrate Kampe's body like a thousand glowing needles. For two seconds, perhaps, he listened. He needed no more. He knew.

"Destroyers approaching from astern," he reported.

Muetzelburg swung the periscope round and saw the destroyer, a bare hundred yards away. She was on the exact same course as *U.203* and was following exactly in its wake.

"Down to seventy feet!" ordered Muetzelburg sharply.

Lieutenant Heyda started. He went as pale as a sheet. He wanted to say something, but young Muetzelburg's quiet, determined smile stifled the words in his throat.

"Has the Old 'Un gone barmy?" whispered the crew among themselves.

The noise of the propellers were now audible and was growing momentarily louder.

Muetzelburg, however, had no intention of seeking the safety of depth. He allowed the destroyer to steam straight over him. Her keel must only have just missed the conning-tower. In the U-boat everyone ducked instinctively. One or two seized life jackets. They held their breath and missed a heart-beat. Any second now, down would come the depth charges.

But not a depth charge was dropped.

"Stand by, number one tube!"

Muetzelburg's order was given in a quiet, almost bored, tone of voice.

U.203 rose again to periscope depth. Muetzelburg saw the stern of the departing destroyer 30 . . . 40 . . . 50 yards ahead. He could see the men standing by the depth charges. The torpedo men reported, "Ready."

Number one bow-cap opened and the glistening monster leapt into blue, crystal-clear waters of the Atlantic. At a speed of forty knots the deadly missile rushed towards the destroyer, caught up with her and hit her. Almost at the same instant as the appalling crash of the detonation the blast of the exploding torpedo hit the U-boat's hull with an impact that rattled and shook her, knocking down the crew like ninepins.

The metal plates rattled. There were sounds of sinister tearing and splitting, the dread noise of the sinking destroyer. Bulkheads could be heard collapsing as the greyhound went down into the depths.

Only with a thoroughly experienced crew, tempered and proven in many actions with the enemy, could Muetzelburg have dared to risk so foolhardy an attack.

One member of this crew was chief engine-room artificer Ivens, a character, if ever there was one. Lack of inches lent emphasis to his considerable girth, and he looked like a little barrel. It is quite likely that a barrel was responsible for his shape—not the tons of shipping which he had helped to sink, but the tuns which he had emptied down his throat. When the alarm went, crawling through the conning-tower hatch was not, thank goodness, one of the duties that devolved upon him. Contrary to the normal practice of men in the presence of the enemy, Ivens, if he was not on duty, used to undress. He used to sleep in his pants, and he slept deeply. Newcomers aboard would never forget the day when the peacefully slumbering Ivens suddenly leapt up, flew from his cabin still garbed in a pair of socks and his underwear, disappeared into the engine-room and proceeded to tear strips off the petty officer on watch.

"Hi! What the hell's going on! Why the hell is the port diesel running on only five cylinders?"

The unfortunate petty officer looked as astounded as if some teetotal enthusiast had suddenly popped up and said that he thought beer was a good and nourishing drink after all!

"Damn it! Can't you hear it for yourself, man?"

"No, Sir. Everything sounds normal."

"It does, does it! Well—we'll see about that."

Together they inspected the diesel. One of the ducts was found to be completely choked up.

And Ivens had heard the engine missing—in his sleep!

On one occasion he was on the bridge enjoying his smoke-time and puffing contentedly at his pipe—a museum piece almost as big and as bulky as himself and consequently a source of perpetual irritation to would-be smokers waiting their turn for a spell on deck. Suddenly he hung his great paunch over the guard rail and gazed thoughtfully at the diesel exhausts. Seeing him there, frowning, Muetzelburg became a bit worried. As far as he himself could see, everything was quite normal. But what was biting old Ivens?

Suddenly Ivens sprang to the conning-tower.

"Diesel engine-room!" he called through the intercom. "I think you'd better gradually get back to using a bit of fuel oil. Scientifically speaking, we can't yet run on sea-water alone!"

And indeed the oil bunker proved to be almost empty of fuel. Oil bunkers cannot remain empty once their contents have been used, because that would disturb the balance of the boat. They are therefore equipped in such a way that water can seep into them through a bottom valve, which is always left open on operations; and as the oil is lighter than sea-water it floats on the top and is thus sucked into the engine. It is the duty of the stokers on watch to keep an eye on the bunker then in use and to disconnect it as soon as it is empty of fuel. In the fumes given off by the exhaust Ivens had noticed just the thinnest of white wisps, which would have meant nothing to any but an expert, but which could be caused only by the presence of sea-water in the combustion chamber.

Once, during an air attack, when Muetzelburg had had to crash-dive, *U.203* had started to submerge at an alarming rate. As calm as a cucumber, the control-room petty officer, Bausch, stood beside his chief engineer.

"Careful, Sir. We're a ton heavier than usual."

As the U-boat approached 400 feet, the chief engineer succeeded in steadying her. On his own responsibility Bausch had taken on an extra ton of weight. He knew a thing or two about this area. He knew, too, better than the chief engineer, who was a newcomer, how suddenly and unexpectedly enemy aircraft were apt to appear out of the blue. He had, of course, no right to act on his own in this way. But in this particular case he had probably saved the ship and the lives of her crew.

*   *   *

There is a similar story of *U.325* when out in the North Atlantic. A heavy following sea was breaking over the bridge, and the men on watch were fastened with belts to prevent them from being swept overboard. The commander came up on deck for a few moments. Just as he arrived a vast roller swept over the bridge, and for some seconds the ship was completely submerged. When the water receded it was found that it had taken the commander with it!

"Man overboard!"

In a few minutes the officer of the watch had completed the tricky manœuvre of fishing his commander safely out of the water. A piece of quiet, heroic efficiency, which was noted in the war-diary in the laconic sentence:

"11·43 to 11·49, commander overboard."

But these short, six minutes were quite enough to start a long paper war at home. One of the entries in the bosun's report on his return read as follows:

"At 11·43 the commander was washed overboard. He was subsequently rescued. In order to facilitate keeping himself afloat, he had divested himself of the following articles:—Trousers, leather, pairs, 2; Jackets, leather, 1; Boots, jack, submarine, pairs, 1; Pistols, automatic, 2; binoculars, 2; sextant, 1; gloves, leather, pairs, 4."

Now, the administrative wallahs are suspicious fellows by nature, and at the sight of this remarkable document they opened their eyes, venomously muttering something about falsification of returns and courts martial.

At Naval Headquarters the document was passed from hand to hand with broad grins. And a few days later, back it came to the flotilla with the remark:

"Losses to be made good. Issue of replacements sanctioned." And at the bottom, scribbled in manuscript, was a little note: "Is this a new type of U-boat? Is it possible to get through the conning-tower in a rig-out like this? It is requested that due consideration should in future be given to this aspect."

CHAPTER VIII

U.74 AND THE TRAGEDY OF THE *BISMARCK*

Situation Report—May 1941.

On 24 May 1941, south of Greenland and to the south-west of Ice-land, the battleship Bismarck, *which had put to sea in company with the heavy cruiser* Prinz Eugen, *sank H.M.S.* Hood, *the most power-ful battleship in the world. A hit forward from H.M.S.* Prince of Wales *reduced the* Bismarck's *speed, and the* Prinz Eugen *was told to proceed independently. While attempting to break through to Brest the* Bismarck *was hit by a torpedo from an aircraft from* Ark Royal. *Her propellers and steering gear were severely damaged, and shortly afterwards she came under the combined and devastating fire of the two battleships* Rodney *and* King George V *and the cruisers* Norfolk *and* Dorsetshire. *At 10.36 on 27 May the giant* Bismarck, *unable to manœuvre, her ammunition entirely expended, sank under the blows of several torpedoes from H.M.S.* Dorsetshire. *Before this happened, Admiral Luetjens, C. in C. of the fleet, who had hoisted his flag in* Bismarck, *had summoned another U-boat to come and take over his war diary. The other U-boats, which Luetjens had alerted, im-mediately after the sinking of the* Hood, *met with no success. Only* U.556 *(Lieutenant Wohlfahrt) sighted the battleship* Renown *and* Ark Royal, *the aircraft carrier whose aircraft had launched the fatal torpedo. Both these great ships sailed at right angles across the U-boat's bows, but* U.556 *had already fired her last torpedo.*

*   *   *

U.74 (Kentrat) was one of the U-boats at sea which had received orders to attack the British forces.

Kentrat proceeded at full speed towards the scene of the action. Towards evening he dived to listen with the hydrophones. The operator immediately reported underwater noises. Kentrat him-self leapt to the hydrophones.

"Unless I'm very much mistaken those noises come from the propellers of a U-boat."

Kentrat surfaced and there, a few hundred yards away, was the boat they had heard. As he had anticipated it was a German U-boat, tossing and plunging in the tumultuous seas. A bearded figure waved from the bridge—Wohlfahrt, commander of *U.556*. Raising his megaphone he shouted something, but it was some considerable time before Kentrat or his men could hear a word he said:

"Kentrat, take over my orders, will you, and go and collect *Bismarck's* war diary."

At last the men in *U.74* understood. Kentrat raised his hand. Wohlfahrt gave the clenched fist signal denoting that he had understood and disappeared into the conning-tower. Soon afterwards his ship slipped like a ghost beneath the waves of the Atlantic.

For a moment a shudder of apprehension gripped Kentrat and his crew. The whole thing had had an air of nightmare unreality, and they could not understand why Wohlfahrt, that ace among the old sea-dogs, should have given this order.

It was only later, when they returned to their home base, that they heard details. Wohlfahrt had run short of fuel to such an extent that, if he were to get back to his base at all, he had had to reckon in terms of minutes and seconds.

Kentrat set off to obey his new orders. An aircraft forced them to submerge hastily, but very quickly everybody agreed that it had probably been a German Condor, and *U.74* surfaced again.

Violent hail storms raged across the Atlantic, followed by equally violent squalls of rain and then more hail storms once again. The hail whipped like needles into the faces of the watch lashed to the bridge. The huge seas foamed up and over the top of the conning-tower. The bows would hover, poised like a lance, in the spray-laden air, as *U.74* was lifted on the back of a gigantic sea. Then down she would come with a thunderous crash, sending cascades of water shooting high into the air.

Night passed and the morning came. *U.74* submerged.

At 10.36 Hallet, on the hydrophones, reported sounds of a vessel sinking on the sound-gear. Kentrat rushed into the W/T office. He saw that Hallet's hands were trembling as they gripped the instruments. When Hallet saw his commander's gaze fixed on his hands, he hastily and shamefacedly withdrew them.

89

"Nothing to be ashamed of, Hallet. I fear we are both thinking the same thing . . . the *Bismarck*. . . ."

He was interrupted by a series of underwater explosions. *Bismarck?* Sunk? Or dared he hope it was one of her adversaries?

U.74 now found herself in the immediate vicinity of the action.

Shadowy forms could be discerned through the periscope, with the unmistakable outlines of battleships and cruisers.

To hold the ship at periscope depth was quite impossible. On the surface the seething, shimmering, green seas thundered and raged like mountains in torment. Whole worlds of water rose in the air and swept onwards leaving in their wake twisting whirlpools that swirled down far beyond periscope depth. *U.74* had the most powerful ships of the British Fleet in her sights, and yet. . . .

For the men in the U-boat it was a hard and testing time. Try as he would, Kentrat failed to get into a position from which he could fire. Not a single torpedo could he launch.

Wreckage now started to flash past the periscope's eye. Kentrat saw corpses. German or British? He didn't know. The lurid yellow of their inflated life-jackets shimmered in sinister contrast to the pallid faces they framed. More corpses—drowned, or torn to shreds by gunfire?

Slowly the British units vanished from his sight. They had turned and increased speed, first the battleships, then the cruisers and finally the last of the destroyers.

Kentrat could now surface. The sea was covered with corpses — they were German seamen.

Evening was already closing in when the bridge watch sighted a large yellow object bobbing up and down between the waves, a blob much bigger than a life-jacket. It was a Carley float and on it lay three German seamen. One of them waved as *U.74* came close alongside, but not close enough to be able to haul the men directly aboard.

"Give me a rope end," shouted Kentrat, "I'll swim across and fetch them."

"Sir, it's madness. You can't leave the ship in a sea like this," ventured the first officer.

" If I'm drowned, you can take her home yourself. But I can't order anybody else to dive into this!" Kentrat's mind was made up.

But in the meanwhile the three survivors had themselves leapt into the sea in the hopes that they would be swept into the clutches of the eager hands aboard *U.74*. It looked as though luck was with them. Two of them yelled with all their might and pointed to their comrade, "Fish him out first," they shouted. "He can't swim." But it did not turn out that way.

The men of *U.74*'s deck first grabbed one of the swimmers as a mighty wave swept him with a crash to the ship's side. By the time they had him safely on deck, he had fainted. Then, aided by good fortune, they hauled the second aboard, wounded and helpless. And finally out of this chaotic wilderness of tumultuous waves they plucked the last and third man, the non-swimmer. They had just got him alongside when there was an air-raid warning. Three of *U.74*'s crew dragged the last of the survivors to the conning-tower. Eager hands below stretched up to give what help they could.

"Quick, lads, quick," urged Kentrat. "Get a move on. You must get that man below."

But the rescued man started to struggle and shout. "Let me go! It doesn't matter what happens to me. You can't let the ship go to hell!"

"Stop it, you mad, barmy ——!" cursed one of his rescuers. "Aye, stop it, you silly ——!" echoed a second and they seized the exhausted man in such a grip of iron that he could struggle no more. . . .

"All clear. Aircraft approaching is a Condor!"

In peace and quiet the three survivors were now shepherded into the boat, if, that is, one can speak of peace and quiet in the midst of this whirlwind of wind and water. Officers' cabins were quickly made ready, and in them the men lay motionless and with staring eyes on the bunks. They were utterly exhausted and incapable of answering any questions. It was only ten hours later that the first of them opened his mouth.

It was only Manthey, the leading seaman, who was able to give a concrete and detailed account of events. The other two were still suffering from the shock of horror at the *Bismarck*'s last hours and the nightmare of their experiences on the Carley float.

Kentrat directed that their statements should be carefully recorded for the later information of the Admiralty in Berlin. According to Herzog, it was Admiral Luetjens who gave the order to abandon ship. Manthey, on the other hand, said he knew nothing about that; all he knew was that the anti-aircraft crews had been ordered to take cover. They took cover behind the two after-turrets, where they thought they would be safe. D turret was still firing and apparently continued to do so, even after the order to abandon and blow up the ship had been given.

While under cover of the turret some of the crew managed to collect a few rafts. But a direct hit blew all but two of them to bits; Herzog and Manthey found a third, jammed between the two heavy turrets. Just as they were about to launch the raft from behind D turret, a shell exploded close against the ship's side and blew Herzog, Manthey, their comrade and the raft into the sea. Close by another raft loaded with survivors was safely afloat. Then Dreyer, the official war correspondent, swam over and clambered aboard their raft. Dreyer had with him the film reels he had taken during the action and the ship's war diary which the Captain had entrusted to his care. At one moment, indeed, the Captain had considered the possibility of flying off these valuable documents in one of the battleship's aircraft. But direct hits had rendered both catapult and aircraft unserviceable.

Manthey stated that he had been able to see how the list of the *Bismarck* became constantly more pronounced. Then when their raft was lifted on the crest of a big wave, the *Bismarck* was gone. All that could be seen on the spot where she had been was a dense cloud of black smoke. Manthey had not heard any explosion. But he saw two cruisers, not far away, which were still firing.

Again and again their raft capsized. First the film reels were lost, and later Dreyer himself disappeared.

They had quickly lost sight of the other raft, and as they had neither food nor water their hopes of survival were meagre in the extreme. About mid-day a Condor flew over them. "Whether they had seen us or not we had no means of knowing. It was only late in the evening that a U-boat surfaced close beside us."

That was about all that could be extracted from the first statements made by the three survivors as they slowly recovered.

U.74 received a signal ordering her to return forthwith to Lorient. Thirty-six hours before they were due to reach the approach-buoy, Kentrat made a signal, according to regulations, giving his position. He was proposing to await further orders and then to submerge, when the chief engineer came up on the bridge. "The whole crew is at its last gasp, reeling like a lot of drunks," he reported. "We cannot possibly dive in this condition. The boat must first be thoroughly ventilated."

The great amount of water they had been shipping had caused the batteries to give off chlorine gas, and this was the cause of the dangerous state into which the crew had fallen.

Kentrat sent a signal saying that the ship was not in a fit condition to submerge and asked permission to enter port on the surface.

They had been proceeding for some four hours when Midshipman (E) Daehne, who was on duty in the control room, heard a series of sudden and rapid orders from the bridge to the helmsman.

"What the hell's up now?"

"That's all right, lad. Don't worry—he knows what he's doing up there," replied the chief engineer quickly.

At that moment there was a hefty explosion. And pretty close, too.

The first officer had suddenly caught sight of torpedo tracks coming straight at *U.74*; and immediately afterward he spotted the enemy submarine dead astern. *U.74* successfully avoided the torpedoes which sped harmlessly by and exploded with a roar at the end of their run.

At last *U.74* reached Lorient.

The three survivors from the *Bismarck* were ordered to report to Naval Group West Headquarters in Paris.

The crew of *U.74*, young Daehne included, were sent off on leave.

Young Daehne's mother was fussing over her son and putting a tasty meal on the table before him when a knife slipped from her hand and fell with a clatter to the floor. The lad leapt to his feet, trembling.

It had been his first trip in a U-boat.

And he was just twenty.

CHAPTER IX

THE HESSLER CONVOY AND THE BETRAYAL OF THE ST. ANTOA RENDEZVOUS

Situation Report—September 1941.

During the ninety-two days between the beginning of March and the end of May British losses rose to a most alarming degree. 142 ships, with a total tonnage of 818,000 tons, were sunk, most of them in bitter actions with convoys. The supply situation in Britain was becoming increasingly threatening. How desperate the situation had become was proved by the fact that the British did not hesitate to sacrifice valuable fighting units in the defence of their merchantmen. With the title "Anti-U-boat Escort", freighters, equipped with catapult launching gear and carrying an aircraft, shadowed the convoys on their way. Once the aircraft had been launched it had to be sacrificed, since it could not land either on the sea or on the "carrier" when the fuel tanks were empty.

However, the British did receive some extra support. Roosevelt gave permission for United States warships to shadow German U-boats, and in September he went so far as to permit them to take offensive action against any U-boat sighted between America and Iceland. In November American merchant ships were armed.

In Berlin there was talk of "Paukenschlag"—the code name for the sudden attack by U-boats on American shipping. As its name denotes this was to be unexpected and as concentrated and forceful as a drum roll. By this time there were between fifty and sixty U-boats on operations. Having already lost three of his aces, Schepke, Prien and Kretschmer, in May Doenitz also had to write off Lemp, who with U.110 followed the victims of his tragic mistake, the dead of the Athenia, into the twilight of the eternal depths. In the meanwhile, of the fifty-three U-boats operating in July not a single one was lost. Even so the U-boat arm was still not numerically strong enough to cope with the ever-increasing strength of the British anti-U-boat organisation in general and with the new frigates with their wide radius of action in particular. Though Doenitz fully realised this he was still reluctant to encroach in any

94

way on the time-devouring period devoted to the instruction and training of the crews of the newly constructed craft. U.67 affords a very typical example of this.

*   *   *

In Bremen *U.67* was nearing completion. Lieutenant Bleichrodt had been appointed to command her, with Pfeffer as his first officer, Trojer as second watchkeeping officer and Wiebe as chief engineer. Navigator Mathiesen, Quartermaster Foerster (Naval Reserve), Boatswain Klocke, Chief Engine Room Artificers Volmarie and Koch, twelve petty officers and twenty-six ratings formed the rest of the crew.

On 22 January, 1941, *U.67* was commissioned. The next months were spent in the Baltic where U-boat and crew were subjected to the most rigorous training and trials in order to prepare them for meeting the enemy.

It was not until August that *U.67*, now commanded by Lieut. Mueller-Stoeckheim, finally joined her flotilla in Lorient on the west coast of France.

It was not until 14 September, nine months after she had been commissioned, that *U.67* proceeded on her first operation.

On 18 September *U.67* was off Lisbon and on 21 September a radio signal was received. *U.107* (Lieutenant-Commander Hessler, Doenitz's son-in-law) reported at 08·00 a small convoy proceeding north and escorted by four destroyers. Because the night had been so clear, Hessler had been unwilling to attack. At 10·00 U-boat Headquarters issued its orders:

"Hessler to maintain contact and attack. *U.68* (Merten), *U.103* (Winter), and *U.67* (Mueller-Stoeckheim) to report position."

20.40 "Get after the Hessler convoy."

Wiebe, *U.67*'s chief engineer, wrote in his diary:

"Off we went. Commander explained position to the whole ship's company. This was it, at last, after we'd been in commission for something like nine months.

"Our position was off Tangiers 24 degrees west.

22 September 04.00. *U.107* reported four misses, and half an hour later said that her cooling water pump had broken down.

11.00 *U.107* reported damage repaired. 17.00 Lt.-Commander Mertens reported first success: 'During the night two ships—15,000 tons—sunk; one ship, 6,000 tons, torpedoed.'

95

"In the meanwhile *U.103* had gained contact with the convoy, which was to be attacked during the night by her and *U.68*.

19.20 Exercise dive. Position west of Agadir.

23 September 03·00. *U.107* reported: '7,000-tonner sunk, two further ships totalling 11,000 tons probably sunk. 6,000-tonner torpedoed. Four ships and escort in sight—course west.'

U.68 reported: 'Five torpedo explosions. There are now only three destroyers. One destroyer attacked—missed.'

09.30. 'Convoy in sight—am shadowing.'

18.20. Signal from *U.67* to U-boat Headquarters:

'Convoy consists of three or four vessels.' Later we found there were more. Course 045 degrees, speed 7·5 knots.

21.00. *U.107* reported she was again in contact with convoy.

"In the evening we went to action stations. Everything was in order and we were ready for anything. I sat in the control-room with the petty officer and a couple of others, playing cards. Although we were every bit as excited as the men, they seeing us sitting and playing so peacefully, came to the conclusion that things couldn't be half as touch-and-go and dangerous as they seemed. We stuck to this little subterfuge later, too. It was a great comfort to the spectators—and to us players, too!

Position Palma, 23·5 west.

"Our game was interrupted by a quiet crack followed by a hissing noise. It was a burst in the main ballast pumping system. It would have to happen just twenty minutes before we were due to attack!

00.10. A few minutes later I had to report to the commander that other minor defects had occurred and that the boat was now not fully fit to dive.

00.28. Attack. Three torpedoes. One hit. 7,000-tonner sunk. It was a copy-book attack, in spite of the three destroyers which fired off thirty star shells.

04.42. Signal to U-boat Headquarters: 'One merchantman, 7,000 tons, sunk.'

09.00. Report from *U.107*: '13,000-ton tanker sunk; one 8,000-tonner and one 5,000-tonner probably sunk. Have been driven off from convoy by two destroyers. All that remains of the convoy is one small steamer, four destroyers, three escort vessels.' "

Here the chief engineer of *U.67* ends his entry.

IN ALL WEATHERS

Top: A glorious morning. The sun makes a golden path across the Mediterranean

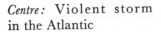

Centre: Violent storm in the Atlantic

Bottom: A patrol in the Atlantic with high seas and a heavy swell

Above: "Shooting" the sun

Right: Emmermann's U-boat taking a torpedo aboard at sea

Below: Air attack on a U-boat

The convoy had been broken up, hacked to pieces and destroyed. In attacks that continued all day, during nights, illumined by the transparent blue light of the star-shells and the brightly flickering flames, five ships, 42,000 tons, were sunk. Six more ships, 36,000 tons were hit by torpedoes, and probably sunk. One solitary vessel remained, protected by seven escorts.

On September 24 came a signal from Doenitz.

"Boats on the Hessler convoy—well done!"

*　　　*　　　*

The weeks that followed the attack on the Hessler convoy afford a very good illustration of the co-operation between U-boat Headquarters and the individual U-boat.

Doenitz had ordered *U.68* (Merten) and *U.111* (Kleinschmidt) to meet at the secret supply rendezvous, a bay in the small island of St. Antoa, the most northerly of the Canary Islands. Kleinschmidt was to hand over to Merten his remaining torpedoes, so that *U.68* could extend her operations into the South Atlantic, and was then to return home.

Merten, who had fired off all he had during the attack on the convoy, was the first of the two U-boats to set course for St. Antoa.

The sun was already setting as *U.68* slowly and cautiously approached the secret rendezvous. According to the international handbooks, the island was uninhabited. But as Merten entered the bay, Lauzernis, his new first officer, pointed somewhat resignedly to the shore. Beside a solitary and withered palm tree stood a cluster of wooden huts, and beside them lounged a number of brown figures. As he got closer Merten thought he could see that some of them were wearing some sort of uniform. Then the darkness fell.

Ashore fires started to flicker, camp fires, which seemed to confirm the assumption that a detachment of native troops were occupying the wooden huts.

Had a radio station been established on the island, Merten wondered, or perhaps a submarine cable station?

Be that as it may, the rendezvous had to be kept. The other boat, *U.111*, had reached the bay some hours before. Kleinschmidt was pressing Merten to get on with the business as quickly as possible.

97

"I've a most uneasy feeling in the pit of my stomach," said Kleinschmidt, and pointed a finger at the figures ashore.

"Get away with you, my dear fellow! Men don't have such things!" replied Merten in an attempt to distract the other's attention. Yet all the time, he too, as he confessed to himself, was not feeling quite happy. Even so, they had to remain in the vicinity, for it was here that *U.67* was to hand over a sick stoker for examination by *U.68*'s doctor and, if necessary, transfer him to the homeward-bound *U.111*. Nevertheless, thought Merten, the sooner we finish with the job, the better.

With the light of small cable lamps the transfer of torpedoes was quickly accomplished. Shortly after midnight *U.111* weighed anchor.

"You and your uneasy feelings, Kleinschmidt!" laughed Merten. But even as he said it he was conscious of an imperative urge to get his boat ready for sea as quickly as he possibly could. Was he, too, suffering from 'funny feelings'?

He gave the order to weigh anchor and proceed at slow speed out of the bay.

With a hand lamp Kokowski, the chief boatswain, made sure that everything on the upper deck was secure. His furry red beard all but outshone the red rays of the lamp in his hand. It was a weird and ghostly picture, quite out of harmony with the palm-fringed, peaceful surroundings of the island shore.

"All correct," said Kokowski, swinging his lamp in confirmation.

As he spoke there was a fearful subterranean roar and a gigantic column of water rose in the air, exactly at the spot where, a few minutes before, *U.68* and *U.111* had been lying at anchor. A moment or two later there was another roar.

Mines, or torpedoes fired from long range by some submarine that had been trailing them? Merten had no idea.

He was about to make a signal warning other U-boats when his radio operator appeared and told him the contents of a signal just made by *U.111* to U-boat Headquarters saying that half an hour after they had left two heavy explosions had been heard in the bay in St. Antoa. The report added that the lights, with the aid of which Merten had been working on his upper deck, had been extinguished by the explosion, and that it was presumed that Merten's boat had been sunk.

"That's the way it goes," said Merten. "You go to bed and the next morning you wake up dead and you don't know a damn thing about it!"

*   *   *

And what of *U.67*?

Here is what Wiebe's diary has to say on the subject:

27 September.

"We'd rigged up a shower on the upper deck, made out of a bit of fire-hose and the suction sieve of the emergency bilge hand-pump, and we were also the proud possessors of a truly feudal bath. We'd taken out one of the valves beside the conning-tower. And now we could sit on the pressure hull and let the fresh sea water spray all over us. All you require is just a little brain. I wonder why U-boat HQ's never thought of it!

"Position. Near St. Antoa.

"02.15. St. Antoa in sight. Horizon misty.

"03.49. Explosion like a depth charge or torpedo.

"03.59. Second explosion. Dived to use hydrophones.

"05.04. Surfaced. All we had heard was a very gentle noise of propellers. It was too dark for us to be able to find the other two U-boats at the rendezvous. The commander decided to lay off and return by daylight. We were not expected till to-morrow, anyway.

"06.17. Report from the bridge: Light of fires observed ashore.

"06.02. A shadow observed on the port bow. Position 90 degrees. Another torpedo boat? It was anybody's guess.

"The commander ordered port engine full ahead, helm hard a-starboard.

"No—it was not an MTB. The silhouette was a U-boat.

" 'Both engines—full astern! Hard a-port!'

"Even that was not sufficient. There was a pretty heavy crack.

"My own first reaction was—close all the watertight bulkheads.

"Thank the Lord, they were all closed. We had hit the U-boat close to its exhaust. Before she sank, she was recognised beyond doubt by the bridge watch to be a British submarine of the Clyde class. There had been tremendous confusion on the enemy's conning-tower.

"Signal to U-boat Headquarters: 'Warn all other U-boats that St. Antoa rendezvous is known to enemy.'

"Later we heard that *U.111*, too, had sighted the enemy submarine. We had suffered a fair amount of damage—nose crumpled; tubes one and two out of action. I went down wearing submarine escape gear, but I could not get at the tubes. The stern had been bent completely round to starboard. The bow caps of tubes one, two, and three were blocked. Tubes one and two were making water. The stem was still hanging by little more than the net-cutter.

"The commander reported the damage to U-boat Headquarters. Signal then received in reply: ' Can damage be made good with means available aboard?'

"*U.67*: 'No.'

" ' Return to base.' "

Merten (*U.68*), sniffed the morning breeze. After this last exchange of signals, which his radio operator had brought to his notice, he asked Doenitz whether he could take over torpedoes and, possibly, some fuel oil from *U.67*.

As Wiebe wrote the last sentence in his diary he made a wry grimace, realising that after her ramming exploit his own U-boat was out of it for the time being. "Merten ought to adopt a hamster or a vulture as his ship's emblem," he grumbled to himself. "The chap grabs everything he can lay his hands on." His mind went back to another occasion at home when Merten, thanks to his seniority, had bagged some beautifully burnished cylinder liners from under their very noses. "This time," he grunted, "as well as our torpedoes and fuel oil, he'll try and bag a complete engine."

It was not until 2 October that Merten was sighted.

Wiebe wrote in his diary:

"When we came within whispering distance, Merten asked the commander: 'How did you crumple your beautiful Aryan nose?'

" 'We were doing our best to follow your own brilliant example, Sir!' was the ready reply he got from Mueller.

"This was an unkind reference to an occasion when, on a tactical exercise, Merten had had the bad luck to ram another U-boat.

"Merten was content to ignore this somewhat caustic retort, particularly as his crew were grinning in sly appreciation.

"17.58 to 20.25. Submerged to avoid a sailing ship that was in radio communication with Dakar.

"21.17. Went alongside *U.68* which had dropped anchor.

"Started to transfer 300 gallons of lubricating oil. As no appropriate hose was available, it all had to be transferred in tins by hand—a laborious and lengthy business which took a full six hours. 50 gallons of distilled water, a ton of washing water and a few torpedoes followed.

"In the meanwhile *U.68*'s doctor had examined the stoker so we now turned to straightening up our crumpled nose and then we were ready to start on the homeward voyage.

"We had been able to give a helping hand to a sister ship. And gladly and willingly we had done so. But it riled us like hell to see our fuel oil and torpedoes being used like lozenges, as it were, to cure the other fellow's sore throat.

7 October.
"Homeward bound."

*   *   *

Thanks to the additional stores and ammunition she had taken aboard, *U.68* now found herself in a position to extend both the scope and the length of her operations. From the Radio Interception Service Merten had heard that a formation of British warships, one of them an aircraft carrier, was patrolling the area between Ascension Island and St. Helena, with the obvious object of intercepting German auxiliary cruisers and other surface vessels. To seek out this force and attack it seemed to Merten an object worthy of exertion. *U.68* first nosed her way into the Ascension roadstead and, as it proved to be empty, then turned towards Napoleon's island, where he hoped he might find the British ships lying at anchor.

In St. Helena harbour, however, there lay but one solitary tanker. Even so, argued Merten, if I can't attack the warships themselves, the sinking of their supply ship will be a significant blow to their fighting potentiality.

Under cover of the night Merten slipped in between the harbour installations and the tanker, unobserved by the sentries ashore. The troops could be heard singing and making merry in their barracks. Then Merten had another idea. He came out again and attacked the tanker from the seaward side. Just as the torpedoes leapt from their tubes a few men on the tanker caught sight of the shadowy outline of the U-boat, silhouetted against the sky line. They had just time to shout "Submarine!" and alert the quayside guard before the torpedoes struck their deadly blows. The tanker's cargo exploded and she sank at once in a pillar of flame reaching to high heaven. Merten turned away at full speed out of the harbour. Searchlights swept frantically in every direction, and the batteries fired salvo after indiscriminate salvo. But all in vain.

The story of the third partner at the rendezvous, on the other hand, had a tragic ending.

A few days after *U.111* had handed over her torpedoes, the commander of H.M.S. *Lady Shirley*, A. H. Callaway, sighted the conning-tower of a U-boat as she was about to submerge ten miles away. This occurred 220 miles off Teneriffe. The British ship steamed to the spot where the U-boat had dived and dropped a shower of depth charges. The badly hit U-boat was compelled to surface, and the British immediately opened fire with every available gun. *U.111* returned the fire. H.M.S. *Lady Shirley* suffered grievous damage. There were dead and wounded on both sides. But after a bare fifteen minutes of desperate combat the U-boat suffered a fatal hit and sank.

Eight Germans, Kleinschmidt among them, had been killed in the fight. The remainder of the gallant crew, forty-four men, were taken prisoner.

CHAPTER X

U.81 SINKS AN AIR SQUADRON
U.331 DESTROYS THE BATTLESHIP *BARHAM*

Situation Report—Autumn 1941.
At the outbreak of war Italy, with 120 U-boats at her disposal,
possessed by far the greatest submarine fleet in the world. But it was
quickly realised, after the occupation of the Balkans and Crete, that it
was essential to put German U-boats into the Mediterranean. In
training tactics and offensive spirit these were infinitely superior to their
Italian counterparts. It was also hoped that this would compel the
British to further disperse their forces and thus put the German boats
in a position to attack those convoys which passed through the Mediter-
ranean. This, admittedly, involved a weakening of the fighting strength
of the Atlantic group. However, Raeder, who was an ardent protagonist
of this Mediterranean intervention, was certain that he would thereby
gain both a military and a psychological advantage over the British.
The passivity hitherto shown by the Italian submarine fleet, an inertia
due less to technical shortcoming than to a lack of morale, had led the
British to underestimate the organisation of anti-U-boat defence in the
Mediterranean. Thus it was considered unlikely that Raeder would
take the responsibility either of withdrawing U-boats from the battle
of the Atlantic or of exposing them to the hazards of an attempt to
force the strongly guarded Straits of Gibraltar. The impressive successes
scored in this very area are well illustrated by the following account
of the experiences of U.81 (*Lieut.-Commander Guggenberger*).

*　　　*　　　*

Approaching Gibraltar.
The night was dark with a new moon. A few clouds swung
lazily across the sky. The swell rose and fell with gentle regularity.
Hugging the coast was a small steamer, ablaze with lights—a
Spaniard. Otherwise there was not a ship to be seen.
But peace—in the vicinity of Gibraltar—was a deceptive thing.
A thick girdle of destroyers, submarine-chasers and aircraft pro-

tected the fortress and the harbour with its concourse of battle-ships and cruisers.

The Straits of Gibraltar still remained one of the vital arteries of British shipping—in spite of Rommel in North Africa, in spite of the German U-boats already cruising in the Mediterranean and in spite of the potential might of the Italian navy.

Inside the U-boat there was absolute quiet. The men on watch kept an alert eye on their instruments. The rest of the crew were sleeping. The look-outs on the bridge seemed to have become part of the boat itself, so harmoniously did they conform to the slightest motion of the ship. Only the automatic sweep of their night glasses, balanced delicately at their finger-tips, showed that these men were alive.

U.81 had long ago had her baptism of fire. On the trail of Allied shipping she had slipped into the narrowest and deepest bays around Murmansk and had taken part in more than one attack on Atlantic convoys.

Guggenberger and his navigator were poring over the chart of the Straits of Gibraltar spread out before them.

"Our best approach would be from the south-west, Sir, I think," said the navigator. "It's the direction from which they'll least expect us to come."

"I agree," replied Guggenberger. "On the surface we can get along three times as fast and, if the necessity should arise, we shall have ample depth of water below us in which to submerge. We'll wait till the tide turns and it can give us a helping hand."

That was his plan for forcing the Straits. Nothing definite had been laid down on the matter, and Doenitz had preferred to leave it to the discretion of the individual commanders.

At half speed *U.81* approached the Straits. "Second watch to be relieved individually at 23.30," ordered Guggenberger. The helmsman passed on the order in a low voice. The control-room rating woke the men, who quickly and quietly prepared to go on duty—leather jacket, glasses, cap, gloves, ready. . . .

The second watchkeeping officer, who was to relieve the navigator, appeared on the bridge, sniffed at the nearby land and cleared his throat "Bloody close," he muttered. He said no more, but seized his glasses and started to polish them. He glanced up at the sky and then disappeared aft. After a few minutes he crawled forward again. His eyes had at last accustomed themselves to the darkness.

"Taking over, navigator."

"Very good, Sir."

The U-boat was about to attempt to force the Straits. She was vibrating gently, nosing her way smoothly through the sea.

Meanwhile in the control-room the navigator had looked at the chart—navigator to commander—"Alter course, Sir."

Guggenberger had all the requisite changes in his head. "Steer 080 degrees!" he ordered.

Thanks to his correct tactical handling of his boat he thus succeeded in breaking through the outer ring without interference from the enemy. On the port side rose the mountains of Spain, clearly visible, and to starboard, dimly silhouetted against the dark night sky, the hills of North Africa.

The Straits were now becoming narrower.

Shafts of light were reflected in long shimmering lanes across the calm waters. The lights to starboard came from the port of Tangier, those ahead from neutral ships, probably Spanish or Portuguese; those to port awoke among the older members of the crew memories of their experiences in Spain.

"Darkened ship to port, Sir," reported the look-out.

"Thanks! For the moment I'm not interested in sinking anything," muttered Guggenberger. He gave his orders for a fresh alteration of course to bring him well clear of the stranger.

The tide was now very noticeable and *U.81* was making good progress.

Tariffa, the narrowest part of the Straits, was already clearly visible.

Seconds, minutes passed, and each one seemed an eternity.

The sea gurgled gently over the bows.

Tariffa was coming nearer and inexorably nearer.

And at last it lay on the port beam.

"Shall I rouse the third watch, Sir?" asked the first officer.

"Not yet. The less disturbance hereabout the better." Guggenberger had no fears that the men on watch had got over-tired; the excitement and adventure of forcing the Straits had kept them all wide-awake and alert.

"Tariffa on the port beam."

Although *U.81* kept to the exact middle of the Straits the shore was so close that it seemed easy to pitch a pebble on to the beach. The revolving light of the lighthouse high above them seemed more like a searchlight, and each time it came round it illuminated the whole ship. The lookouts on the bridge were so dazzled by it that for a moment Guggenberger wondered whether he ought not to dive. He decided, however, to remain on the surface. "Steady! Just keep your eyes skinned. And above all keep them on the sea."

The actual Straits were quickly cleared. But the most difficult phase was now only just beginning. To port the land had started to recede as it swept back into the bay of Gibraltar. The famous fortress showed up jet black against the dark blue of the night sky.

What could those lights ahead be? Ah! They came from a line of boats strung right across the Straits. The important question was—had they got nets or hawsers stretched out between them?

U.81 veered a little to port.

The lights came nearer and nearer. Guggenberger held course mid-way between two of the boats. He reached them. Nothing happened. He was through, and very soon the buoys and boats were well astern.

"God grant you deep, refreshing sleep, gentlemen," laughed the second officer derisively. His laugh worked wonders. It was like the key to the door of confidence.

Gibraltar—the Rock—was now astern, rising abruptly and menacingly into the night.

The Straits widened out and visibility improved. Once more silhouettes loomed up ahead. Another line of boats? In fact, two destroyers, patrolling to and fro, steaming first towards each other and then turning and steaming in opposite directions.

U.81 made for a point midway between them as they gradually drew further and further apart. The destroyers saw nothing, suspected nothing.

U.81 was through.

The way to the Mediterranean lay open before her.

U.81 turned in to sleep.

Not all the U-boats got through so easily. More than half of them ran into trouble.

As dawn came *U.81* submerged.

A signal from the Radio Interception Service reported that a British squadron consisting of the battleship *Malaya*, the aircraft-carrier *Ark Royal*, the carrier *Furious* and escorting destroyers, which had attacked a German convoy en route for Africa, was now steaming on a westerly course.

U-boat Headquarters ordered *U.81* and *U.205* (Lieutenant Bürgel), to attack.

"If we find them at all, we ought to find them just about here, near Gibraltar. The information is already five hours old, and there are a dozen courses they could have followed in the meanwhile," thought Guggenberger. *U.81* accordingly turned back towards Gibraltar, back into the lion's mouth. The wind had freshened, and now a bit of a sea was running, short, choppy, and unfamiliar.

Aircraft forced *U.81* to dive.

13 November—a Friday, of course—dawned.

Aircraft . . . alarm . . . crash dive. Destroyers . . . alarm . . . submerge.

More aircraft.

According to Guggenberger's reckoning, the British ships should reach this spot at about 15.00 hours.

14.10 Aircraft approaching from the east.

14.11 *U.81* at periscope depth.

14.15 More aircraft approaching from the east.

14.20 Foremast of a battleship appears over the horizon.

Shortly afterwards Guggenberger sighted the three great warships steaming squarely towards him.

Fritz Guggenberger's reactions were reflected by his train of thought:

"What's the point of all this David and Goliath stuff? Why not beat it while the going's good? It's too easy—just one little order and you can easily think up a plausible explanation later. After all, no one but you aboard this ship knows that you've sighted those so-and-so's over there. . . ."

Guggenberger was pale and deadly earnest. His lips, tight pressed, conformed to the mathematical formula of a straight line—the shortest distance between two points.

"Action stations!"

As he gave the order all other thoughts and preoccupations flew out of his head. His sense of duty gripped him.

"Commander to ship's company. We are about to attack a British battle group."

The force was approaching nearer and nearer. It was steaming echeloned to port, with the *Malaya* leading followed by *Ark Royal* and then *Furious*. Six destroyers with foaming bow waves formed a protective screen, the white fountains giving proof of the high speed at which these greyhounds were travelling.

An aircraft came roaring down, aiming, seemingly direct for the U-boat. Guggenberger waited till it passed and then raised his periscope for a brief second.

But the aircraft's crew were not thinking about U-boats. They were delighted at the prospect of being home again soon, and the pilot was just stunting for sheer joy.

Guggenberger gave a hasty glance round. He had no time to bother about aircraft. What were the destroyers doing? One of them was bearing down directly on the U-boat. Damn and blast it! And the battleships? Grand! They had zigzagged! And the destroyer, following suit, passed harmlessly astern of him.

Where were the rest of them? All clear! Right!

"Down . . . up!"

A quick look round, a pause.

"Down . . . up . . . down! Keep her at 45 feet!"

"Tubes one to four ready!"

From the fire control the estimated course was passed to the torpedoes. Then the bows of one of the ship's came in view in the periscope.

"Salvo. . . ."

"Down . . . up . . . down . . . both slow! . . . down . . . up . . . fire! . . . down . . . *down*! Half speed ahead both!"

Whoof! With a coughing sound the first torpedo left the tube, and the remaining three followed at regular intervals.

"All torpedoes running!"

The ship, relieved of a considerable burden, at once began to rise. It requires a great deal of practice, a very cool head and a steady hand to prevent a U-boat from breaking surface when a four fan has been fired. The Commander leapt to the control-room. *U.81* continued to rise.

"All hands for'ard! Jump to it!"

Only very slowly the stern began to rise.

34 feet . . . 33 feet.

"Crash dive to 300 feet!"

The U-boat tumbled down into the depths. Why hadn't there been any depth charges?

At 360 feet she levelled off.

"How many explosions were there?" asked Guggenberger, now thoroughly exhausted. He had so concentrated on executing the dive that he had not even heard how many hits had been made.

"Two, Sir. Two hits," answered the first officer. At slow speed the U-boat slipped away. Why no depth charges came down no one could make out. Both radio operators were seated at the hydrophones. One of them pointed to the scale of his apparatus.

"Here—a loud noise, receding. Destroyers here . . . here . . . and here."

Guggenberger could not make out exactly what had happened. Two hits, eh? Well, since the torpedoes had been set for sixteen feet, it must have been one of the big ships that had been hit, for at that depth the torpedoes would have passed beneath the destroyers.

From nearby Gibraltar fresh destroyers appeared on the scene. They too, started quartering and using their hydrophones. On the submarine's hydrophones the Asdic could be clearly heard. It was a wonder that the operators remained so cool and calm.

"Destroyer closing on the port side."

Down came the first depth charges.

U.81 shook.

Nothing serious. She slid slowly on her way.

Again the destroyers stopped.

Now their Asdic could be heard, without recourse to instruments, by everybody. The situation now became critical.

"Destroyer closing on the port side," reported the operator.

"Full ahead both!" ordered Guggenberger.

Immediately above the U-boat the depth charges fell crashing into the sea. The second destroyer had arrived on the spot. The splash of the depth charges was plainly audible. A whole carpet of charges had been dropped directly above the U-boat and they were sinking down deeper and deeper. Guggenberger set his stop watch going.

Each second that passed brought the depth charges ten feet nearer. Already they had reached a depth of well over one hundred and fifty feet. The U-boat was proceeding at maximum speed. Would she manage to slip away from beneath the deadly carpet coming down on her?

Then the crashes started. *U.81* bent like a sword of tempered steel. There was a splintering of glass. Electric light bulbs leapt out of their sockets.

And then the game began again from the beginning. The single combat between destroyer and U-boat continued.

Guggenberger had quickly come to the conclusion that even though the destroyer commanders were not sly old foxes, they certainly knew their job. More than one of their runs in had been unpleasantly accurate. And the depth charges had been both very numerous and unpleasantly close. Even so, the distance between the U-boat and the destroyers continued to increase steadily. And at the end of three hours the destroyers dropped their one hundred and thirtieth depth charge—two and a half miles away.

The coxswain had counted them. He always did, and he used prune stones to keep the score. He was always indefatigable in his chewing to produce the requisite number of stones. He'd put up some pretty shows on previous occasions. But this time the demands had proved beyond his powers. And before the final whistle went, he was replete.

*　　　*　　　*

On 14 October the British Admiralty officially admitted the loss of *Ark Royal*. Guggenberger first heard of his success in a signal from U-boat Headquarters.

What, however, was not known at the time was that Guggenberger had also hit the *Malaya* below her forward turret, and that the battleship had been towed the twenty miles into Gibraltar harbour. The damage she had suffered was severe but she did take further active part in the war.

Ark Royal, which was commissioned shortly before the outbreak of war, was a ship of 22,600 tons and carried seventy-two aircraft. She had a complement of 2,000 naval ratings and airmen and was commanded by Captain Maund. Curiously enough Maund had served in every aircraft carrier that had been sunk to date. This was seized upon by the British Press as a bad omen.

According to British figures *Ark Royal* cost three and a quarter million pounds to build—and her armament and the seventy-two aircraft she carried must have swallowed up another million or so.

The fighting value of *Ark Royal*, from the air point of view, corresponded to that of an air squadron; in terms of artillery it was equal to that of a well-equipped anti-aircraft and artillery regiment. Her high speed of 30 knots, more than double the speed of the U-boat which attacked her and four times the underwater speed of a submarine.

It must not, however, be overlooked that the British force had also included the 22,450-ton carrier *Furious* and the battleship *Malaya*. The *Ark Royal*, incidentally, was lost during the thirteenth month after leaving Britain, on the thirteenth of the month—and on a Friday to boot.

But it had, after all, been one of her aircraft which had scored the fatal hit on *Bismark*'s steering gear. In addition *Ark Royal* was regarded as the most enterprising of all Britain's aircraft carriers. Between October 1939 and February 1940 alone, her aircraft had covered four and a half million square miles of the Atlantic Ocean.

*   *   *

Among the thirty-six U-boats which were detailed for duty in the Mediterranean at the end of 1941 was *U.331*, commanded by Freiherr von Thiesenhausen.

To the east of Raz Assaz, where the coast from Tobruk turns south towards Sollum and Bardia, *U.331* was waiting for a target, on this her second operation.

For days on end she had been surfacing by night and had remained submerged during the day. But nothing had shown up except aircraft, which drove the U-boat underwater each time she had surfaced during daylight. *U.331*'s orders were to try and prevent British supplies reaching Tobruk. These supplies were being sent from Alexandria by warship or in small, heavily escorted convoys. For at least a month the British had been trying to get a convoy through from Gibraltar to Alexandria.

On 25 November the radio operator aboard the submerged *U.331* picked up a faint noise on the hydrophones. It appeared to be coming from a formation of ships somewhere to the north.

Thiesenhausen rose to periscope depth to have a look round. In the Mediterranean conditions vary so greatly that one can never be sure whether noises of this kind are coming from close by or from afar off.

Through the periscope nothing was to be seen; the surface of the sea was empty, and in the sky there was no sign of any of those troublesome bees. The commander gave the order to surface, and just as he opened the conning-tower hatch he saw an aircraft, almost on top of them.

Alarm!

But the aircraft failed to spot *U.331* and no bombs came down.

For the next few hours the U-boat remained submerged. At moderate speed she proceeded in the direction of the echoes, which now seemed to have veered a little to the north-east. What sort of a formation was it—warships or a convoy? That was the big question.

If it were a convoy, its presence would certainly have been reported, and Doenitz would have concentrated all available U-boats against it.

If they were warships, it was more than likely that Thiesenhausen would fail to catch even a glimpse of them. Be that as it may, the echoes were strong and audible, and the great thing was to see that they remained so.

At full speed *U.331* proceeded in the required direction, which was now N.E. There was still not a thing to be seen. Weather conditions were ideal. A light north-east wind ruffled the surface in a way that made it very difficult for any hostile aircraft to pick up the thin wake left by a cautiously raised periscope; and the shadows of clouds, scudding across the surface of the water, further confused the issue.

At last at 14.30 something was sighted to starboard. At first it seemed no more than a little smear above the horizon. But ten minutes later needles appeared on both sides of the smear.

Destroyer masts! So that was that!

In the yellowish mist a darker kernel was beginning to take shape, big ships, obviously, but it was not clear whether they were warships or merchantmen. One thing, however, was certain; there, to the E.N.E. was a big formation of ships sailing south. In spite of the high speed at which the U-boat was travelling, the concourse began to fade from view. It must have altered its course to east. So, thought Thiesenhausen, they're probably warships either zig-zagging or altering formation. But there was always the danger that they would disappear completely from sight and that a unique opportunity of attack would be lost.

Thiesenhausen rose to the surface to make full use of the surface speed of his diesels. *U.331* hastened eastwards in pursuit of the formation.

A MERCILESS WAR

Right: Twenty-five thousand feet of wood, destined for England, fly into the air when a torpedo strikes home

Centre: The last man to leave a sinking destroyer

Bottom: Survivors

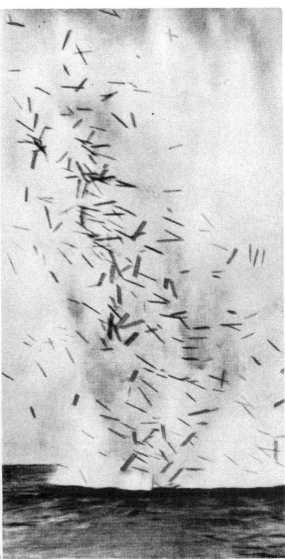

IN THE MEDITERRANEAN

Top: *U.77* off the coast of Palestine. Her forward tanks are flooded and she is ready to dive. The eight white rings on the barrel of the gun denote the sinking of eight sailing ships off Beirut

Centre: Against the background of the Rock of Gibraltar, from left to right, *Ark Royal, Malaya, Renown*

Bottom: *Ark Royal*, after she had been torpedoed by Guggenberger. The crew is being taken off by a destroyer

To the south, but a long way away, was another aircraft, but it, too, failed to spot the U-boat.

Then, suddenly, the mist became stronger, clearer and more sharply defined. The warships had again zigzagged and were now steering a westerly course, directly towards the advancing U-boat. Then things began to happen quickly.

Following some instinctive impulse Thiesenhausen swung his boat through an arc of well-nigh 350 degrees. Only later did it become apparent how important the resultant loss of time was when seconds meant the difference between life and death. "Crash dive! Action stations!" were the commander's next orders. At last there was "something doing". The nervous tension which had held the whole ship's company in its grip all day—though an outsider would probably not have noticed it—now relaxed, or rather was replaced by a different kind of strain.

Each man had his own job on which he had to concentrate, which claimed his whole, undivided attention and which left him no time to think about anything else.

Now that there was "something doing" Thiesenhausen, too, became calm and relaxed. It was just after 16.00, about tea-time for the chaps over there.

The weather was ideal for an attack. The sun stood in the south-west, behind the U-boat. The periscope was practically invisible; and so it had to be.

The U-boat and the formation were approaching each other rapidly on reciprocal courses. Through the periscope three battleships could be recognised. They were steaming line ahead and were protected on each side by four destroyers steaming line abreast. Signals were being exchanged, obviously denoting a change of formation. The two destroyers on the port side and nearest to the leading battleship increased speed and raced ahead. They were a bare 500 yards apart, and *U.331*, submerged, was heading midway between them. Every now and then her periscope emerged for a brief flash a hand's breadth above the slightly choppy surface. The commander watched each of the destroyers in turn until both were on the beam. "Down periscope!"

The duty of following the movements of the two destroyers now devolved upon the operator on the hydrophones. When he reported them abaft the beam, Thiesenhausen again raised his

113

periscope. Both destroyers had continued on their course. They were away and no longer a source of danger.

Now for the battleships. The U-boat was by now fairly close to them and still on a reciprocal course.

The torpedo tubes had long ago been made ready. Everything was absolutely quiet, concentrated.

Then—the first battleship! And what a magnificent ship she was!

The U-boat was so close to her that she overflowed beyond the periscope's field of vision. Thiesenhausen did his best to turn hard towards her. But with the first ship the manœuvre failed. The combined speed of the two vessels was too great.

"Keep your eye on the whole picture," Thiesenhausen abjured himself.

"Quicker, man, quicker. Have all three battleships passed me? Or haven't they?" Was that really the leading battleship? If so, where were the others?

"Up periscope!"

A quick look. A steel colossus of rather antiquated design was bearing down mightily on him. What class, what ship she was, there was no time to see. Not that it mattered much. The important thing was to hit her.

The U-boat would have to haul off a little, or she would be too close. Then . . . with every means he had Thiesenhausen turned.

The orders cracked out like blows from a hammer. The battle-ship was in the sights and getting bigger every second.

"Stand by to fire!"

Everything was now ready. Only the angle of fire still remained too great. More than 90 degrees.

By Neptune's head—what a target!

"Salvo . . . Fire."

Swish . . . swish . . . swish . . . swish! Like a demonstration shoot the four torpedoes leapt at regular intervals from their tubes. With one last, swift sweep of his periscope the commander had just time to see the third battleship, a mighty grey mass of steel turn and bear directly down on him.

Down—down as quick and as far as possible! It was a devilish awkward situation for the chief engineer. The ship was at half speed, and four torpedoes had been discharged.

The U-boat at first responded, and down went her nose. But

then in spite of the chief's best endeavours she started to rise again. But he knew his job. Everyone on board felt his stomach sink as the ship continued to rise.

"Conning-tower's broken surface!" shouted the chief engineer from the control-room. As surely as thunder follows lightning only one possible thin gcould now follow—a collision.

"Clear conning-tower! Jump to it!"

Chief Quartermaster Walter hurled a few odds and ends into the control-room and closed the hatch between it and the conning-tower. Thiesenhausen hoped that, if he were rammed, only the upper conning-tower would be damaged, and the pressure hull would escape unscathed.

The control-room was now the scene of the most tense and desperate concentration. First three, then a fourth explosion. That must have meant hits on the targets. But at the moment even that seemed of little importance. Then the churning of propellors audible . . . the third battleship. The really important thing was to get down.

Still no collision.

At last the U-boat began to submerge again. It had seemed like an eternity. And, indeed, for forty-five seconds *U.331* had been on the surface, and the third battleship, *Valiant*, had done her utmost to destroy her.

The needles of the depth gauge flickered past the 90, 120 and 150 foot marks. At 220 feet they moved more slowly. At 250 they stopped. Something, obviously, was amiss. Feverishly some explanation was sought. Desperate situations demand desperate remedies, and they banged against the glass and tubing. In vain.

Thiesenhausen suddenly remembered a previous situation and a possible explanation occurred to him.

"What's the reading on the for'ard depth-gauge?" he asked.

With horror all eyes were riveted on the scale. Some men swallowed noisily, as fear gripped them by the throat.

820 feet! ! !

Never before had *U.331* been as deep as that. Indeed, no German U-boat had ever gone to such a depth.

There followed yet another period of almost unendurable tension which Thiesenhausen broke with a calm, almost monotonous voice. For the space of a heart-beat he thought of Otto

Kretschmer, who had been his teacher and master. What would Otto the Silent have done in a devilish situation like this?

"Ah! well," he said nonchalantly, "we must just wait and see whether the old cylinder can stick it—or not."

But the pressure hull held out. There were no leaks anywhere. *U.331* was the first U-boat to have been constructed in the private yard, Nordseewerke, in Emden. The ship's company could well be proud of their shipbuilders.

At last the chief engineer regained control. He succeeded in bringing *U.331* to a more "civilised" depth. Even so, at 750 feet she was still very deep. 820 feet was certainly a record. It meant that every square centimetre of the pressure hull was exposed to a pressure of more than half a hundredweight.

Thiesenhausen grinned. "There's this about it—no one can get at us down here!"

"Did you hit the destroyer, Sir?" asked the chief engine room artificer, who came striding into the control-room. Then for the first time it was explained to him that the target had been a battleship. There had simply been no time to give the ship's company any information on either the attack or the target. The range, when the torpedoes were fired, had been 1,200 yards.

Very few depth charges had been dropped. A few could still be heard in the distance.

Without being seriously molested by any destroyer, *U.331* turned north.

*   *   *

Here are a few more interesting details concerning the loss of the *Barham*, gathered by the author from the other side.

The signals that had been observed by *U.331* had, indeed, denoted a change of formation, and the two destroyers had been in the process of acting upon them. The three battleships, *Queen Elizabeth*, *Barham* and *Valiant*, which had been steaming in line ahead had to turn slightly to port to get into the newly ordered echelon formation. As she started to turn, *Valiant*, the last in the line of the three battleships, observed a violent explosion on the middle ship, *Barham*. *Valiant*, then, was already turning to port when suddenly the conning-tower of a U-boat broke surface on her starboard side, about 130 yards away, seven degrees to starboard, and crossing her course to starboard. It remained visible for

forty-five seconds. The captain of *Valiant* immediately gave the order:
"Hard starboard—full ahead!" hoping to ram the U-boat.
The U-boat disappeared, however, before she could be got at.
Had the torpedo attack occurred just a little early, the U-boat
would, at that short range, undoubtedly have been rammed.

Barham had in the meanwhile turned hard to starboard and
then, four minutes and forty-five seconds after she had been hit,
disintegrated in a series of terrific explosions. Of the four torpedoes
fired at her, three had hit their mark. One of them must have hit
the magazine. That and that alone can have been the fourth
explosion which had been heard aboard *U.331* and which had
swiftly sealed the fate of the 31,110-ton battleship.

A year later, when *U.331* was lost, Thiesenhausen and his men
became prisoners of war. One afternoon—it was in January 1943—
he was taken from the Interrogation Camp to the Admiralty in
London to be interviewed. On the way he had tea in the crowded
Regent Palace Hotel with the Air Force and naval officers
escorting him, just as he might have done in times of peace. They
all got on splendidly together, particularly so because his hosts
made no attempt whatever to persuade Thiesenhausen to give
away any military secrets. Yet even so, it was a test, a sort of
psychological experiment to try, in an ostensibly friendly atmosphere, to analyse the character and outlook of a U-boat commander.

*   *   *

More light is shed on submarine warfare in the Mediterranean
by Lieutenant Schonder who was aboard *U.77* at this time. He
was later, as commander of *U.200*, lost off Iceland:

Owing to the extreme activity of the British air reconnaissance,
operating for the most part beyond the reach of German fighters,
our U-boats were unable to operate by day on the surface off
the hostile coast of Africa. Apart from that, destroyers galore
and a whole heap of other patrol ships were sculling round these
narrow waters. And these little fellows, of course, took full
advantage of the fact that the U-boats were waiting for a bigger catch.

Often, and particularly during the long summer days in the
Mediterranean, operations off the coast necessitated remaining
submerged for fourteen, even sixteen, hours. That meant that a
commander had to take steps to ensure that his men were not

exhausted beyond endurance. In spite of many clever installations the air in a U-boat quickly becomes foul. The commander therefore has to see that all work and all movement is reduced to a minimum. There must be very little cooking also for the fumes add considerably to the vitiation of the air. In practice this means that the men have to go without hot meals. The mid-day meal is transferred to the middle of the night, when the boat can proceed on the surface. Day becomes night, night becomes day, and the afternoon becomes morning. In the "morning" the air is thick; it hangs in a clammy, damp mass that you can all but grasp with your hands. It flows like melted gelatine over everybody and everything. The walls sweat and run with water. Everything is clammy and damp. Silver pearls glisten on the men's foreheads and their eyes are sunken deep in their pale faces, framed in a stubble of beard.

For those not on watch, no orders to keep still are required. Everyone is so exhausted, so utterly fagged out by the heat.

In this way the day passed—or, rather, the "U-boat night"— in the Mediterranean. Only after the sun had set did Schonder prepare to surface. The cook prepared breakfast, a fine, solid breakfast, that would be eaten in the early hours of the evening. It was a topsy turvy life that the men were being called upon to lead. Soon after the sun had disappeared came the welcome order: "Blow tanks". Wheels turned and whirred, and a hissing, muttering noise filled the boat. The commander was the first up the ladder in the conning-tower. He opened the hatch.

In a moment he was out, casting a keen look round the clear, starlit night. To port stretched a long, thin shadow—the coast of Africa. The beautiful fresh air could be heard rushing into the U-boat, and all but audible, too, were the eager lungs of the crew as they inhaled in copious, hungry gulps. The ventilator fans whirred, driving the sweet, clean air into every nook and cranny of the boat.

And the red light was burning brightly—as usual!

But on one occasion at least this routine was disturbed.

Suddenly the commander paused, motionless. He turned to the officer of the watch.

"D'you hear anything?"

"I thought I did, Sir. A plane? . . ."

"You bet it's a plane."

"Alarm! Diving stations!"

The rumble of the engines in the sky drowned the trampling of the men as they descended the conning-tower. A shadow swept across the ship, and for a second the light of the stars was cut off. A short whistling noise, a hissing splash nearby that hurled spray all over the commander, who had remained fast, clutching the rim of the conning-tower. His legs were swept away beneath him. The U-boat leapt bodily out of the water, twisted and seemed about to burst asunder. Below, the glass faces of the gauges and indicators were smashed to pieces. The men off duty were hurled violently from their bunks. The lights went out. Very soon the flickering beams of torches revealed a scene of wild desolation.

"Stop! Stop the dive!" shouted the commander. He had no intention of exposing his ship to further bombs while she was diving or just as she completed her dive. He had decided to try and drive this pestilential bee away with his A.A. armament.

The hard, staccato crack of machine guns then started.

"Ammunition! Up ammunition!" the men on deck shouted to those below. And the shout re-echoed throughout the boat. But the ammunition supply was cut off. The watertight door separating the control-room from the rest of the boat had jammed. The chief engineer was shut in. Others were there with him, tearing and wrenching at the bulkhead.

"Now—heave! All together, heave!"

Slowly, reluctantly, the bulkhead opened. However, another obstacle presented itself. The conning-tower ladder was down. With swift, sure hands the men set to, to repair the damage.

At last the way was clear. As a matter of fact, it was still only a matter of seconds since the attack had occurred. But the work had been expertly handled, with a maximum of speed and a minimum of fuss. Ammunition was being passed by hand up the conning-tower. The A.A. guns had a good target. All they had to do was to aim off the silver threads of the tracer with which the aircraft was bombarding the ship. Hastily the Britisher slipped out of the field of fire of the German A.A. gunners. He dropped a few flares over the scene of the attack, only to see to his chagrin that the German U-boat was afloat and proceeding calmly on its way.

Within *U.77* light had been restored, and the men had a look around. Some of them looked pretty pale. They'd had a real slice of luck. With their sleeves they swept the beads of sweat from their faces. Shoes crunched everywhere over splintered glass. Reports from various parts of the boat began to reach the commander.

"We aren't fit to submerge," reported the chief engineer.

"Do you think your men can do the necessary repairs, Chief?"

"We might, Sir. But it may well take a long time."

"Right! Go to it!"

The bombs had fallen within fifteen feet of the U-boat, had exploded at a depth of some sixty feet directly beneath her, and had shaken her from stem to stern.

"I'd like to shake hands with the lads who built this boat," said the commander.

"And I'd like to shake yours, Sir," the men heard the chief engineer say quietly. "If you hadn't stopped the dive, we shouldn't be here."

The radio was out of action, so Schonder was unable to inform his base that he was moving to another sector, and this nearly had disastrous results.

At eleven o'clock in the morning, *U.77* was again in the midst of shrieking, whistling bombs—a shattering and breath-taking experience. To right and left, ahead and astern, all round her, gigantic spouts of water rose out of the sea. Then those aboard recognised the aircraft which were attacking them, flying at a great height. They were five German JU88's, which were flying to Africa, and had spotted the wake of a submarine.

No German U-boat had been reported to them as being in this sector, and at the great height at which they were flying it was of course impossible for the airmen to differentiate between German and British submarines. It was sheer good fortune that the bombs were no worse than near misses.

U.77 proceeded on her way. She was attacked by a British submarine. The torpedoes were heard quite plainly on board. But they, too, missed their target.

Night came. Yet another submarine attack.

A British torpedo leapt out of the water like a playful dolphin. It landed with a crash on the afterdeck, bucked back into the sea with its tail unit all twisted and disappeared.

"Well, my lads," sighed Schonder with relief, "the good God must certainly have kept *all* His fingers crossed for us on this trip."

CHAPTER XI

NEW BRITISH DEFENSIVE TACTICS

Situation Report—December 1941.
Vice-Admiral Gilbert Stephenson had assumed the difficult task of training the crews of the new anti-submarine vessels. He had selected for the purpose the harbour of Tobermory on the west coast of Scotland. Hundreds of A/S craft passed through this special school of instruction. The British realised that, in spite of the urgency of the situation, the men must be given a thorough training. The same applied to the air crews of Coastal Command and to the freighters which had been hastily converted into MAC's—as auxiliary aircraft carriers, in an effort at long last to cover the "Black Pit". The convoys were now getting added protection both on sea and in the air. There was also Captain Walker to be reckoned with. Just as the German submarine ace, Otto Kretschmer, surprised the enemy with new offensive tactics, Walker, as the Officer in Charge of A/S defences, sought new and better methods. With his "Killer Groups" he scored a success off Gibraltar which was most disturbing to the Germans.

* * *

The Gibraltar convoys were now being protected by from anything between eight and eighteen warships. Early in December an aircraft from the carrier H.M.S. *Audacity*, sighted a U-boat twenty-two miles away from a convoy which had just sailed from Gibraltar. Walker at once directed five of the escorts to the spot and these, with a stream of depth charges, damaged the U-boat so severely that it was compelled to surface. Commander Baumann, *U.311*, did his best to drive off the carrier-borne aircraft by gunfire. He shot down one aircraft which was trying a low-flying attack, but he could do no more. His U-boat received fatal damage and began to sink.

There can be no more vivid description of how things looked in the vicinity of this convoy than the terse sentences of the log kept by Lieutenant Wiebe, *U.67*:

11 December.

"11.13. Heyda reported convoy in sight. Hastened towards it at full speed.

12 December.

"00.26. Destroyer was coming up at speed from the port quarter. Speed 16 knots. Multiple salvo fired. Immediately after discharge, one of the torpedoes turned in a circle and came straight back at us.

"00.45. Destroyer opened fire at a range of 600 yards. Its shells all passed over us. At full speed and zigzagging all the time we made for a favourable position from which to attack a corvette which was approaching. The destroyer followed hard on our heels. Visibility good, and we offered a fine target.

"00.55. Helm jams at port 270 degrees. Insufficient power. My shout to crash dive came too late.

"The hands on the bridge hurtled down into the ship. If the destroyer had held her course, she must inevitably have rammed us. Hand steering out of action.

"00.56. Alarm—enemy less than 300 yards away. We crash dived to 550 feet. Four groups of three depth charges each exploded above us. Minor damage to glass, etc. Several hours later we surfaced. All quiet, nothing to be seen or heard.

"02.50. Proceeded in search of convoy.

"04.45. Crash dive. Low-flying aircraft.

"10.09. Crash dive. Flying boat.

"10.30. On surface.

"10.35. Bristol Blenheim a long way away.

"10.38. An aircraft, 230 degrees.

"11.00. Crash dive. Flying boat, 120 degrees.

"11.15. Surfaced.

"11.29. Land based aircraft.

"11.48. Cruising at periscope depth. Patrol vessel. Submerged.

"12.48. On surface. Smoke bearing 340 degrees, patrol vessel, 270 degrees, another, 100 degrees, and a destroyer's tripod mast, 080 degrees.

"14.28. Low-flying aircraft.

"14.47. Flying boat 080 degrees, apparently covering convoy from S.W.

"16.30. A mast dimly visible.

"16.45. Two more masts.

"17.40. Convoy sighted.

"17.41. Aircraft.

"17.52. Crash dive.

"17.56. Two escort vessels very close.

13 December.

"03.08. Small steamer showing lights. Neutral. U-boat Head-quarters reported convoy's whereabouts. Müller (that's us) Hansmann, Baumann, Scholz, Gelhaus, Gengelbach ordered to attack. This group to operate under code name 'Seeräuber'— 'Pirates'. Our position—170 sea miles west of Tangier.

17 December.

"04.47. Baumann reported: Contact established.

"06.05. One of our own U-boats sighted. Presumably Baumann.

"07.45. Baumann reported: Contact lost.

"08.26. U-boat Headquarters detailed a Condor to shadow.

"10.12. Smoke.

"10.47. Scholz reported convoy's position.

"12.10. Eight or ten explosions heard.

"13.45. A U-boat.

"13.55. Three smoke clouds steaming directly towards it.

"14.04. An aircraft, bearing 150 degrees, dropped bombs and turned away.

"14.10. Aircraft dropped another bomb. On the horizon, bearing 160 degrees, course 090 degrees, a U-boat. Presumed to be Baumann.

"14.15. Baumann reported that his ship was unseaworthy and that he was being chased by four destroyers (Walker).

"14.46. Crash dive. Flying boat. Could not, alas, help Baumann.

"15.55 Surfaced.

"15.59. Crash dive. Flying boat was approaching.

"17.45. Returned to surface.

"18.19. Gelhaus reported contact with convoy.

"18.41. Crash dive. A number of aircraft.

"19.55. Surfaced. U-boat Headquarters asked Baumann and Hansmann for their positions. No reply from either.

Sunday, 22 December.

"00.05. A large silhouette. Behind it escort craft. It was a large

10,000-ton vessel, high out of the water, with a very long forecastle. Presumably a catapult aircraft carrier.

"00.23. Tubes five and six fired. Miss. Ahead of us there were now the aircraft depot ship and six escort vessels, astern in their wake were two patrol craft. A corvette was firing a series of star shells, some of which came unpleasantly close to us. Bridge watch ordered below. Patrol vessel 900 yards away. Crash dive.

"00.48. Eight depth charges. No effect.

"00.55. Twelve more. Nearer this time.

"01.30. Confused echoes from destroyer and corvette.

"01.44. Fourteen excellently aimed depth charges.

"02.09. Five more, equally well aimed.

"02.38. Two more, ditto. Ship severely shaken.

"02.48-02.56. Enemy movements plotted by hydrophone.

"03.08. Corvette was departing.

"04.30. Surfaced. All contact with convoy lost.

"10.36. Present position—600 sea miles N.W. of Finisterre.

"16.28. Flachsenberg reported contact with convoy.

"When we rose to the surface, we noticed that we were leaving a twenty-yard wide trail of oil behind us. Damage traced and repaired. Seeing the oil, the corvette presumably thought she had sunk us. Hence her departure.

23 December.

"09.21. Signal from U-boat Headquarters: Break off operations against convoy and return to base."

*　　*　　*

What, in the meanwhile, had happened to *U.131*?

True to the traditions of his service, Commander Arendt Baumann remained on his ship. As he stood by the conning-tower, the water was already lapping over the gratings of the upper deck. His gaze turned to his crew. They had all managed to get into their life jackets and were now swimming in the warm water, free from any further danger.

Did his ears deceive him? Mingling with the soft swish of the gentle swell and the murmuring melody of the trade wind came the sound of the national anthem. At first softly and then louder and louder as every man in the water joined in.

Baumann picked up his binoculars. They, at least, must not be allowed to fall into enemy hands. As he hung them on the periscope mounting, he felt a stab of pain in his heart, as though he were parting from a dear friend.

"Why don't I abandon ship?" The thought passed like a flash through Baumann's mind. "Tradition? Is it so holy, so noble, thus to sacrifice oneself?"

To that he had no answer. He was hardly conscious of the warm water, lapping gently over his feet and slowly rising higher and higher. His right hand was still clutching the strap of his binoculars. Through those very glasses he had seen quite a lot of the peaceful, multi-coloured world around him. But that was before 1939. In those days. . . .

"Jump, man. Save yourself. The suction will take you down and you'll drown like a rat. Why do my legs seem powerless? My body incapable of movement? Whether I drown or not is in God's hands."

Baumann saw the waters close over his binoculars. Were they the only thing he loved? They were not merely a possession, they were part of his very self.

Still Baumann did not jump.

The U-boat was sinking and with her sank Baumann.

He was dragged down by his ship and then thrust violently upwards to the surface again. Instinctively he struck out.

Half an hour later he was safely aboard the British destroyer. He was given a good and courteous reception and he was well looked after.

The next morning while Baumann and his officers were having breakfast in the ward-room, a messenger appeared.

"The captain's compliments, Sir, and will the German officers please come on deck?"

"Tell the captain with my compliments that we are at breakfast and will come as soon as we have finished."

The messenger departed, and five minutes later he was back with a further request that the German officers should go up to the bridge. Baumann remained polite but firm.

"Please tell the captain," he said quietly, "that in our service we do not disturb people at meals. We will come later."

The messenger appeared for the third time.

"The captain's orders, Sir. The German officers will go up to the bridge."

Baumann laid down his knife and fork. "Very well," he said. "Let's go." Slowly and without haste they went on deck.

On the bridge there was quite a commotion. All eyes were turned to starboard. Baumann followed their gaze. Before him he saw a German U-boat, men struggling in the sea, and a motor boat from the destroyer hastening towards the submarine.

Baumann glanced at the contented face of the British commander.

"We're going to board her and tow her home," said the latter with a confident smile.

Suddenly there was a violent explosion. Baumann saw the U-boat disappear in a cloud of smoke and sink like a stone. The motor boat turned away in time. It has only just escaped reaching the U-boat and being blown to bits with her. Baumann smiled. But the British captain was furious.

"Thank you, captain."

Baumann and his officers were dismissed.

A quarter of an hour later Heyda clambered aboard. He met Baumann.

"Boat sunk. Crew safe." he reported.

"A double consolation, Heyda, even though a bitter one."

In the attack on this convoy, which was commanded by Captain Walker, Lieutenant Endrass, who had been Prien's first officer at Scapa, was lost. Doenitz had sent Endrass, in whom he had great confidence, to reinforce the U-boats already detailed to attack.

"Hold on to that convoy. I'm sending Endrass," had been the text of his signal. But it was in vain. The British counter-measures had been so excellent that the U-boats had scored no success and suffered grievous loss:

U.127 (Lieutenant Hansmann), sunk on 15 December by H.M.S. *Nestor*. No survivors.

U.131 (Commander Baumann), sunk on 17 December by H.M.S. *Exmoor*, *Stanley*, *Penstemon*, *Stork* and aircraft from carrier *Audacity*. Commander and some of the crew rescued and taken prisoner.

U.434 (Commander Heyda), sunk on 18 December by H.M.S.

Blankney and *Stanley*. Commander and crew rescued and taken prisoner.

U.574 (Lieutenant Gengelbach), sunk on 19 December by H.M.S. *Stork*. Part of the crew rescued and taken prisoner.

U.151 (Lieut.-Commander Hoffmann), sunk on 21 December by aircraft. One survivor.

U.547 (Lieutenant Endrass), sunk on 21 December by H.M.S. *Deptford* and *Sapphire*, with all hands.

It is probable that *U.208* (Lieutenant Schlieper), was also sunk in the same action. No details of her loss, however, ever became known.

In view of the severe losses and meagre success Doenitz had called off the attack on this convoy. The new, concentrated A/S tactics had passed their first test with flying colours. Try as they would, the German U-boats had been unable to pierce this massive defence.

CHAPTER XII

THE DRAMA OF THE U-BOATS AND *ATLANTIS*.

Situation Report—December 1941.
The year ended with heavy losses. The principal factor behind these
losses had invariably been the British aircraft. In all, Germany lost
35 U-boats in 1941—an average of little less than three per month,
in comparison with the twelve to eighteen which monthly entered the
service. British losses, according to their own figures amounted to
2·2 million tons. In the meanwhile America had entered the war with
the result that the strength of the anti-submarine forces on sea and in
the air was multiplied many times over. In the U.S.A. shipbuilding
yards the Henry Kaiser programme was beginning to take shape. The
first mass-produced ships, called Liberty Ships, were being launched.
In all only six U-boats could be detailed, under the code name
"Paukenschlag", to operate against United States shipping. But,
thanks to the advent of the supply U-boat, the field of U-boat activity
was now greatly extended to include the Caribbean and the South
Atlantic. The submarine war was like a forest fire. Scarcely had it
been extinguished in one place, than it broke out in another. The wider
the field of operations became, the more the Allies were forced on to the
defensive. The U-boat was not always visible, and he enjoyed all the
advantages of the guerilla.
Even so, good fortune had at least one warm smile for the Allies.
A few weeks before the Gibraltar convoy catastrophe another dramatic
event ocurred in which the German Navy also suffered grievous loss.

*　　*　　*

U.126 (Lieutenant Bauer) was operating against shipping off the
Gold and Ivory Coasts of Africa. In the still virgin stretch of sea
off Freetown Bauer had luck. He sank six merchantmen and a
tanker, and then, since he had been at sea for ten weeks and was
running short of fuel and provisions, he asked Doenitz if he might
return to base.
Wireless message from U-boat Headquarters:

"Ship 16, Auxiliary Cruiser *Atlantis* will supply your needs."

"Grand!" said Bauer. "So much the better."

Bauer was given a precise rendezvous and was ordered not to use his wireless for four days, in order to prevent the German overseas supply sector from being betrayed by sound location.

On board *U.126* not a soul, of course, had ever heard of Ship 16.

First the tips of masts, then funnels and finally the superstructure of a merchantman appeared at the rendezvous as punctually as an express train.

Was this the ominous Ship 16—or an enemy freighter?

"Ship 16. Captain Rogge. Welcome," came the swift answer to Bauer's morse signal.

The date was 22 November, and Ship 16 had been at sea for exactly 622 days.

For 622 days, nearly two years, the auxiliary cruiser had been operating in distant waters without once docking or entering a harbour. During this period she had sunk 145,000 tons of shipping and was thus able to claim the second highest aggregate of any ship, after Ship 33, the auxiliary cruiser *Pinguin* (sunk, after twelve months at sea, on 9 May 1941 in the Indian Ocean).

"Follow astern of me," signalled Rogge by semaphore, "and prepare to receive stores."

The transfer began without any fuss. That suited Bauer. The quicker he could get his stuff aboard the sooner he'd be able to get back to his beat. A hose was passed over the stern of the auxiliary cruiser, and through it flowed the liquid gold into the oil-fuel tanks of the U-boat. Everything went splendidly. A telephone line was also rigged between supply ship and U-boat, and, in the middle of the Atlantic, the phone aboard *U.126* rang, just as if she were alongside in a home base.

"Chief Engine-room Artificer Reinhard Koenig, auxiliary cruiser *Atlantis*, speaking. Have you got a bloke named Schlumberger aboard? . . . You have? Tell him to come over to Ship 16. I've got a nice little bit of something wrapped up for him. Message ends."

The commander, the U-boat's doctor and one or two others who found they had friends aboard the steamer accompanied Schlumberger across to this mystery ship, which bore the number 16.

They stepped on to the snow-white teak deck of an ordinary merchantman. Nowhere was there anything to be seen which gave the slightest indication of the real nature of the ship.

Two worlds seemed to meet head on. . . .

The men on the auxiliary cruiser wore snow-white shorts, snow-white tropical shirts and Panama hats. They were bronzed by the sun, fit and radiant with good health. No luxury private yacht could have boasted of a better turned-out crew.

The submariners were in their grubby, grey-green U-boat jerkins, which smelled of oil and sweat. They were unshaven. Huge, tangled beards framed their faces, which were gaunt and hollow-eyed. Their complexions had taken on an unhealthy yellowish-green colour after the long weeks spent under water. The youngsters among them, eighteen or twenty years of age, looked infinitely older, and seemed to have lost all trace of youthful insouciance.

"This is just like the Kiel Week," chuckled Schlumberger, beaming at his opposite number, Reinhardt Koenig, who was later destined to become a U-boat chief engineer. He gazed contentedly round the spacious petty officer's mess of the *Atlantis*. Appreciatively he filled his lungs with the sweet, fresh air. On the table stood a bottle of Black and White, booty from some British merchantman.

"You're all right here, Schlumberger, you can pour a couple down the hatch, and no need to worry about anything. We're a long way off the beaten track here. You'd be surprised at the number of ships, some of 'em warships, too, which have taken on fuel, ammunition and stores and so on from the supply ships since the war began. *Admiral Graf Spee* has been here, and *Admiral Scheer*, too, and any number of auxiliaries like *Thor*, *Pinguin*, *Michel* and *Kormoran*."

Here, too, had been that fabulous egg-ship which the *Admiral Scheer* had captured shortly before Christmas 1940. With her fourteen million eggs aboard, the British ship *Duquesa* had become a supplementary food office for *Wilhelmshafen-Sud*. And it was from this spot, too, that *Pinguin* sent back to Germany the Norwegian whaling fleet which she had captured by ruse and without firing a shot in the Antarctic.

"To look at this lovely blue meadow of water you'd never

believe it! And who'd expect to find a lively base like this in the middle of the blooming Atlantic!" said Schlumberger. He stood up and stuck his head through a porthole—unlike the poor submariners, the crew of the *Atlantis* had a constant source of air and light.

One of the ship's cooks appeared and plumped down some freshly baked rolls, appetisingly garnished with slices of meat, gherkins and little onions. Schlumberger's mouth dropped open in astonishment.

"Oh—we do a bit of farming on board," explained Koenig. "We've got a few beasts, first and foremost some little pigs, which do pretty well on the pickings and leavings and in the fresh sea air. When you're at sea as long as we are," he added, "you want something decent to eat, especially plenty of fresh meat. You poor blokes in the U-boats don't do yourselves that proud, so, in your honour, one of the little piglets has been struck off the ship's roster."

"Fine!" cried Schlumberger. "Let's get down to it!"

With his mouth full and his jaws champing he asked Koenig what he intended to do after the *Atlantis* had got home again.

"U-boat, of course!"

Schlumberger leant forward and banged the table with his fist. "You're barmy! Look at us, poor miserable ——s! With us it's attack, attack, attack all the time. And you know what that means in the engine-room—see nothing, know nothing, stick it and hope! And responsibility! You're responsible for the safety of the boat and all the blooming ship's company. Not like on this packet here, where there's so many of you, you have to look after each other!"

"That's just the point, chum."

"D'you mean to tell me you're coming back to U-boats?"

"I am. Of course I am. Before, when I volunteered, as cocky as a lord, I was terrified I'd be frightened. And the first time I stepped into a U-boat I'd have run like hell if I could. But now? Well, there's only one job at sea for me. Anyone who has served in a U-boat knows what I mean."

An hour later the alarm gongs clanged throughout the ship. Koenig leapt to his feet and rushed to action stations. Schlumberger hurried on deck.

Two masts and three funnels were rising over the horizon.

"Cruiser," shouted Bauer and he leapt to the port rail, urging Schlumberger and the rest to get back to their boat as quickly as possible. But the U-boat too, had heard the alarm, and Bauer just had time to see his *U.126* submerge and disappear from view.

An aircraft came sweeping down and dropped two bombs ahead of the suspicious-looking ship warning her to stop. A British cruiser was approaching at speed.

"All *U.126* personnel below! Beards will give the show away!" came the order over the ship's loudspeaker.

In spite of the ticklish situation, Schlumberger could not help laughing.

"That's all right, Sir," he said to the First Officer. "No one'd recognize us with these beards!"

"O.K. Schlumberger—get a move on. This is serious. Our job is to play the innocent cargo-boat."

When they got below the submariners were given life jackets.

"A hell of a fine mess we've got ourselves into!" cursed Bauer.

"What ship?" signalled the British cruiser. Rogge gave the name of an American merchantman.

"Where bound?" asked the cruiser.

"U.S.A." replied Rogge.

Between the questions flashed repeatedly the demand for the secret code signal, which, of course, Ship 16 could not give.

Nearly an hour passed in this game of question and answer, which Rogge deliberately dragged out as long as he could.

The cruiser persisted in her demand for the code signal. Although the U.S.A. was not yet at war, it was obvious that here there was some sort of secret understanding such as usually exists only between combatant allies.

Rogge passed the word to be ready for all eventualities.

Hardly had he done so than the cruiser—it was the heavy cruiser *Devonshire*, armed with eight eight-inch and ten four-inch guns—opened fire. She was some eleven miles away from *Atlantis*, and at that range *Atlantis'* armament was useless. *Devonshire* disappeared at high speed over the horizon. Rogge followed and did his utmost to close the range. But *Devonshire*, mindful no doubt of the destruction of the cruiser *Sydney* by the auxiliary cruiser *Kormoran*, kept well out of range of *Atlantis'* guns.

Aboard the latter everyone had but one hope and prayer—

that the U-boat even with her officers absent, would be able to come into action.

Devonshire's third salvo was on the target and tore open the *Atlantis*' bows, which started to burn.

Rogge, however, would not give in.

Again shells crashed into the ship. The port side was shot to bits.

"A hopeless situation," Bauer was heard to mutter. And Rogge, too, admitted it. No ruse or subterfuge, an auxiliary cruiser's most potent weapons, could help him now. . . .

Rogge gave the order to abandon ship.

Before surrendering themselves to the merciless seas the crew of *Atlantis* made sure that their ship would not survive them.

She sank quickly.

Devonshire disappeared for good.

For seven hours the survivors drifted with the sun almost vertically above them. The majority were but scantily clothed. Where, they wondered, was the U-boat? The burning rays of the sun were even more painful than the pangs of thirst.

U.126, in its vain attempts to close and attack the cruiser, had lost sight of the survivors.

Suddenly a glad, many-throated shout rang out across the South Atlantic. With foam pouring and cascading from her, *U.126* had unexpectedly emerged quite close to one of the lifeboats. Bauer hastened to take over his ship again and immediately made a signal to U-boat Headquarters, asking for help.

He managed to get perhaps a couple of hundred of the ship-wrecked men on his upper deck. They were packed together like herrings in a net, quite unable to stir, and the thought that the cruiser might come back again did nothing to improve their spirits. Every one of them realised full well that disaster had overtaken them.

Had the *Devonshire* been aware of the presence of a U-boat? Assuredly, yes, otherwise she would have returned to pick up the survivors.

The rest of the *Atlantis*' crew remained in the lifeboats and on the rafts, which *U.126* now took in tow. In each boat were 120 men—far too many, and far more than the boats were designed to carry.

But not a soul complained.

In the U-boat itself all the cabins were filled with wounded. The officers, warrant officers and petty officers slept on the deck.

Rogge and Bauer between them divided up the water and food. They had to reckon that they would be faced with a long voyage. Ten days' towing, they hoped, might bring them to Pernambuco in South America.

A handful of vegetables, a small piece of meat and one tea-cupful of water per man was laid down as the day's ration. The days were glowing hot and the nights bitterly cold.

From home came a comforting signal. All surface vessels in the vicinity and a few U-boats had been directed to proceed to their assistance. That all sounded very comforting and hopeful. But— did naval staff know the exact whereabouts of all these craft? After all, they only used their radio in case of necessity or emergency.

But five days after the disaster a surface vessel did come in sight.

It was the German ship, *Python*, an auxiliary vessel operating with the warships at sea. However, not even the blandishments of senior officers could persuade Bauer to pay a visit to *Python*. He soon made off for his operational sector just as fast as God would let him. . . .

Even so, a capricious fate had not yet played its best, malevolent card. What followed was in the nature of a chain reaction.

Merten (*U.68*) who had lain alongside *Atlantis* a few days before Bauer arrived, in order to let his men stretch their legs a bit, had received the SOS signal broadcast by U-boat Headquarters. On his way to the scene of the disaster he heard by radio that Bauer was trying to tow the survivors in boats to South America. Shortly afterwards he received another signal: *Python* had, in the meanwhile, taken over the *Atlantis'* crew. U-boats in the vicinity were to avail themselves of the opportunity to obtain any stores they required from *Python*, before the latter set course for home.

Merten required no second invitation. More fuel meant more sea miles, more chances of scoring a success.

On the way to the rendezvous he ran into a real pea-souper. Griese, the navigator, felt like a mole, blindly burrowing its way through the earth. Even so, not only did they reach the exact spot indicated, but they got there ahead of schedule. Merten was full of praise.

Griese grinned: "Anyone can navigate in clear weather, Sir," he remarked. And by "anyone" it was clear that he was having a cheeky dig at the commander himself. Merten smilingly accepted this. After all, he knew full well that when the navigation was in Griese's hands it was not only in good hands, but probably in the best hands aboard.

The second U-boat which had been ordered to rendezvous with *Python* had not yet arrived. This suited Merten's book and he started taking in stores at once. He took more fuel oil than he really needed—why, exactly, he could not himself explain. Nevertheless, he did so. He had what is always regarded as the characteristic of all great captains—a sixth sense of approaching danger. The next morning the second U-boat arrived and made fast to the stern of the supply ship.

"I'd get a move on, if I were you," Merten shouted.

The other commander waved an airy hand.

Merten meanwhile was urging his men on.

"Get a move on, lads, get a move on. I want those torpedoes stowed away and the hatch closed just as quickly as possible."

Indeed it was no easy job, in that sweltering heat, to get the heavy and bulky torpedoes inside a heaving U-boat.

U.68 was rolling heavily in the swell.

Merten had taken up his position by the conning-tower rail, with Griese beside him. Both remained silent. Both continuously raised their binoculars and swept the horizon. It looked as though they were doing damn all, while others laboured and sweated. But Merten had his reasons.

Suddenly he ducked down. Griese did likewise. At the same instant the alarm sounded on board *Python*.

"Cast off!" yelled Merten. And as he said it the *Python*'s propellors began to churn the sea.

Three funnels had appeared over the horizon.

The survivors from *Atlanis* did not require to be told what ship was bearing down upon them.

It was the *Devonshire* once more.

Treachery? Where? At home? How had the British got to know of this new, secret rendezvous? Was it by chance? Coincidence has a fairly long arm, but not, surely, as long as that. . . .

On Merten's U-boat the situation was enough to make one's

hair stand on end. All the hatches were open, quite a number of the crew were still paddling about on Carley floats. His first job was to get them back aboard. He cleared his upper deck as quickly as he could. In the control-room below the chief engineer was desperately trying to work out the new trim dependent upon all the stores they had taken aboard.

In the meanwhile the whole of the *Devonshire* was now visible above the horizon, and she was approaching at speed. The captain of *Python* turned away. He was trying to get the U-boats between himself and the cruiser, in the hope that they would engage the enemy's whole attention—particularly as they were on the point of submerging. It was a bit of very quick thinking and a cunning manœuvre on the part of the old fox on the supply ship.

In spite of the chaotic position as regards the trim of his boat, Merten gave the order to crash dive. *U.68* hurtled down in a truly terrifying manner. Although Merten had put the best men he had on the hydroplanes, and although the chief engineer in person gave the necessary orders, *U.68* could not be brought under control. She danced about like a ballerina, and nothing they could do would keep her on an even keel.

For quite a time they threshed about in the water. Every now and then, when the periscope emerged for a few seconds, Merten was able to catch a glimpse of what was happening. The British cruiser, he saw, had set about her work of destruction, while he himself remained helpless, powerless and quite unable to launch an attack.

Perhaps the other U-boat could do something. . . .

But her commander had no luck. He completely miscalculated the cruiser's speed, and his torpedoes sped harmlessly away behind her stern. A wonderful chance had gone down the drain.

Then Merten took a completely mad decision.

"Surface!" he roared. "Blow tanks and up!"

The chief engineer, the officers on watch and the crew looked at him in consternation. Surface? Now? Had the Old Man gone completely off his head?

Python was sinking. Her crew and that of *Atlantis* whom she had rescued had already taken to the boats; and between these life-boats and the British cruiser Merten surfaced. He did more. He steered straight at the *Devonshire*. At all costs he wanted to save the crews of *Python* and *Atlantis* from falling into the hands of the British; and he staked his all on one desperate throw. And it came off.

The cruiser, seeing the U-boat, put sharply about, made off at high speed and soon disappeared below the horizon.

Rogge now assumed command. He detailed as many of the survivors as possible to the two U-boats, each of which took on 120 men.

The rest were divided between the lifeboats, a few of which were taken in tow by each U-boat. And those that still remained had to make shift on the U-boats' upper decks. They were given inflatable rafts which might (or might not) be some consolation to them if the U-boat were forced to submerge and leave them paddling about in the water. There were plenty of sharks about in these regions, and to have a raft handy was at least of some comfort to the men.

A signal from U-boat Headquarters said more U-boats were hastening to help and that two large Italian U-boats had sailed from Bordeaux to come and pick up survivors. Whether the Italians would successfully get through the rigorous air patrol over the Bay of Biscay was, of course, quite another matter.

But the men at least had the comforting feeling that they had not been completely abandoned. They knew that something was being done for them and that no effort would be spared to bring this somewhat unique rescue operation to a successful conclusion.

Meanwhile, in the U-boats' galleys they even managed to cook a meal for everybody. The hoary old Atlantic now witnessed perhaps the strangest scene in all its long years. With a pinnace, which they had luckily been able to lower from the *Python* before she sank, meals were ferried across to lifeboat after lifeboat.

The tow-ropes luckily proved equal to all the demands made of them. That was thanks to Rogge, for these hawsers had come from the *Atlantis*. Rogge had always been at great pains to keep his ship and her equipment in first-class order; and now his seamanlike thoroughness was paying good dividends.

Everyone, of course, was cursing like hell—about the heat, the food, and everything else they could think of.

"As long as they go on cursing I don't mind," thought Rogge. "It's a sign that their spirits are all right. It's only when they get obstinately silent and hang their heads that I don't like it."

At night, the men in the lifeboats and on the upper decks felt frozen and they envied their mates, tucked up snugly inside the U-boats. But the latter, too, were miserable. The atmosphere was thick, much thicker than usual, even in a U-boat, and that's saying something.

And to crown it all, when at long last a steamer hove in sight, she turned out to be British! Fully laden, she sailed past and away on her lawful occasions.

This was too much for Merten's equanimity. Even Rogge thought it a bit hard. For a week they'd been longing for the sight of a ship, and. . . . "Well," he thought, "we'll be lucky if she doesn't use her radio and give us away."

The British ship did not use her radio. Decency at sea was not, after all, quite dead and buried. She might, perhaps, have made enquiries about wounded and so on. But she preferred to close her eyes and see nothing; and that, in all conscience, was decent enough of her.

Five more days passed. The new rendezvous given to them had almost been reached. Here two further U-boats were awaiting the advent of this strange convoy making its way across the ocean.

One of the two U-boats had already almost run out of fuel.

"My hunch was a good one. It's not a bad idea to play the hamster sometimes," said Merten contentedly to himself, thinking of the considerable surplus he had taken aboard.

Fuel oil was transferred, gallon by gallon in drinking-water containers, from one U-boat to the other.

To accelerate their progress all the survivors were now divided among the four U-boats. The work of transfer was still in full swing when heavy black clouds began to gather in the west and sweep swiftly over the horizon. In no time a real storm came down upon them, developing rapidly into a regular tropical tempest. In the midst of a wildly tossing sea they had to work for five long hours before every man had been brought to safety aboard the U-boats.

A little later they met the Italian submarines which were sufficiently roomy to relieve the congestion and make everybody reasonably comfortable.

It was on Christmas Eve that the U-boats berthed alongside the pier of their home base; and the men that stepped out of them were as grey and as weather-beaten as the ships themselves. But the submariners could not have brought a better Christmas gift for the hundreds of families waiting to greet the survivors.

*   *   *

On that Christmas Eve *U.645*, commanded by Lieutenant Ferro and acting as a weather ship, was sunk by an American destroyer bearing the German name *Schenk*. *U.645* was the first ship to be sunk by the American forces in this war. There were no survivors. The *Schenk* searched vainly all round the scene of action but found no one. In the evening, with the candles on the Christmas tree alight, the men on the ship with a German name drank a toast to their success over other Germans.

Another incident at the end of 1941 was, or should have been, cause for considerable misgiving:

In December a U-boat operating in the Mediterranean reported that in the middle of a completely dark night she had been accurately bombed by an aircraft.

"Just chance," said the experts, nodding knowingly to each other.

Competent authority did not for a moment believe that the enemy had succeeded in building into an aircraft anything comparable to the German DeTe radar apparatus. It was much too big and much too heavy.

"Quite impossible!" asserted the experts. They consulted the astronomic charts for the month.

"There you are—a full moon, and most probably there was such a bright reflection over the sea that the aircraft would have no difficulty in spotting a U-boat by night."

The commander, however, insisted that the enemy must have had some new device.

Doenitz, too, found it rather hard to believe in radar location from the air. He agreed that the attack must have been just a coincidence.

"If they had had anything of that sort," he declared, "we should certainly have received news from other commanders, reporting similar experiences."

Part Four

1942

CHAPTER XIII

WAR WITH U.S.A.

Situation Report.

Japan had attacked U.S.A. Germany honoured her obligations to her ally. Hitler decided to put "Operation Paukenschlag" into action off the American coast. For this operation, however, which had been planned in the greatest secrecy, there were at the moment only six U-boats available. The success of this operation was largely due to the enterprise, the boldness and the efficiency of the commanders and crews who carried it out—and, in a measure, to American ignorance of anti-submarine defence. One of the "Paukenschlag" commanders was Lieutenant Hardegen, who was on leave in Italy when war was declared on the U.S.A. Without waiting to be recalled Hardegen hastened back to his base and reported to his Flotilla Commander, Viktor Schütze.

*　　*　　*

"Glad you've come, Hardegen. I knew you would, so I didn't bother to send you a telegram," said Schütze, as they shook hands.

"What sort of preparations ought I to make for the next trip, Sir?" asked Hardegen, hinting obliquely at the U.S.A. It was not mere idle curiosity; he was thinking primarily about the problems which would face his watch-keeper, von Schroeter, who simply had to be told whether the boat was to be fitted out for the Arctic regions or the tropics.

"I'm sorry—I can't tell you any more than that you should be prepared for everything . . . for the frozen north and the blazing south . . . the rest must come from the chief himself."

So that was it. Now Hardegen knew where he was, and decided to prepare for "everything". He stuck to the electric fans which had been such a godsend during his last trip in the tropics, and he stuck, too, to the electric heaters which were an "Arctic issue".

The cook, Hannes, worked hard and long into the night. Like a hobgoblin, he crept into every nook and cranny of his ship to see whether he could not find, here and there, odd corners for just a few more tins of stores. There was nothing old Hannes didn't know about the particular fancies of all the crew and he was determined, somehow, to have everything their hearts could desire.

With eager enthusiasm the crew made ready for sea.

Torpedoes were checked, ammunition and fuel oil were taken aboard, and finally there came a few bulky sacks of presents for the men, for once more they would spend Christmas at sea. The first officer grabbed these sacks. It was his secret, and not even the Old Man knew what was in them.

Hardegen was one of the first three commanders to whom Doenitz issued his orders—and pretty terse orders they were, too: "Submarine warfare on Roosevelt's door-step."

The ships were ordered to take up their positions off various American ports and to deliver a simultaneous and energetic attack.

Six ships would take part initially. Others would follow later.

"Have at 'em! Sink 'em! You mustn't come home empty-handed!" were the words with which Doenitz took leave of the first three commanders. The flag-officer looked long and searchingly into the faces of his young officers as he shook them by the hand, holding their hands perhaps just that second longer than usual.

*   *   *

"Course—west."

Hardegen's boat fought her way through the rough, wintry seas of the Bay of Biscay and, following the prescribed secret route, reached the broad, open spaces of the Atlantic unchallenged. There followed days of ant-like activity on board. The Christmas spirit was rampant. In the narrow control-room the biggest of the Christmas trees they had taken aboard was bedecked and decorated with electric lights; and that was the right place for it—in the very heart of the ship. It was a real tree, from the Harz Mountains redolent with the scent of home.

Hardegen said a few words to his crew and von Schroeter, his watch-keeper, played a few Christmas carols on his concertina.

Then came a real banquet, letters and parcels were distributed, greetings from home, Christmas presents. . . .

"First watch—stand by!"

"Prepare to surface, chief."

The presents disappeared. The lights on the tree were extinguished. Like a dream picture of another world, peaceful and happy, the typical Christmas scene faded and died. The air hissed and whistled as it was pumped into the diving tanks. Through the control-room mummy-like figures, muffled up to the ears, tramped upwards.

Tramp, tramp, tramp. . . .

In no time the bridge watch were soaked to the skin.

In those days the Atlantic was a no-man's-land, a dead land, a land of shadows.

Hardegen's radio kept on picking up signals asking for help— but his boat ploughed on westwards, steadily westwards.

Close under the coast off Halifax a 10,000-ton ship of the Blue Funnel Line came in sight. Hardegen paused. "Operation Paukenschlag" had not yet begun, so, if he were to sink her, he must give her no chance to use her radio. Tricky—but he'd take a chance, thought Hardegen. But he had to fire two torpedoes before the ship finally sank. And while she sank her radio went on transmitting to the last! The American Press was in an uproar over this first sinking, which had occurred within sight of the Canadian mainland.

* * *

The moon was new. Hardegen was off New York. The harbour lights were burning as usual. Unsuspecting America!

It seemed incredible. Surely even the American naval authorities should have realised that some danger existed, that, with the outbreak of war, some German U-boats might well appear off the coast. What was it—sheer irresponsibility? Overwhelming self-confidence?

Manœuvring cautiously, Hardegen edged in closer and closer to the coast. The echo sounder showed a bare 130 feet of water.

And over there lay New York, the city which Hardegen had visited when on a cruise as a cadet. He was the first German fighting man to see it in wartime, even though he could but see its reflected lights, flickering red and yellow on the surface of the water.

Off Sandy Hook, the small island that divides New York's

shipping lanes into the Ambrose Channel and the main channel, tugs and pilot craft were puffing industriously to and fro. Fishing boats were sailing in and out, and Hardegen was hard put to it to avoid all the numerous little craft hurrying in all directions about him. Not for a moment, however, did he think of submerging. With the utmost calm, he and his first officer reconnoitred the harbour, checked the soundings taken with those given on his chart and made their plan of attack.

Zero hour in 'Operation Paukenschlag' was at hand.

Hardegen and his first officer, Hoffmann were intently observing a large motor tanker. Fully laden, she had left New York harbour and was now steering for the Nantucket Lightship and the open road to the Atlantic. Hardegen's torpedo hit her amidships. The explosion rent the night sky like some huge beacon. As it died away and the water became calm again, a thick black mushroom of smoke hung like a pall over the ship, whose masts were all awry. Feebly her radio flickered its message: "Tanker *Norness* struck a mine to the south of Long Island."

Hardegen expended yet another of his precious torpedoes to hasten her end. It hit the stricken ship aft, just where, in a tanker, the engine-room is usually located. That finished her. Her stern sank to the bottom, and her bows remained sticking out of the shallow water.

Hours later the American radio issued a warning to all shipping about the wreck of a tanker which had sunk off Long Island as the result of an explosion as yet unexplained. . . . For some queer reason they did not give the name of the ship concerned.

"Well—well!" grinned Hardegen. "A clean conscience makes a nice soft pillow. These Christmas revellers don't seem to think it might have been a U-boat." He waited.

When daylight approached he put out to sea and lay on the bottom. The next night he went even deeper into New York's harbour approaches. Here the water was so shallow that there was no point in even thinking of submerging. In spite of all the harbour lights and the innumerable small craft steaming hither and thither, he had to make up his mind to attack on the surface.

There was no trace at all of any anti-submarine defences. "U-boats? Here? Quite impossible!" said the American experts.

Hardegen went in to the attack. He fired and hit. The night sky was as light as day. The first tanker he attacked was burning furiously. A second shot finished her off, and she, too, sank with her bows and masts sticking out of the shallow water.

"The sinking of the *Norness* can only have been accomplished by a U-boat," declared the American Vice-Admiral Kalbreus, S.N.O. Newport, in the American Press. The ship, he added, had been sailing under the Panamanian flag, and two of the crew had been killed.

The next day Press and radio made a big story out of the sinking of the second tanker. The ship had had no chance to use her wireless before she went under, and as the wild and furious accounts in Press and radio made no mention of names, the men in the U-boat had no idea what ship they had destroyed.

After this Hardegen decided to wait for the enemy ships which, according to the astonishingly accurate reports of the German radio interception service, were on their way to New York.

This allowed him to ignore without misgiving the smaller vessels that passed. The only big ship which came in sight the next morning turned out to be of friendly nationality—a Spaniard.

As soon as war had been declared, the Americans had, of course, mobilised all available destroyers. But sea reconnaissance is not only a matter of textbook training, it has also be to practised constantly. Time and again Hardegan's practised eye caught sight of the enemy before he was himself spotted.

American aircraft were a little more unpleasant. But the bombs they dropped, compared with those of the British, were somewhat futile little things. New York, however, was in a ferment of excitement. In the Press and on the radio they announced that the U-boat which had had the impertinence to penetrate into the approaches to New York harbour had been attacked and destroyed by aircraft.

A few days later they were compelled to correct the report. Even after she had been officially destroyed, the phantom U-boat was still using live torpedoes. In one mighty bang a 4,000-tonner from New York went down and like the others she, too, remained with her masts above the shallow water.

"We're saving our pals over there a lot of money in lightships," said Hoffmann derisively. "We're marking out a first-class channel for them."

After that it was blow after blow.

At point-blank range a torpedo tore asunder a medium-sized freighter close off the American mainland. Its blast rocked the U-boat. The night air was filled with fragments of iron, lead, steel and wood from the vessel's superstructure. Hardegen's bridge look-outs crouched horrified under cover of the gunwale.

Then ship after ship came in sight. The leader was a small tanker. But Hardegen now had only two torpedoes left. A pity to waste one on a dwarf like that.

He decided to attack the little fellow with gunfire. In order, however, to be able to get at the big merchantman as well, he decided on the almost foolhardy plan of simply sailing slap bang into the midst of them all. His gunner officer stood first on one foot and then on the other in his embarrassment.

"Well—what about it, Guns?" Hardegen asked. "I've never done a gunnery course and I don't know anything about it. But it sounds O.K. to me. What we must do is to take full advantage of those first few seconds of surprise and consternation. Those fellows over there don't even know what a conning-tower looks like. The more impertinent and improbable the line of attack, the greater will be the consternation."

"Hm," muttered Schroeter quietly. "It's not what I'd call a snip, Sir."

"I know, I know. And next you'll tell me you've a wife and family to think of!"

Schroeter laughed and said he thought the gunners might prove equal to the occasion. "Even so it's . . ." he added, with a dubious shake of his head.

"Commander to ship's company. We are just going to attack the tanker with gunfire, and then the freighter with torpedoes. The ships are steaming line ahead at the moment. So far all is clear. We are following in their wake and gradually overhauling them," said Hardegen. Then he turned and gave his orders. His voice was at first calm and quiet, then he became abrupt, decisive:

"Range 500. Port ten—meet her—midships!" To the crew: "We're now getting into position for the first attack."

"Full ahead both. Hold on tight, on the upper deck. . . . Half ahead both. . . . Ten rounds. . . . Fire!"

The gun roared.

145

The very first shells burst in the tanker's engine-room. She stopped. Further shells tore open her bunkers, shot her superstructure to pieces. Burning oil began to pour out of her. Hardegen let his boat drop astern. The burning tanker was already settling deep in the water.

"God looks after drunks and fools, Sir," said Schroeter dryly. Hardegen frowned. Then he laughed and gave Schroeter a dig in the ribs. This was no time for long dissertations.

The remaining ships had meanwhile split up like a herd of frightened sheep at the appearance of a wolf. Hardegen was about to turn to bring his torpedo tubes to bear when the port diesel failed. One of the cooling water feed pipes had burst.

"Patch it up! Get a move on, chief!"

There were steamers everywhere; and in the midst of them sat Hardegen, like a lame duck.

Then in the shimmering darkness of the starlit sky a shadow loomed up ahead—straight into the line of fire. "Torpedo! Fire!"

Hardegen's reaction had been instantaneous. Without a pause he let drive—and hit. The ship ahead disintegrated, and 5,000 more tons were added to the tally.

What, meanwhile, had been happening to the hard-hit tanker which had fallen astern? Hardegen turned and went slowly back on his tracks. He zigzagged first towards the coast and then out towards the open sea.

He suddenly caught the smell of burning wood. He turned his boat into the wind and followed the scent, which grew momentarily stronger. Like a gun dog he sniffed the air and then raised his night glasses again. Damn it! He was certainly on the right trail. At last! Two silhouettes slowly began to take shape, dead ahead. As he got closer, Hardegen saw that the two ships were just getting slowly under way. The tanker seemed to have decided to try evasive action; it could either stand out to sea or beach itself. Hardegen decided to try a trick. He turned sharply away, as thought the ship did not interest him in the least. The captain of the tanker immediately fell into the trap. He, too, turned. With full helm Hardegen drew his boat round again into a good firing position. He fired. The torpedo struck the tanker aft, in the engine-room. It was Hardegen's last torpedo.

"Hard a starboard! Home!"

"Object on the port beam," came the report almost at the same time as Hardegen had spoken.

"She's probably sailing independently and she'll certainly cut and run for it when she sees us," said Hardegen unperturbed.

In the meanwhile it had been getting lighter. At any moment the stranger would be bound to see the U-boat. Hardegen could not submerge, the water was still too shallow.

The silhouette coming out of the still dark western sky loomed bigger and bigger.

"The skipper of that old tub has got guts," thought Hardegen. "He shows no sign of running for it." The ship looked like a whaling-factory ship, and Hardegen put her down as about 16,000 tons. But he had no torpedoes left—so what!

"Commander to chief engineer. Get that port deisel working as soon as possible. When you've done so, put both to full ahead without further orders. Knock the last ounce out of her, chief."

"O.K.!" The men below needed no bidding to do their damnedest.

The giant ship continued to bear down directly on the U-boat, which could neither submerge in the shallow water nor proceed at speed. The bridge watch gripped the guard rail tensely. Nearer and nearer crept the colossus. Her bow wave looked like the slavering jaws of some antedeluvian monster. 300 yards . . . 280 . . . 250 . . . 200.

At the last possible minute the chief engineer did the trick. The port diesel sprang to life, and in no time was running at full speed. But the giant whaler, too, had plenty of speed and was hot on the trail. But a short two hundred yards behind she chased after the U-boat. The sea was now beginning to get rougher; and dearly as he would have loved to use it, Hardegen could not bring his gun into action. And still the water was too shallow. Every few seconds soundings were reported to the bridge.

Hardegen fired off a few signal lights in the direction of his pursuer's bows. But her captain was not be put off by any little firework displays. His radio was chattering unceasingly, giving the U-boat's movements and position. "The U-boat," it added, "must presumably have run out of ammunition, as she is making no attempt to attack."

"And even if I had one," thought Hardegen, "what's the use of

147

a solitary torpedo against a 16,000-tonner? And the next thing I suppose, is that we'll have destroyers and aircraft buzzing round us like bees."

It was now quite light.

"This could be rather fun, if it weren't so bloody dangerous," said Hardegen. "Keep a sharp lookout for aircraft—and watch the horizon."

Yard by yard, the U-boat began to draw away.

After a while the whaler saw that further pursuit was useless and turned away. As she did so aircraft came zooming over the horizon.

"Another hundred yards and we'll be in deep water," yelled the navigator.

A hundred yards, two hundred, and the bees were becoming alarmingly and menacingly bigger. The U-boat was poised, ready on the instant to crash dive, and as the aircraft wheeled to deliver their attack, she plunged headlong and disappeared into the protecting depths.

Just before she did so, the operator picked up one last signal—from the stricken tanker.

"SOS! SOS! Urgent. Sinking rapidly."

It was evening before Hardegen ventured to show his nose above water again, and he ran straight into black thunder clouds, lightning, squalls, rains and hail.

"Just what the doctor ordered!" grinned Schroeter.

"An appropriately theatrical finale to 'Operation Paukenschlag'," replied Hardegen. He could not know that this was in reality a prologue, a portent of the grim hazards and heavy losses which hung in secret like a pall over the future of the grey wolves of the ocean.

Hardegen had sunk 53,000 tons. The other two U-boats had sunk 75,000 tons between them. In all, 'Operation Paukenschlag' had accounted for eighteen ships in American and Canadian waters, with a total tonnage of 125,000 tons.

"Anti-submarine defence was in the elementary stage. It was not organised, and where we came up against it, we found it untrained and inefficient," reported Hardegen modestly. In the meanwhile he had been decorated with the Knight's Cross. But the keen ear of his Admiral did not fail to detect an undertone of misgiving behind his words, a worried hint that further grazing in these rich and lush pastures might well be impossible, and that 'Operation Paukenschlag' had been launched with too few U-boats.

Doenitz, however, was—or appeared to be—content.

On his next operation off the American coast Hardegen found that things were already very different. . . .

Patrol craft were guarding the main shipping lanes. Aircraft circled over wide areas of the sea, and submarine traps abounded, ready to snatch the hated "Nazi U-boats" and send them to the bottom.

One evening Hardegen attacked a small and seemingly quite harmless freighter. She had been emitting such volumes of smoke that she could not have failed to attract his attention, and she paid the penalty for her lack of forethought. A torpedo hit her in the after hold.

"She's had it," said Schroeter who was now first officer.

Hardegen thought so, too. Great, however, was their astonishment to see that the little vessel made no attempt to scurry from these troubled waters. She listed a little, and small fires were observed. But that was all. The crew seemed to be in no hurry to take to the boats. They lowered them quite calmly, as if to abandon ship were the most natural thing in the world. Strange, very strange.

"Either those chaps have nerves like a rhinoceros or . . ."

"Clear the gun for action!" ordered Hardegen, his eyes fixed on the enemy. He saw that she was still steaming slowly and had turned a little, and now, as it happened, was coming straight towards the U-boat. Hardegen thought it better to depart at full speed. Scarcely had he given the order than hinged flaps fell away from the decks of the suspicious-looking craft, tarpaulins were torn aside, guns and machine guns became visible and in a trice the U-boat was deluged in a hail of shell and bullets. A few struck home, and Hardegen winced as though stabbed by a thousand knives when he heard the crash of these hits which could so easily prove fatal to the vulnerable pressure hull. With a groan the midshipman beside him sank to the deck.

Then came depth charges. The sea reared and foamed. Mountains of water rose out of the depths. The U-boat was tossed hither and thither like a cork in a cauldron of boiling water.

149

The commander and Schroeter alone remained on the bridge, deafened by the roar of explosions under water and in the air, and surrounded by a hail of whistling bullets. Red, green and white tracer shells rushed towards them. Gradually, however, as the range increased, the firing became more sporadic and finally ceased.

Hardegen's first concern was for the young officer who had collapsed beside him. He had been taken gently below. His right leg had been almost completely severed by a shell that had penetrated the double thickness of the bridge plating. He had been given two injections of morphia, and he lay, uncomplaining and seemingly at peace.

"The ship, Sir, the ship," he murmured, as Hardegen bent over him. "You must drive that fellow away."

Schroeter coughed and sought his handkerchief.

The "panic party" from the Q-ship had meanwhile returned aboard. Hardegen, who by this time had submerged, crept cautiously towards this uncanny opponent.

As the torpedo struck its mark, the midshipman closed his eyes. The terrific explosion on the Q-ship set off the depth charges which lay primed on her after-deck. Shells stacked beside the guns also exploded and the ship was blown to pieces.

Hardegen was soon to have yet further proof that the Americans had become very alive to the U-boat menace and were taking energetic steps to meet it.

After he had attacked another tanker, which he left blazing like a furnace, the hydrophones gave a screaming echo of fast-approaching propellers. Hardegen saw a small submarine chaser bearing down on his periscope. It was a very fast motor-boat, carrying depth charges and it hurtled past the periscope, missing it by only a few yards. Depth charges were dropped, and Hardegen just had time to see another pattern being got ready as the enemy boat turned to run in again.

Then he disappeared as fast as he could into the depths below. He had to leave the tanker, which was burning fiercely but not sinking, to her fate. There had been no time to give her the *coup de grâce*.

Yes—things had changed a great deal off the coast of the U.S.A. Go where he would, Hardegen invariably came up against destroyers and aircraft. This, however, did not deter him from stubbornly continuing the chase, thrusting his way into harbours and close inshore in search of his prey. And what he sought above all were tankers and yet more tankers. For fuel oil is the heart's blood of modern warfare.

One of his next victims was a tanker, which went up in flames immediately off the fashionable seaside resort of Jacksonville Beach, and whose fuel streamed forth and left a wide and fiery road upon the waters. Then came aircraft and, hot-foot after them, the destroyers. The water was most unpleasantly shallow, and Hardegen could do no more than lie doggo on the bottom, cautiously changing position when the chance occurred.

In these shallows the effect of the depth charges was correspondingly more violent. The U-boat sprang a leak. The compressed air began to escape. Even a child could have put its finger on the spot where the U-boat lay.

More bombs. More damage.

Suddenly the U-boat stopped dead and refused to move. A depth charge had put both electric motors out of action.

"Chief, do you think there's any chance of getting out of this mess with a whole skin?"

"Not much, Sir. But while there's life there's hope. The blokes up above make mistakes, too."

"Mm. Shouldn't count on it. Get the life-saving apparatus ready. Destroy all the secret matter. Prepare to scuttle."

The chief engineer did not allow himself to be rattled by these alarming emergency orders. He gave his commander a quietly confident look, took a hitch at his pants in the seaman's manner and calmly went on with the job which demanded his and his men's full attention.

After hours of work they completed the job, and the motors were once more in order.

The last torpedo struck down a freighter and on the way home the gun, too, claimed a victim. With the small 2-cm. shell it took some hours to riddle a big 5,000-ton vessel. Hardegen circled round and round her, to "let the air in." And she actually sank. Results of this operation—79,000 tons. The thanks of a grateful nation and Oak Leaves to the Knight's Cross.

CHAPTER XIV

IN THE CARIBBEAN—DYNAMITE

Situation Report—Spring 1942.
   The salient feature of the battle off the American coast was the destruc-
tion of a large number of tankers. Hampton Roads, North Carolina and
Cape Hatteras were the focal points for the concentration of U-boat
attacks, where tankers sailing independently could be intercepted. The
mobile pipeline constituted by the Allied tanker fleet and stretching
across the oceans started from the oil depots in and around the Caribbean
Sea. It was there that Doenitz sent the new, big U-boats, among them
U.68 (Merten).
   During the period 15 January to 10 May Allied losses in the American
area of operations amounted to 303 ships with a total tonnage of
2,015,252 tons. Of these ships 112 (927,000 tons) were tankers.
Doenitz regarded these tanker losses not merely as the destruction of
enemy shipping but also, and far more important, as a direct blow to
the American armament and shipbuilding programmes. On the other
side of the picture, the American system of rationalisation, notwithstand-
ing this vast loss of oil, constituted an immense danger. The full impli-
cations of this were appreciated by very few of those in authority in
Germany. While German thoroughness seemed to be incapable of
abandoning the old, well-tried methods (U-boats, for example, were
still being built and equipped as in peace-time) the Americans im-
provised, simplified, standardised and changed over to mass pro-
duction—in shipbuilding as in everything else.

*   *   *   **

U.68 was sixty miles off the Panama Canal. When the day ended
and darkness came, suddenly and without any period of twilight,
the heat within the U-boat remained as oppressive as that in a
hothouse. Each day was just like any other in the intensity of its
heat. This particular day happened to be a Saturday, a week-
end.

In *U.68* Saturday, even on operations, was always regarded

as the week-end. It was the day of the bottle of iced beer. On Saturdays Merten used to grant a bottle of beer to his men—and to himself. He was himself very partial to a drop, but he thought it was no fun to drink alone. So everyone on board used to look forward for exactly 160 hours to this moment.

The beer had been issued. Merten was standing on the bridge. As he was about to take that first, appreciative sip, the officer of the watch reported to him:

"There's something funny over there, Sir," he said, "a queer light over the sea."

Merten exchanged his drink for his night glasses. Through them he discerned two dimly shining Vs and above them a barely visible silhouette. There was no doubt that they were two ships, big, heavily laden freighters, sailing without lights.

"Stand by for a salvo of three!"

Course, instructions to the torpedo fire control were rapped out in brief, terse orders. All hands reacted instantly. Everything was done with the speed and precision of a press-button electrical operation.

When *U.68* had manœuvred into an attack position ahead of the merchantmen and when all the necessary firing data had been worked out—own speed, speed of target, range, angle of lead and so on—then came the order to fire.

Hearts in the U-boat thumped like muffled drums. Everybody thought they could hear the tick-tick-tick of the stop watch with which the navigator was timing the torpedoes' run.

Ra-BAM! Ra-BAM! Two heavy explosions in quick succession.

Two torpedoes had hit the second ship. The third torpedo had missed its mark. But there was still time. Merten swung his boat round and fired his stern tube at the leading vessel—a lightning piece of thinking and shooting.

Hit. The ship caught fire and flames enveloped her. On the 10,000-tonner, the crew were abandoning ship in the wildest panic, rushing and yelling like madmen.

"That's curious, very curious. Our noble opposite numbers don't usually get the wind up as quickly as that," said Merten thoughtfully.

"Well—they probably read some sensational yarn in the yellow

153

Press about us 'bloody submariners' just before they sailed and had the guts frightened out of them," suggested the officer of the watch.

"I hope you're right," answered Merten.

Freighter number one was sinking. The second one, however, was still afloat, her engines stopped, and rolling slightly in the gentle swell. She looked as helpless as a fatally wounded elephant rocking to and fro in the waving grass of the jungle.

The dark night swallowed the overloaded lifeboats as they pulled frantically away. Only the metallic creak of the rowlocks, growing fainter and fainter, reached *U.68* through the still air. Suddenly a light flashed in the sea, followed immediately by a gurgling cry.

"Help! Help!"

"There's someone in the drink. He must have jumped overboard with life-jacket, emergency light and all. There he is—bobbing about in the swell," said the officer of the watch, with outstretched hand.

"Pretty poor show to leave their mate in the drink and beat it," said Merten angrily, and turned his boat in the direction of the survivor. They hauled him aboard—an iron-grey old mariner, at least sixty years old. Merten handed the trembling old man his opened but as yet untasted bottle of beer—best Dortmund Union beer—and the cooling draft refreshed the old man.

"You must have had the wind up," said Merten kindly, giving him a friendly dig in the ribs.

"Oh! Yes, Sir."

"Engineer?" asked Merten pointing to his oil-smeared jersey.

"That's right, Sir—donkeyman." The old man gave a shiver.

"You're a pretty old hand, I bet."

"Yes, Sir, I've turned sixty-nine."

"About time to pack up and stay at home."

"That's what I meant to do this year. Then your damn war came along and they asked me to serve on. So I signed on again, but. . . ."

Suddenly the words came tumbling angrily out of the old man. He had been sitting in the engine-room when the bloody torpedo exploded. Everything was smashed to hell. Pipes had burst, hissing and belching. One of them had pinned him down, helpless and unable to move. But he'd managed to get free. He'd rushed up on deck. But all the boats were away.

"So I jumped overboard. Anything to get away from that God-awful ship."

"Steady, old boy," said Merten gently. "A big ship like yours doesn't sink as quickly as all that. I'm an expert, and I know what I'm talking about. One torpedo isn't enough. . . ."

"Oh, yes it is—for that one there!" Again the old man began to tremble violently, and then with a groan he collapsed.

"Exhaustion," thought Merten. He had really no more time to bother about the old man, but he turned to a seaman and ordered him to bring up the bottle of ship's brandy. "And a real, strong middle-watch coffee, too," he called after him.

Merten's immediate task was to finish off the damaged freighter. He was far too close to Panama. The ship had to be sunk as quickly as possible. Slowly he started to circle round his stubborn victim. At a range of a bare three hundred yards he gave his warning order.

"Hähnert," he said, turning to the officer of the watch, "just watch this—it'll come in useful to you when you get a ship of your own. To sink a ship like this one, the best thing to do is to hit her between the two after-holds, just below the mast aft. As you know, that's where the shaft tunnel runs. And when that gives way the most solid of old tubs will sink at once. . . . Now, watch. . . ."

Hähnert paid the greatest possible attention to this "lesson" in the presence of the enemy.

Merten gave his orders.

The torpedo flashed into the sea. But it failed altogether to hit the spot that Merten had indicated. Instead it sailed away harmlessly past the freighter's stern.

"Damnation!" cursed Merten. "Did y'see the bloody thing jink right off course?"

The young officer under instruction grinned. "The Old Man had to find some excuse for his blob," he thought.

Not that it mattered very much, for the vessel had started to sink, anyway, slowly but quite surely.

U.68 was now about a thousand yards away. The sea had already closed over the scene as though nothing had ever ruffled its surface. Nowhere is the end so utterly final as at sea. Merten decided next to turn towards the lifeboats. He was anxious to have a word with that captain. As he was about to give his orders, he seemed to hear once again the shouts of panic that had followed the explosion of the torpedo. Why, he wondered, had no one made any attempt to fish the old donkeyman out of the water? Why had they pulled away in such frantic, panic-stricken haste from their ship? There had not been the slightest reason for it. Did they think he was going to murder them as they sat in their boats? Or was there some other reason, and if so, what?

This philosophic little interlude had delayed the giving of his final orders. It did more. It saved the U-boat and the lives of Merten and his whole ship's company.

Scarcely had he turned his head to give the helmsman and the engine-room their new orders, than a terrific rumbling explosion occurred deep down, near the ocean's bed.

At the same instant the U-boat was lifted clean out of the sea. Merten felt the bridge arch under him, like the back of a horse gathering itself to take a jump. His stomach seemed to sink to his knees. He fell from the edge of the conning-tower on which he had been sitting and landed with a crash on the groaning old donkeyman below.

Torpedoed! The thought flashed through Merten's head. Like a drugged man he heard, as from afar, the thudding crash of the water as it descended again after the explosion. "So that's what it feels like when a lousy torpedo hits you," he thought.

Merten shook himself free of the old Yank, who in his fear had clutched him in his arms. With a tremendous effort, he pulled himself together. "God!" it dawned on him, "she is still afloat." He grasped the guard rail. His hand sought the periscope mounting. It was all there, real and solid. He wasn't dreaming, then. Who had fired at *U.68*? Where was he? And what was happening to his men and inside his ship? These questions flashed in rapid confusion through his mind. But now he must act, and act fast.

"Hallo, below!" he shouted down the conning-tower. "What's happened below there?"

"Captain, Sir—is that you?" Timorously, almost incredulously, the question rose from the darkness below. All the lights had been blown, and the emergency lighting was not yet functioning. Then report followed report in rapid succession:

"Port diesel out of action."

"Both diesels out of action."

"Electrical plant on strike."

"Gyroscope broken down."

"Any water in the boat?" asked Merten sharply.

"No, Sir. Only unfit to submerge. We're doing what we can to repair the damage."

"Only unfit to submerge!" thought Merten with a grim smile, "and the lad said it as if it were a mere nothing!"

"Hähnert, take over the watch and keep a sharp lookout," he ordered and hurried purposefully below, so that his men should know he really was still there.

Lord! what a mess! His sea-boots crunched across splintered glass. All the gauge glasses had been smashed. Sextants lay on the deck. Fragments of coffee-cups, the old and well-loved coffee jug, "Virtuous Helen"—dumb comforter of many a midnight watch—all smashed to atoms and strewn all over the ship. Charts, binoculars, broken crockery, all in a chaotic heap. . . . And in the midst of it all stood his men, their faces registering fury rather than fear. Grimly they had set to work to repair the damage and restore order in the boat. Merten was conscious of the enquiring look on the face of his chief engineer.

"I don't know what hit us. Probably a torpedo. Chief, can you get the diesels working again? You must. We don't want a second one like that."

As Merten hastened up the conning-tower again and swung himself on to the bridge, his eye fell on the old donkeyman. "Of course! He's still there," he thought. "I'd forgotten all about the old boy."

The old man was just staggering to his feet. Swaying a little and with his arms hanging dejectedly at his sides, he leaned against the camouflaged conning-tower. When he caught sight of Merten he raised his hand with outstretched fingers. "Five thousand tons, Sir," he murmured.

"What five thousand tons? What d'you mean? I don't follow," said Merten.

"Dynamite," groaned the old man.

157

"What!"

"Five thousand tons of dynamite, that's what our cargo was, Sir."

And that, indeed, among other things had been the cargo of S.S. *Surrey*, 10,000 tons, bound from the U.S.A. for the American theatre of operations against Japan. By some miracle the hellish cargo had not exploded, even though the ship had been hit by two torpedoes. But as she sank deeper and deeper the increasing pressure had compressed not only her hull but also the dynamite, packed in cases in her hold. At a depth of about two thousand five hundred feet it had exploded. Mere words cannot adequately describe the fury of that explosion. But those who have seen depth charges explode will have some idea of what happened.

Merten felt an icy shiver run down his spine. What would have happened, he thought, if that final torpedo had not made that extraordinary jink and missed, if it had really hit the after-hold, as it had been meant to do?

So that was why the crew had abandoned their ship in such panic-stricken haste. That, too, was why the old donkeyman had been frightened out of his life.

The first freighter, incidentally, was S.S. *Ardenvor*, 5,400 tons, bound for Australia from Baltimore, via the Panama Canal, with a cargo of arms, ammunition, tanks and aircraft.

Merten was now in a hurry to get the torpedoes out of the upper-deck compartments and the work of transfer started at once.

Within seventy minutes the first torpedo was ready to be up-ended and passed through the torpedo hatch.

At that moment the starboard lookout reported a silhouette on the starboard beam. The ship was fast—much faster than Merten had expected. He had thought she was probably a straggler from the convoy to which the others belonged, and on account of which Merten was now so hastily preparing his ship for action.

With his torpedo hatch open, however, he could not proceed at speed, but had to content himself with proceeding slowly along a parallel course.

It seemed an eternity before the obstinate steel cigar, as smooth as an eel, consented to leave the deck and the hatch could be screwed down. Even as the last turns were being given to the screws, Merten rang for full speed. At his best speed Merten set off in pursuit of his target, which by this time had disappeared from sight. A little later the lookout spotted something to the west. It was a mere whisp, a minute spot of light against the dark sea— the stern wash of the freighter.

Fifty minutes after the first orders had been given the torpedo-men reported the torpedo loaded.

But the range to the freighter was decreasing at a snail's pace, hard by yard.

Merten held a council of war with the navigator and the torpedo officer.

He was determined to try a shot. The range, admittedly, was long, and the inclination—140 degrees—gave so acute an angle of fire that a hit was unlikely. . . .

But behind them the day was awakening. In the east the sky was changing colour, shafts of pale, golden light heralded the advent of the sun; and in front of them, on the still, dark waters, his quarry still trotted along its course. Her captain was certainly still tucked snugly in his bunk, and at this very moment the cook was probably preparing breakfast for him and his crew.

All aboard *U.68* knew that with every minute their U-boat would become more clearly visible against the lightening eastern sky.

To try and sweep round out of sight and then deliver an under-water attack offered no prospect of success; the quarry was far too speedy for that. So, there was nothing for it, but to have a crack from where they were.

"The chances are about a hundred to one against," muttered Hähnert, more to himself than to the commander. Merten gave him a dirty look. "He would, of course, start croaking now," he thought to himself.

With his eyes glued to the freighter Merten gave his orders. . . .

". . . Fire!"

The press of a button, a cough, a slight jerk in the boat, and the torpedo was on its way. Shot from an inclination of 140 degrees it sped through the crystal clear waters of the Caribbean. The slightest hint of a deviation, the most minute error in the calculations, the merest deflection caused by the unruly sea, and the torpedo, the last available torpedo aboard, would miss the target.

Merten stood on the conning-tower. He appeared to be perfectly calm, but his heart was in his mouth. And it was the same with everyone else.

05.40. 30 . . . 40 . . . 45 . . . 50 seconds. . . .

05.41. . . .

Where, a moment before, the stern of the freighter had been visible a volcano burst forth. Like a giant fist a vast column of water, foam, smoke and debris rose out of the sea.

Still proceeding at speed they watched the ship sink, bathed in the golden glory of the rising sun. She sank by the stern. For a moment she righted herself as if in a last endeavour to say farewell. Then down she plunged.

Her crew saved themselves by hanging on to the great cases which had been her deck cargo and the lashings of which had burst asunder with the explosion. Everything had happened so swiftly that they had had no time to lower a boat. The sea was covered with broken pieces of aircraft, the content of the great cases on her deck. For she, too, had been carrying war material. *Port Montreal* was her name.

Three freighters—20,000 tons of shipping—and 30,000 tons of cargo had been the fruits of this one single night in the Caribbean.

CHAPTER XV

MORE INEXPERIENCED AMERICANS

Situation Report. Spring 1942.

The average sinkings continued to increase. In January 1942 the average was 209 tons per day per operational U-boat, in February it was 378 tons, in March 409, and in April it rose to 412 tons.

The U-boat Command advocated that the submarine warfare in American waters should be continued for as long as it proved fruitful; with the reservation, however, that the situation might well change any day. Notwithstanding the tremendous efforts being made by the Americans, it was thought that for the time being at least the American A/S forces would not constitute any grave menace. The American air reconnaissance was regarded as extremely poor; the destroyers and corvettes steamed far too fast to be able to locate the U-boats and drop their depth charges with accuracy. This had been proved by the experiences of U.71. The American crews were still untrained and lacking in experience. But for how long?

*   *   *

Let Lieutenant Flachsenberg, commander of *U.71*, tell the story of his fifth operational trip, in the spring of 1942, in his own words:

"When we sailed on 23 February it was unpleasantly cold, even for the Atlantic coast. At the mouth of the Loire a filthy sea was running, with thick patches of fog scudding above it. In such weather, we did not find it exactly easy to get out of St. Nazaire. Our A.A. escort very soon turned back, but I managed to persuade the mine clearance vessel to accompany us as far as the gap in the barrage.

"Then we were alone.

"By day we travelled submerged through the Bay of Biscay, and by night we surfaced and proceeded at full speed, in order to get through the danger zone unchallenged and as quickly as possible. We were already very familiar with the bombs which

British aircraft used to unload on return flight after an unsuccessful sweep after U-boats; but at the nice, snug depth we maintained, these did not worry us at all.

"On the third day the weather was unbelievably fine. The sun shone, and visibility was excellent. We had a following sea which was just what we wanted. According to my orders, I was to make for the area off Cape Hatteras, if my supply of fuel oil permitted; if not, I was to operate further eastwards.

"I proceeded at the 'most economical speed'—which, incidentally, was bloody slow. Not that that mattered, we had plenty of time. . . . Quite apart from that, the amount of fuel we used largely depended upon the weather—and that is a matter of luck. So far, luck had been with us.

"But not for long. This lovely day was the last fine weather we were to see for a very long time. We were following the Great Circle, the shortest navigational way, but one which in the North Atlantic was notorious for its bad weather at this time of year. Our luck with the weather was, as I have said, short-lived.

"The next morning was still fine, and I was able to carry out my usual exercise, action stations—a thing I always did on the way out, because on each trip I found that twenty-five per cent of my new crew were quite inexperienced.

"The next day the wind changed and it started to blow from the north-west, west, or south-west, always, that is, in our teeth. I ought, of course, to have taken a more southerly route. . . .

"We pitched, tossed, rolled, went up hill and down dale with every conceivable possible contortion. Giant waves, fifty feet high, came roaring steeply at us. The ship quite literally had to clamber up, only to slide down the other side with giddy speed.

"Life on the bridge was only possible in storm-kit, the nearest thing I know to a diver's outfit, and even then we had to be lashed fast. But we could do nothing to prevent the icy cold water from pouring down our necks. The conning-tower hatch had to be kept permanently closed, with the usual result on the air below.

"The fore compartment was a regular thieves' den. The reserve torpedoes took up every inch of available space. It was impossible to stand upright. The men took their meals squatting on planks laid across the two top torpedoes.

"Plates, mugs, knives and forks slipped away and disappeared into the bilges. It was a hard life and the worst place of all was the engine-room, with its noises and oil fumes.

"Then there were the sea-sick. I had on board a young midshipman who was pale and haggard, and had eaten practically nothing for a fortnight. Most of the time he lay apathetic and completely exhausted on his bunk. There was nothing I could do to help him if his own stomach wouldn't co-operate. But it worried me, of course.

"In the midst of all this, the ship's cook worked with astonishing skill and was always punctual with meals. By the eighth day our fresh supplies, except for the lemons which provided our vitamins, came to an end, and the tinned stuff, which was much easier to dish out, dominated our menus.

"I envisaged a fairly long trip and I therefore introduced a system of rationing in ample time.

"Between meals we lounged in sea boots or rubber trousers on our bunks, wedged in between the side of the ship and the boards which we used to stop ourselves rolling out. The men call it 'The Kindergarten'. You can't sleep and you don't want to read. You doze a bit, and you have much too much time to think about yourself—and that is not a good thing.

"The fuel oil situation remained the decisive factor. If we could not push along on the surface—and high speed at the price of increased consumption would not be any advantage in the end—then we proceeded submerged until our batteries were exhausted or the atmosphere became saturated with carbonic acid and we had to surface again. I had to keep my potash cartridges until we reached our operational area, of course.

"Proceeding submerged at the appropriate depth had at least the advantage that the boat was steady. The crew immediately livened up; in the control-room desperate chess battles were fought out, cards slapped crisply down on the table in the petty officers' mess; in the wireless office crossword puzzles were solved with the aid of dictionary and atlas; in the forecastle a seaman strummed on the piano; the tattered and oil-smeared illustrated papers for the last three months passed from hand to hand, to be, quite literally, read to bits.

"I myself tried to read a French novel. And as I followed the old approved method of my schooldays and read half-aloud, my crew eyed me suspiciously and wondered whether after a fortnight at sea the Old Man had gone bats.

"Below the surface everything was quiet and peaceful. We were more or less on our own; and neither the raging sea, the wicked enemy nor U-boat Headquarters with its unceasing signals, could get at us for the time being. . . .

"We were now in our third week at sea, and progress had been painfully slow. The crew were pale, patience was in short supply. The nearer we got to the Newfoundland Banks, the worse the weather became. The barometer hopped about like mad, and it was getting colder and colder every day. A U-boat further north had already reported icebergs. That would be the last straw, if we bumped into one of those things on a dark, foggy night or when we were submerged. The electric heaters were consuming too much current. P.T. as the universal specific against cold isn't too easy aboard a U-boat, so the only remedy is to dress as warmly as possible.

"My first officer was the champion in this respect. Somehow he managed to get on five pairs of pants and/or trousers, and with the rest of him equally well protected he found getting through the conning-tower hatch quite a manoeuvre. But his feet, poor fellow, were always cold.

"As a finale to the run of bad weather we ran into a storm depression that beat anything I've seen. The night was as black as pitch. A wild thunderstorm raged with rain and hail and a tempest that squashed the sea flat and left our conning-tower almost in the water on the lee-side, like the sail of a yacht. It was with a sigh of relief that we dived deep into calmer water to recover. There are, after all, some advantages in going to sea in a U-boat.

"At last we passed the meridian of 55 degrees west. I reported that I still had a large stock of fuel oil, and I was ordered to operate along the American coast between Cape Tear and Cape Hatteras.

"But we had not yet arrived.

"The weather improved. It got warmer. We were now in the Gulf Stream.

"My first officer had just celebrated his birthday. As he was also messing officer we had two feasts, one at midday and one in the evening. The cook even managed to conjure up a birthday cake. So that we could all enjoy all these good things in peace, I submerged. Once more it was good to be in the Navy.

"Unexpectedly soon, on the afternoon of 17 March, we sighted our first steamer. We were in waters traversed by British ships coming from South America and proceeding to their convoy assembly point south of Nova Scotia. But I had not expected to see any of them here. When I first sighted this vessel I was in a hopeless position far astern of her, and I was about to proceed on my course westwards when she suddenly zigzagged and turned towards me. Provided she held her new course, all I had to do was to submerge and go forward to meet her. I was a fair distance off, and with the sea that was running she could not possibly see my periscope. Then I realised that she was a tanker of about 10,000 tons, and, of course, armed. I'll need two torpedoes for her, I thought, and I waited till she came within easy range.

"Away went the torpedoes. . . .

"Time's up!" reported the navigator, and a few seconds later came the sound of two heavy explosions. Both torpedoes had found their mark. Flames and columns of smoke rose a thousand feet and more into the air. As there was no immediate danger of air attack, we surfaced. One by one the crew were allowed time up on deck for a breather.

"The tanker was still steaming. Her rudder apparently had jammed to port, and she was steaming slowly in a circle. She looked like some mortally wounded monster.

"The burning fuel, probably petrol, poured out into the water, and the wreck steamed through the middle of this sea of flame.

"Not one of the crew remained alive. Their end, thank God, had been mercifully swift.

"When an hour had passed and the tanker still showed no sign of sinking, I let her have a third torpedo, and at last she seemed to have had enough. Her foremast and bridge collapsed and she was afire from end to end and listing heavily to starboard. I did not wait to see her sink. It might have taken hours.

"We continued westwards. Until darkness blotted it out we could see a black column of smoke on the horizon. At its summit the column fanned out into a plume, reminding me of Vesuvius.

"During the next few days the weather made any operations

impossible. It had not improved very much when, three days later, we sighted our second steamer. I could hardly expect my torpedoes to run true. But I had to do my best. But now the steamer was on the other side, and a good chance of a shot had been lost owing to the heavy seas. Suddenly I saw a flag at her stern. Could she be a neutral, I wondered? To make sure I rose to the surface. No, she was an American without any doubt, and unarmed.

"She was sailing innocently along. She must have seen me, but she gave no hint of having done so.

" 'Look out!' I thought to myself, a U-boat trap.

"At last she really did spot me and sought to escape by taking really skilful evasive action. I had to go full speed into the weather. I opened fire with my machine guns. That helped things. A fully laden lifeboat was launched and fell with a splash into the sea. But the captain was not going to throw up the sponge yet. He was wirelessing desperately for help.

"The ship was the *Oakman*, 5,766 tons, bound for New York. She seemed to be steaming a little more slowly and I went after her. All we want now, I thought, was for a few American aircraft to put in an appearance!

"The first torpedo missed; and in such weather I was not surprised.

"I opened fire again on the bridge. A second boat was lowered, but empty. Two men leapt down from the upper deck into it.

"The second torpedo broke surface but hit just forward of the bridge. In the immediate vicinity of the hit the water was stained bright red. What on earth are they carrying in the way of cargo, I wondered.

"By steaming on as she did till the last moment the *Oakman* literally encompassed her own death. Her bows swiftly settled deeper, and a few moments later the ship plunged headlong into the depths, her stern poised vertical for an instant and her propellers still revolving.

"The next day we were given the expected greeting from the mainland. A land-based aircraft forced me to crash dive but it dropped no bombs.

"Now, I thought, we can get cracking. I must close in nearer to the coast and get further south, where, according to the latest reports, the best opportunities for attack were to be found.

"In the middle of the night the first officer woke me. In his excitement he had mistaken Jupiter for a red signal flare. Contrary to the information given in the Atlantic charts for the month, which had predicted stormy weather in these waters, the weather for some days had been set fine. The sea was like a mirror, and the sky was blue and cloudless. The sun shone brilliantly all day. Over the horizon on the coast of Virginia people would be basking in the sun on the beaches. War seemed far away.

"But we had to remain underwater by day, for the American pilots were now getting pretty slick with their bombs. The temperature inside the ship rose accordingly. In the engine-room the thermometer registered over 100 degrees.

"The next morning, 24 March, as we lay on the bottom in American waters, the hydrophones picked up the noise of propellers. So up we rose at once to periscope depth.

"Beyond the range of my torpedoes and too far for me to stand any chance of getting into an attacking position, a fully laden tanker was steaming north, guarded by a destroyer. Her escort looked splendid. Involuntarily my mind conjured up a picture of the American athletes at the Olympic Games in Berlin in 1936. The destroyer was spick and span and well aware of the fact. But she was not a very efficient escort. Once, indeed, at high speed she passed straight over us. If only she'd known!

"The next night, too, brought nothing. Far and wide everything was peaceful and still. The lights ashore shone brightly as in times of peace. At first light I sighted two patrol vessels setting off on their allotted task. I had taken up a position, submerged, of course, in the middle of the shipping lane.

"The entries in my war log run as follows:

" '13.26 (for technical signalling reasons we had adhered to German summer time). Tanker proceeding S.W. fully laden. Decided to attack. Tanker's estimated speed 12 knots. Underwater attack delivered at 800 yards' range.

" '13.26. Sighted a second tanker.

" '14.59. Fired two torpedoes set for 6 feet. The first hit amidships, the second between mast and funnel. Exceptionally heavy explosion caused, presumably, by the shallowness of the water. Two high columns of fire observed. Estimated size of tanker,

167

7,000 tons. Type unknown. Unarmed. Tanker stopped with a heavy list and burning furiously. Proceeded further out to sea.

" '15.05. Martin flying boat observed circling over stricken tanker.

" '15.12. Destroyer, Anderson class, bearing 010 degrees, observed approaching burning tanker at high speed. The flying boat was screening her to port and dropped two bombs not very far from me. I went down to 130 feet.

" '16.00. Destroyer dropped a number of depth charges haphazard. She stopped to take a sweep round with her hydrophones and then steamed away southwards, presumably to protect the second tanker sighted at 13.26.

" '16.30. Destroyer returned, dropped a few more depth charges and then steamed away north at high speed.

" 'Final observation at scene of action—Wreck burning hard, upper deck awash. Heavy curtain of smoke. Cargo—petroleum or light oil.'

"During the night I transferred my sphere of activities further northwards. Once for a few seconds my heart was in my mouth. In the brightly phosphorescent water I suddenly saw the tracks of two torpedoes, flashing like two streaks of light straight for our bows. Nothing, it seemed, could possibly save us. Fortunately, however, the two torpedoes were only a couple of dolphins which had nothing better to do than to frighten the life out of us.

"By day, in order to save fuel, I remained most of the time on the bottom, coming up only for one brief period to ventilate—and was immediately chased down again by a couple of bombs from a very vigilant aircraft. At night I moved close inshore.

"The weather had once more become unfriendly. The thick clouds prevented the moonlight from shining through.

"Throughout the night we remained on the bridge, staring out into the darkness. The first wave of fatigue can be overcome by a good, strong cup of coffee. When one reaches the second phase, a cigarette, anxiously screened to prevent its glow being seen, is a great help. And, finally, a cup of steaming hot broth puts one on one's feet again.

"Ashore we could clearly see the lights of a town. It must be Wilmington, and on the other side was the wireless station on

Currytuck Island. Lucky fellows! The only thing we could not see was a ship.

"I had just gone below, and a signal reported a British landing at St. Nazaire, when a destroyer was sighted. The officer on watch had at once altered course, and the destroyer, clearly silhouetted, steamed slowly across our bows. I was in a good position to fire, but I could not afford to miss; if I did, things would be pretty sticky for us in the shallow water. After careful thought, I deliberately refrained from attacking. Later on we found that the torpedo which would have been fired at that destroyer was a dud.

"For good measure the destroyer was now joined by two anti-submarine craft.

"The explanation for this rather unexpected concourse was contained in a signal which we received the next day. On the previous day, apparently, another U-boat had sunk a patrol craft very near this spot, and now the balloon had gone up! Hence, too, the innumerable depth charges and aircraft bombs which went off all round us while we lay on the bottom. They were never a source of danger to us, but they thoroughly disturbed our period of peace and quiet.

"On 30 March I turned east once more, as my supply of fuel oil was running low. When we emerged from the American cold water belt into the Gulf Stream the temperature of the water rose thirteen degrees in a quarter of an hour. First we were in woollen jerseys and mufflers, and a quarter of an hour later we were in shorts and shirt!

"A cool west wind was blowing offshore and a thick, steamy mist was rising from the warm water. We seemed to be sailing through a vast washing tub.

"Scarcely had the visibility improved than the aircraft were back on the job. On the last day of March, in perfect weather for an attack, a tanker ran straight into my arms. At least, so it seemed. I immediately submerged. Through my periscope I could see that she was zigzagging violently and at very frequent intervals. I did all I could to get into position for a shot. Sweat poured down my face. At last, after two hours of juggling I let drive a couple of torpedoes at fairly long range and from a rather difficult angle. Contrary to my expectations both hit the ship aft. I observed two broad but not very high columns at the point of explosion, and two

169

dull detonations resounded. The torpedoe;, however, must have severely damaged the tanker, which I estimated to be of some 8,000 tons. She stopped with a heavy list and then very quietly, within five minutes of the shots, she slid stern first into the sea and disappeared. My periscope had cut under for a few minutes, when my radio operator, a lad of vivid imagination, reported that something was on fire above us. But the cracking and crackling he heard was nothing more than the horrible noise of bursting bulkheads.

"When we surfaced all that remained on the spot where the tanker had been was a gigantic patch of oil.

*   *   *

"We were seated at our usual evening game of skat—the best thing I know for calming our nerves and dismissing from our thoughts the beastly scenes we had just witnessed—when for the second time in one day a steamer was sighted. This was certainly proving to be a very fruitful area!

"Darkness had fallen. The moon was hidden behind a thick bank of cloud, and I hoped fervently that it would stay there! Our first night surface attack had begun. I rapidly made the necessary calculations.

"The first shot missed. The torpedo was a dud! I hoped very much that the ship—a 6,000-ton merchantman, laden and armed —had not noticed anything; and apparently she had not, for she steamed along with, if anything, less alteration of course than before. Gradually I worked my way ahead and sought a position for a second attack, a laborious and long business, and a race with time before the moon appeared again.

"This time I ran in close. Even without glasses we were able to pick out things on the ship's deck, and one of my men swore he could see the ship's gun being cleared for action. If he'd been right, they could have swung round and blown us to hell in an instant. But nothing of the sort occurred; the ship steamed serenely on. My second shot, too, went astray. We waited and waited, but nothing happened.

"I had a third shot, and this time I scored a hit—with the last torpedo ready for action. Then everything followed the normal pattern. The ship stopped and listed heavily. The crew took to the boats with a swift smoothness that denoted old hands at the convoy game. Then the ship disappeared for good and all.

"Ten minutes later, as we quite fortuitously passed over the spot where she had sunk, there was a heavy underwater explosion, which shot the boat up into the air and sent us all flying.

" 'They've got us!' I thought instantly, though to the 'how' and 'with what' I confess I gave no thought.

"On life-jackets! Emergency stations!" I shouted, though what good that would have done us if we'd been really for it I don't know. Then the reports began to come in. The damage, thank God, proved to be very minor.

"The explanation? As the steamer had sunk slowly beneath us, her boilers had burst.

"We now still had two torpedoes on the upper deck. But we were compelled to wait for better weather before transferring them below. On the first fine night we started on the laborious task. But the luck, which had so far stood so staunchly by us, now deserted us. The forward torpedo was faulty and presumably unserviceable; and while we were unshipping the after torpedo the hoisting gear collapsed. It took us until dawn to get the torpedo back into its container on the upper deck.

"Of course, a steamer had to choose that very morning to come sailing gaily into my sights. We had examined the faulty torpedo, and as far as we could see there wasn't a hope of its functioning properly. Even so, I felt I must have a try. My target was another heavily laden 6,000-tonner, armed as usual.

"Conditions and position were perfect when the torpedo left the tube, but it hit nothing. From the hydrophone echoes, it would seem that it veered away to starboard. The steamer noticed nothing. In fact, she zigzagged straight towards me. I had no option but to let her go; in such weather a dubious attack with guns was out of the question.

"Easter. We had been nearly six weeks at sea. The announcement over the loudspeaker: 'Boat is now returning to base!' was greeted with great joy and loud cheers. As it was already April, and the icebergs were now much closer, I chose a course well to the south of our outward course. In good weather and with a following wind we made good progress.

"I now allowed a couple of men at a time, in addition to those on watch, to be on the bridge. At long last we were able to stretch our stiffened limbs again. I even indulged in a little sunbathing—and got thoroughly and painfully burnt!

"Provisions were beginning to run short and had to be carefully watched. Stew figured prominently on the menu most days.

"The water around us was a mass of Saragossa weed, brought up by the Gulf Stream. With us, too, were innumerable jelly-fish, trailing long, white plumes behind them. When the current catches them they roll over and shine like large, shimmering, blue balls of glass. Flying fish, dolphins and whales took our minds off aircraft, columns of smoke and torpedoes.

"After a tiring time submerged, which, in anticipation of our imminent home-coming, seemed much longer than it really was, we sailed at speed and with literally our last drop of fuel through those dangerous coastal waters patrolled by enemy submarines and infested with mines.

"On 20th April *U.71* ran into La Rochelle. In eight weeks at sea the U-boat had covered 7,906 miles—7,065 on the surface and 841 submerged—without refuelling. With no casualties and only very minor damage she had sunk five ships—three tankers and two merchantmen—totalling 35,200 tons."

CHAPTER XVI

U.134. OUT OF THE FRIDGE INTO THE OVEN

Situation Report.

Doenitz was most unwilling to accede to the demands from Fuehrer Headquarters that convoys proceeding to Russia should be attacked. This meant splitting the forces detailed for the battle of the Atlantic. Of the 288 U-boats at his disposal, only 125 were front-line craft, and of these only a third at a time could be actually operating against the enemy. He was, however, forced to compromise and to agree to organise one U-boat flotilla to attack convoys carrying arms and ammunition to the Soviet forces via Murmansk and Archangel.

Doenitz contended that the battle of the Atlantic was in any case affording relief, albeit indirect relief, to our eastern front, and that therefore a direct cutting of the Russian line of supply in the Polar regions was unnecessary. The crucial point, he asserted—disregarding the few craft detailed for operations in the Arctic Ocean—remained in the Atlantic off the coast of America. It was here that after four months of war with America, the first German U-boat, U.85 (Lieutenant U. Greger), was sunk by American anti-U-boat forces.

In all, the Russians received four million tons of war material during the war by the northern route. This may well be the key to the German defeat in the East. However, it should be remembered that it was the same Fuehrer Headquarters that had obstructed U-boat construction and in the ignorance and short-sightedness of its naval policy had limited the naval budget to what was left after the other services had been provided for.

*   *   *

The commander of *U.134*, transferred for service in the Arctic Ocean, was Lieutenant Schendler. His bos'n's mate, Hofmann, was a submariner of ripe experience, who had already had his baptism of fire in *U.48*. *U.134* was on her way to Kirkenes, her new base of operations.

The Northern Lights shimmered, distant and aloof, over the vast expanse of the Polar horizon. It was bitterly cold and wet, and the men could not stop shivering; nor was it long before the aches and pains of rheumatism gripped the bones of even the youngest of them.

On the way to Kirkenes the look-out sighted a convoy. It was guarded by a few escort vessels, and in the misty weather *U.134* went straight in to the attack. Schendler first made a brief signal to U-boat Headquarters and at once sank one of the ships. Then he left the bridge, went below and, to the bewilderment of his ship's company, set a course which took him right away from the rest of the convoy. His face was ashen and grim, and he spoke not a word.

The convoy was sailing under the German flag, and Schendler had only spotted the fact after the fatal torpedo had been fired.

From Kirkenes *U.134* proceeded on her first operation in the Arctic. The winter of 1941-42 was the most severe winter for many years. After standing on watch for four hours a man was conscious of a job well and truly done; or perhaps he wasn't, for as often as not he would be so frozen that he hardly knew who or what he was, and when he descended into the boat, crusted with ice and creaking, he looked like Father Christmas.

Those going on watch assumed twice their natural size, clad in two sets of underclothes, a woollen track-suit, uniform and sou'wester, crowning the whole with a "Mickey Mouse", a cape designed to protect head and shoulders. But all to no purpose.

Two minutes on the bridge . . . and the man was soaking wet. Very soon his beard became encrusted with ice and his fingers went numb and stiff. Thawing out took half an hour. The electric heaters aboard helped in the process, but they did not warm the boat right through. The only way in which the crew could get a bit of sleep in comfort was to dress in as many of their clothes as were dry enough to put on. Outside it was always night. The months of unbroken darkness got on everybody's nerves.

U.134's operational area was the White Sea, the coast off Murmansk and Bear Island. For some curious reason, on their first trip they found that the Russians were very obligingly turning on their lights. As soon as *U.134* had passed one lighthouse and was faced with the unknown, another light would spring up ahead. Both air and water were becoming clearer, and the smooth sea afforded a wide field of vision. To the north they noticed some curious oil patches on the water. Had a tanker been sunk? Or even, perhaps, a U-boat? The little patches came nearer and nearer, joining together to make big patches. Soon *U.134* was sailing through the middle of them. They were obviously not oil, for the shimmering rainbow colours of oil on water were not evident.

Suddenly they saw that these patches were formed by minute crystals of ice floating, like specks of dust, on the chilled water. Gradually the crystals became bigger, and were soon quite clearly visible as small, white patches. Then the little patches joined together into groups, at first the size of a small plate, then growing larger and larger, crunching, grinding and always coagulating.

U.134 had become an ice-breaker; and it was here that navigation ended and polar exploration began.

At last a ship was sighted. Bos'n Hofmann had spotted her with the naked eye.

The remainder of the operation—after the sinking of this ship— was without incident. There was very little shipping in those Arctic waters and it was more or less a question of the U-boat being on the spot—just in case. . . .

U.134 returned to base, was ordered to proceed to La Rochelle and there received orders to proceed to the central Atlantic and the Gulf of Mexico.

"Cold's bad enough, but this heat's worse," wrote Hofmann in his diary on a page bespattered with drops of sweat. When the boat was submerged, sailing up and down off the coast of Florida, the heat became well nigh intolerable. Between the refrigerator and the mess the fresh, cool butter was transformed into greasy oil. To try and spread it with a knife on bread was just silly. Everything aboard was clammy and sticky. Everything was wet and damp. The bacon was rancid, the sausage was rancid, the butter was rancid, and the water was foul. Boils had now become the badge of the ship's community.

The Gulf of Mexico was deserted. The Americans were sending their ships along the coasts, well aware that the U-boats would hesitate to follow them into these shallow waters, which afforded no opportunity in submerging. *U.134* had a look at the estuary of the Mississippi. Not a ship. Not even a wisp of smoke. By boycotting the shipping route the Americans hoped to blunt the enthusiasm of the U-boats and wear down their morale. Indeed, this endless and fruitless searching did have considerable effect on the spirits of the crew, who seemed to slip from one slough of despond into another. The news that a ship had been sighted acted like an electric shock.

Schendler decided to attack while submerged. His target was excellently placed, and he could get into a firing position without any difficulty. Over the ship's inter-com he gave a running commentary on what he could see . . . till finally:

"The ship is now coming into our sights." Immediately afterwards came the old, familiar orders.

As the torpedo left the tube, the chief quartermaster pressed the knob of the stop-watch which he was holding in the hollow of his palm. He and those around him followed the jerky progress of the second hand with eager intentness. If the torpedo had been well and truly aimed it should reach its mark just as the second hand reached the point the quartermaster was marking with his thumb nail. Suddenly the commander threw his arms in the air, and at the same time the dull thud of an exploding torpedo reached the ship.

The quartermaster gave a start. He gazed down at the watch in astonishment. 'Damn it,' he thought, 'Have I taken leave of my senses? Is the watch faulty?' What was happening? The explosion had occurred a good five or six seconds before it was due. Had the Old Man made a mess of it? And why had he flung his arms up like that?

"——!" shouted someone—and the whole crew recognised the voice of their commander.

"Here, blast it, take a look for yourself. Either I'm right in what I can see, or I've gone crackers!"

"No, Sir—you're quite right."

After the torpedo had left its tube the commander had remained at the periscope to observe its effect. But several seconds earlier than he had estimated he saw a bright flash and a great fountain of water rise behind the merchantman. When the water fountain subsided the usual familiar sight greeted his eyes. The ship had broken in two. And while he was trying to puzzle things out— why the torpedo had exploded several seconds before its time, and why the column of water had risen from the other side of the ship, as though the torpedo had circled round her and then hit her from the opposite direction—he suddenly caught sight, far off in the distance behind the sinking ship, of the unmistakable outlines of a U-boat conning-tower.

Another U-boat had beaten *U.134* by a few seconds and had literally snatched the eagerly awaited prey from under her very nose. The only consolation for *U.134*'s crew was the knowledge that they were not alone in this deserted part of the ocean.

A few days later. . . .

"Smoke dead ahead!" yelled the look-out excitedly.

Binoculars swiftly confirmed the presence of two plumes of smoke, or possibly even three. It could be a convoy. *U.134* went at speed into the attack.

"Bloody funny, those smoke columns," muttered Hofmann to himself. "They're not moving. It looks as though the whole lot are anchored."

"No, no!" answered the commander. "The convoy's sailing on the same course as we are, obviously."

That certainly seemed a reasonable enough explanation.

The columns of smoke grew much more rapidly than Schendler had anticipated; but he could see no sight of mastheads or hulls coming up over the horizon.

When they had approached a little nearer, Schendler was able to see the awful truth for himself. The smoke was coming from the two fussily puffing chimneys of some factory built on one of the smaller islands of the Antilles group. A glance at the chart would have told them that long before. But who could be expected to think of a thing like that in such blazing heat!

CHAPTER XVII

LACONIA

Situation Report.

By the spring of *1942* it seemed certain that the enemy had succeeded in developing a radar set small enough to be fitted into an aircraft. Up till then the German scientists had declared that it was impossible to adapt the *DeTe* set for such purposes. However, when the High Command became convinced that direct night attacks on U-boats could only have been implemented with the assistance of radar, the German scientists produced the Metox search receiver. This was a warning device which gave a rough bearing based on the enemy's radar impulses. Since the Metox aerial (raised when the U-boat surfaced) emitted radiations, it was thought that this was responsible for later heavy losses. However, it was proved, eventually, that Metox had not betrayed the position of the U-boats and that the British success was based on a centimetre waveband radar in the aircraft.

In the direct combating of the U-boat menace, too, the enemy was searching for better methods. "Hedgehog" was the name given by the British to a new weapon which was used against U-boats for the first time in January *1942*. With "Hedgehog" it was possible to continue to operate Asdic while depth charges were actually being dropped. "Hedgehog" consisted of a container, rather like a packing-case, in which were 24 thirty-two-pound charges, loaded with the new explosive, amatol, and so arranged that they could be discharged singly, in series or in a single salvo. It also included other improvements on the earlier depth charges.

From the beginning of May the Americans gathered their shipping into heavily escorted convoys and kept them close inshore. These tactics not only increased the difficulties of the U-boats, but eventually, thanks to the shallow water, rendered any U-boat attack virtually impossible. The U-boats withdrew from American coastal waters, and it was left to the mines to score a few, isolated successes.

In the Atlantic itself the battle was reaching its climax. In May, for the loss of four U-boats, 600,000 tons of shipping were sunk; in June 700,000 tons were destroyed and three U-boats were sunk.

*From early June the British added further aircraft, all fitted with
the new radar equipment, to their forces over the Bay of Biscay. This
area was now patrolled day and night.*

*In a device called "Bold" the Germans thought that they had found
an adequate antidote to Britain's Asdic. "Bold", admittedly, did not
cut out underwater location, but it confused the enemy and caused him
considerable irritation. It consisted of apparatus which caused reflection
of the Asdic impulses and acted as a decoy.*

*In Germany there was no dearth of eminent scientists, but there was
a lamentable lack of sense in the attitude of the High Command.
Many specialists were popped into uniform to serve as privates or
ratings.*

*In the midst of all the rigours of the Arctic ocean, in the bitter attacks
on convoys, and in the lonely wastes of the South Atlantic, there were
still a few light-hearted interludes.*

*   *   *

U.68 provides a good example.

Off the British naval base of Freetown a floating sack was
sighted. It was first spotted by the navigator, Griese. Thoughtfully and in silence he and Merten eyed this dumb witness of a
force that had been destroyed, as it rolled slowly and wearily in the
steel-blue sea. In times of peace imagination could have conjured
up whole volumes on the fate of the ship from whose hold it had
escaped. But now, in war, to deduce its origin made no strain on
the imagination. Without any doubt it had come from some
sunken merchantman.

"Sack of flour," remarked Merten, and Griese saw his eyes light
up as he said it, just as though the Old Man had had a bright
idea. The others on the bridge kept their eyes fixed on their own
sector of the sea. Sacks of flour were no concern of theirs.

"Wouldn't it be nice, Sir?" said Griese significantly, at the same
time sketching on the bridge coaming with his finger something
that looked rather like a nice fresh loaf of bread.

"What do you think, Griese? But even if it is flour, it won't be
much good now, will it?"

"We might have a look, Sir."

U.68 turned towards the sack. With the help of a couple of
hands, only too grateful for any novelty which broke the mono-

tony, Chief Petty Officer Bitowski hauled it aboard. It was a smooth, slippery, two-hundredweight sack. Hoffmann, the cook, deftly slit it open, as though it were a pig's stomach. Under the sacking was a greyish-looking porridge of slimy, wet flour. He drove his knife deeper into the sack. Here he struck snow-white, dry flour. "Made in Canada." The slimy outer casing peeled off like the skin of a sausage.

"Hoffman, keep on with the good work—and let me know as soon as possible if the stuff's any use."

Five minutes later the cook's beaming peasant's face with its crinkly fringe of red, fuzzy beard popped up through the hatch.

"It'll do, Captain. First-class flour."

In all, five sacks were fished out of the sea. In the evening the cook got busy with his mysterious rites, and that night the crew had Berlin pancakes for supper.

There were two other members of the crew who were jubilant at the treasure trove: Grecian, the ship's champion baker of bread, and Geest, a master in the art of pastry-making. Their talents, coyly hidden, had been discovered by Merten himself, who had a reputation throughout the U-boat service for making excellent use of any and every thing that came to hand.

There is another rather amusing story connected with Merten. At one stage his cook had unearthed a rusty tin which contained magnificent Australian fruit. It was a relic from that unfortunate rendezvous with the auxiliary cruiser *Atlantis*.

"Pity we don't ever get the chance to fix our hooks on a ship carrying this sort of thing," said Hoffmann. "Those blokes in the auxiliaries don't know when they're well off."

This remark of Hoffmann's, flippantly though it had been made, was a signal for the younger officers on board to drop a number of more or less subtle hints to the Old Man. At first Merten remained strictly unresponsive, then, however, he began to lend an ear.

U.68 was in very peaceful waters, far from the grim and stubbornly protected convoy route on the Great Circle. Here there was peace, perfect, unbroken peace. Aircraft were things unknown; so were steamers—or nearly so.

Merten decided that he would give the next vessel sighted just a tap, enough to stop her, but not enough to sink her. Then they would see how things turned out.

One night the eagerly awaited steamer was sighted and sailed blissfully across the stern of *U.68*. Petty Officer Buttke, who was responsible for the look-out aft, spotted just a faint, thin silhouette. Merten gazed intently in the direction indicated.

"Hallo—it's getting smaller! Now it's gone, damn it! No, by God! We're in luck. She's steaming on a reciprocal course and now she's come slap into our after sector!"

Buttke received a pat on the back, and the chief engineer was asked for full speed. Within ten minutes the silhouette was in sight again. After that everything went like a demonstration at the U-boat Tactical School.

The torpedo hit, but not in a vital spot. It just gave the ship a tap, as Merten described it. But the British aboard her seemed to be a hard-bitten set of toughs. They made no attempt whatever to abandon ship. Why should they, indeed? The ship was still afloat, and whether the U-boat had another torpedo after the "miss" she'd scored remained to be seen.

"Well—we'll have to ginger 'em up a bit," said Merten.

A few bursts of machine-gun fire went whistling over the steamer's bridge; and then the crew did start to move. The scene looked like a film shot, even to the ship's boats pulling towards instead of away from, the U-boat.

"Captain Hawe," a tall, thin figure in the boat nearest *U.68* introduced himself. The man sitting on the thwart beside him was his chief engineer.

To Merten's question the captain gave a short, terse reply: "General cargo."

That, of course, could have included anything—trouser-buttons, razor-blades, cigarette-lighters, safety pins or even five billion pairs of suspenders. Merten was at first inclined to show anger, but he controlled himself, recalling that had he been in the British captain's shoes he would himself have given much the same answer.

In the meanwhile, some of the crew were clambering back aboard their ship, for all the world as though the presence of a German U-boat didn't worry them at all. What the hell could the damn Germans do, anyway? They couldn't ram with their tin-pot little ship!

The U-boat opened fire with her light A.A. weapons.

The crew, thinking that the Germans really meant business, again abandoned ship, this time a little more quickly than before. Their boats disappeared swiftly into the darkness, and only the noise of their rowlocks broke the silence of the night. Every now and then a loud and violent curse rang out across the water.

Merten decided to send a prize crew aboard; he was anxious to find out what the somewhat ominous phrase "General cargo" covered. When he called for volunteers, his whole crew responded, and he was rather at a loss to know whom to send. Eventually the boarding party stepped into the unsinkable and un-capsizable boat (at least, that's how the makers had described it), manned by the best seamen. Merten watched them cast off and then was horrified to see the boat overturned by the powerful swell when it was a bare ten yards from the U-boat.

He cursed the designer and the makers of the boat, he cursed the ham-fisted idiots in it and above all he cursed himself. All this did not worry the men of the boarding party; the water was lovely, and a swim was most refreshing.

Merten's mind, however, was on the sharks and the responsibilities he had assumed in staging this adventure.

He shuddered to think of the dressing-down Doenitz would give him if he lost a man in the process.

However, they all clambered safely back aboard.

From the expression on his face, it was obvious that Merten had little inclination to repeat the experiment.

"Well—what now? How are we going to get at the cargo without boarding the ship? Any man got any ideas on the subject?"

The men stared glumly at their commander. His poor joke did not go down very well.

"No ideas? Right—listen. You, too, chief, with your mechanical turn of mind. It has suddenly struck me that if we can smash up the hatch covers over the hold with the 2-cm., then, when we sink her, some of the cargo will bound to be left on the surface—provided, that is, the old tub is kind enough to sink on an even keel."

"You're right, Sir!" exclaimed the chief engineer.

And so it was done. A stream of tracer bullets flashed through the night. There was a splintering of wood, and shreds of tarpaulin flew through the air. The iron linchpins shot out of their sockets.

Two of the holds were already open. Where before there had

been a grey surface of tarpaulin protecting the cargo from rain and seawater, there now yawned a black hole.

A carefully placed torpedo ensured that the ship would sink on an even keel. She was a bit down by the stern when she disappeared. Then one after another packing cases were spewed up to the surface from the bowels of the 6,000-tonner.

Vast, enormous cases! The men gazed at them in astonishment.

"And how the hell are we going to get a thing as big as a house on the deck of our little boat?"

"Easy! Money for old rope!" snapped the chief. "Flood her forrard, push her nose under a crate and then blow. It'll work like a Hamburg crane."

"Good! Carry on!" said Merton.

Half an hour later one of the great cases was resting securely on the U-boat's deck, its ends protruding a good two yards on each side. The excitement was tremendous. Everyone wanted to take a hand in opening it up. The artificers, accustomed by long habit to working with conscientious and meticulous precision, started drawing nail by nail with the aid of pincers. The seamen got down to the job with hatchets.

An air of Christmas-like expectancy pervaded the boat, and Merten was as pleased as Punch at having been able to give his crew this bit of fun. Bit of fun? No—it was the treat of the century!

To the chief engineer fell the honour of lifting the lid and exposing the hidden treasure. Necks craned and stretched. The contents were still shrouded from their gaze by oiled paper.

"I've smelt something like this before," said the chief petty officer.

To cut a long story short; the crate contained eight hundred oilskins. Nothing for mother or the girl friend at home, nothing for the pot, but only a lot of gear, of use only to seamen and only in dirty weather.

The next crate was slightly smaller. Contents—sou'westers. The next—again sou'westers. And the next, again a bit bigger—oilskins.

Merten gave up. The men were more downhearted with disappointment than exhausted by their labours, and it was quite a time before they could see the funny side of things.

That evening on the little wooden rectangle that served as a table in the ridiculously tiny officers' mess, at the place where Merten normally sat, was a visiting card in copper-plate writing:

Karl Friedrich Merten
Traveller in Oilskins & Sou'westers

*   *   *

"Tomorrow we must sight a ship, if only as a birthday present for August Maus," said Merten one night as with a shout of 'Gangway below' he disappeared down the conning-tower to snatch a few hours sleep on his hard bunk.

"She'll show up, Sir. You can put your shirt on it," called Maus, his first officer.

That was a little before midnight. After a brief inspection of his boat, Merten flung himself fully dressed on his bunk. He had just intended to snatch a few hours' rest, but before he knew where he was he was fast and sound asleep. Nor did he stir when his first officer walked into the cabin.

"Sir, I beg to report that the steamer you ordered is waiting!"

"If this is his idea of a joke . . ." thought Merten crossly in his sleep.

"Sir, ship in sight, dead ahead!"

"Oh, yes? And next I suppose you'll tell me that the British have already abandoned ship in panic and, please, will I come up and give my celebrated imitation of Santa Claus. No thank you. Good night—and—get to hell out of here!" Maus was non-plussed. He shook Merton pretty roughly and said in an urgent voice.

"I'm not kidding, Sir. It's a ship—a 6,000-tonner."

Merten woke with a start, shook himself and, wide awake now, dived through the round watertight door that led into the control-room. In two swift strides he reached the conning-tower. Below the glittering disc of the rising sun, he saw a ship, very close indeed, and at least a 5,000-tonner.

Had the U-boat been spotted? There was no time to ponder over possible plans.

"Crash dive!"

The ship was brought down to periscope depth. The trim was atrocious. But it was not the chief engineer's fault and there was nothing he could do about it.

"Can't hold her at periscope depth, Sir," he warned.

184

But there was no time for anything. Without pausing to make any calculations Merten seized upon the last chance and let drive with a torpedo.

A slight shudder rumbled dully round the pressure hull. Merten decided to raise his periscope and at the same time called for increased speed in order to be able to use his hydroplanes to help him to surface more quickly.

Suddenly there was a violent, explosive jolt. The U-boat bucked and twisted, almost as though she had hit a rock at full speed, and had been brought to an abrupt standstill. The chief engine-room artificer was hurled head first against the overhead tank and knocked unconscious.

A rock? Nonsense—there were no rocks in mid-Atlantic. Or was it a submarine?

The periscope gear was humming softly, and Merten already had his eye glued to the eye-piece. The periscope broke surface. What on earth . . . ! Before him was a black wall, flecked with patches of rust and red lead. The side of a ship, obviously; what else could it be?

It was so near that it seemed to Merten that he only had to stretch out his hand to touch it. How had it got there? Perhaps the ship had altered course at the last moment, he thought, and then, after she had been hit, had swung violently towards him.

"Full astern."

The order was given calmly, and the men breathed a sigh of relief. One or two were scratching their heads pensively. Meanwhile a series of fantastic pictures passed before Merten's eyes. Vertically above him lifeboats were being lowered. Men were tumbling into them with panic-stricken faces. One seemed to be completely mad. Another was waving naked, hairy arms and appearing again and again in the periscope. The fellow was trembling like a jelly. The bridge was afire and enveloped in thick, black smoke. On the stern Merten could distinguish quite clearly two heavy guns. But they were not manned. The crews had abandoned them. Merten could not understand the reason for all this panic. When a ship was as heavily armed as this, the crew didn't normally abandon her in this fashion, but stuck to her, at least for as long as she promised to keep afloat.

In a flash his mind reverted to the dynamite ship in the Caribbean. . . .

U.68 submerged as quickly as she could. A quarter of a mile further on, Merten cautiously raised his periscope again. It was just possible that those fellows over there had pulled themselves together again and had manned their guns.

Merten had not yet got the ship in the periscope's eye when a murderous explosion rent the air.

"So that's it, by God!" cried Merten.

"Surface!"

Merten leapt up to the bridge. A vast mushroom of thick black smoke covered the spot where the freighter had been. The force of the explosion must have been terrific, for the columns of water rose well nigh three thousand feet into the air. The ship seemed to have burst like a soap bubble.

It was only later that *U.68* obtained any details. The ship had been the *Bradford City*, with a few thousand tons of aviation petrol aboard! That, then, was the reason for the panic-stricken flight.

*   *   *

It was not always to bombs and depth charges that the U-boats fell victim. Sometimes a technical fault was the cause of disaster, something which would seem trivial to the layman, but which to submariners were of vital importance. . . .

Here is an example.

It is the duty of the technical personnel to measure water densities at precisely specified intervals. In *U.128* this duty devolved upon Midshipman Ossadnik. *U.128* was one of the new big Type IXc boats. In March 1942 she proceeded on her first operation and came back with pennants fluttering. She then underwent a test as an anti-aircraft U-boat, put to sea again in September and was ordered to proceed to Africa to attack a cruiser reported by Naval Intelligence to be operating off Freetown. She failed to make contact with the cruiser. Lieutenant Heise was annoyed because he had been forbidden to fire at anything else and had consequently missed many a golden opportunity. After a long and fruitless search Heise was called off and directed to proceed to the coast of South America. Twelve hours after these orders had been received an Italian submarine (Captain Rossi) sighted the cruiser and sank her.

U.128 had meanwhile set course for the shipping lane between

Bahia and Trinidad. Every twelve hours Ossadnik measured the water density and entered the results. This data then went to the chief engineer, who required it when making his calculations for submerging. Ten hours had passed since the last measurement had been taken, when suddenly *U.128* had to submerge in a hurry. The chief engineer based his rapid calculations on the last available information. The ship sank like a stone to a depth of nearly 500 feet.

The water had become lighter, for *U.128* had run into a channel that was not marked on the charts.

The electric motors hummed. The commander gave the order, "Full ahead." The hydroplanes were set hard to bring her up, but the boat failed to answer. She was plunging downwards at an angle of 45 degrees. Everything that was not properly secured went bumping and clattering into the bows, adding to the weight forward and increasing the danger.

The boat had already reached a depth at which, in theory, the hull should have collapsed under the pressure. Only the commander and the chief engineer knew that the new German U-boats were able to withstand this pressure without any grave danger.

In a U-boat diving depths are taboo as a subject of discussion. That is entirely the captain's affair. *U.128* continued to go deeper. The pressure hull groaned. A dull, singing noise, an ominous creaking and cracking filled the boat. Meanwhile, the diving tanks had been blown. The fatal plunge was at last arrested. The U-boat started to rise, at first slowly, then faster and faster. . . .

And the reason for this nightmare plunge had been "only" a difference in water density.

*　　　*　　　*

U.128 took on fuel and provisions at sea and was able to continue her operations. In January 1943, *U.128* returned to base, after nearly five months at sea and after having used her fuel oil to the last drop.

*　　　*　　　*

On 12 September, 550 miles from Las Palmas, *U.156* (Lieutenant Hartenstein) sank a 19,965-ton transport, the former Cunard-White Star liner *Laconia*. There were 3,000 on board—463 crew, 286 British troops proceeding on leave, 80 women and

187

children and 1,800 Italian prisoners of war from North Africa. One third of the survivors were rescued by Hartenstein and the other U-boats of the "Polar Bear" group ordered by Doenitz to the scene of the disaster. These included *U.507* (Lieutenant Schacht) and *U.506* (Lieutenant Würdemann). Some survivors were taken aboard the U-boats themselves, others were put into lifeboats which were taken in tow. For five complete days the German submariners looked after friend and foe with equal care. On 17 September all the survivors were handed over safely to ships of the "Darlan Fleet," which Doenitz had summoned by radio to go to their assistance.

In spite of U-boat Headquarters' orders of 17 September precluding the future rescue of survivors except in special circumstances, which must have subjected all U-boat commanders to an immense moral and psychological strain, these latter still continued to do all that was humanly possible to save life, as the following exploits of *U.71* and *U.207* will show.

*   *   *

U.71 was under the command of Lieutenant Flachsenberg.

The increasing numbers of patrol vessels and aircraft had greatly added to the difficulties of the tasks assigned to him. Steamers, in this area, were becoming a rare sight. He did, however, manage to surprise one tanker, sailing independently. Weeks later a sailing vessel unexpectedly hove in sight. It was a cutter, a typical ship's lifeboat, a fragile nutshell on the tumultuous waters.

"Keep a sharp eye open for aircraft," Flachsenberg warned the bridge look-out and turned his U-boat in the direction of the cutter. He approached her from astern, and when he was near enough to read her name he was horrified. The boat belonged to the tanker he had sunk three weeks before!

Under a tarpaulin he discerned human figures. They were inert and motionless. Even when the heavy seas caused the U-boat to bump violently into the side of the cutter, they showed no sign of life. "Nothing much we can do for those poor devils," murmured the officer on watch.

Flaschenberg cast off. Was there nothing he could do? Once more his eyes turned back to the cutter. Through his binoculars he saw three figures crawl painfully from beneath the tarpaulin, waving feebly.

He turned back again. The three men were Norwegians. One of them, younger than his companions and seemingly less exhausted than they were, had grasped the tiller and slumped beside it. The other two presented a terrible sight. Their gaunt, hollow faces were salt-encrusted and smeared with oil. Their cheek bones protruded, and above them glaring, feverish eyes gazed at the U-boat commander. Their bodies were little more than animated skeletons. Even had they been capable of coherent thought, they would never have dreamed that this was, indeed, the U-boat which had sunk their ship three weeks before.

Flachsenberg had to strain his ears to catch what the youngest of the trio feebly shouted across to him . . .

. . . originally there had been eleven men in the boat; they had been the sole survivors from the tanker. . . .

They did not ask for help. But their red-rimmed, pleading eyes were more eloquent than any words.

Flachsenberg was deeply moved. The others on the bridge felt themselves trembling at the knees.

In spite of U-boats Headquarters' clear orders, in spite of the very real danger that at any moment an aircraft equipped with the new radar might plunge through the clouds and attack him with bomb and machine-gun, Flachsenberg gave the men food and water, cigarettes—and a generous drop of drink for good measure.

"Have you got a chart?" asked the officer on watch.

They shook their heads.

They were at once given a chart, with their present position marked on it and their exact course to Greenland, which was only a hundred miles away. Only . . .?

U.71 went about her business. Watching the cockleshell through his glasses, Flachsenberg saw the youngest of the trio, the only one capable of thought or movement, rise to his feet and then as suddenly collapse from sheer exhaustion as surely as though he had been struck with a hatchet.

Flachsenberg literally shuddered with horror.

"Once they've had a drink and a good feed and regained their strength, they'll make it all right," said the officer on watch; but

189

his tone was that of pious, albeit sincere, hope rather than that of conviction.

"Let's hope so. With God's help, everything is possible."

"Beg pardon, Sir! Shall I—er—shall I enter that issue of stores in the log?" asked the chief quartermaster a little later.

"What d'you mean? Of course you'll enter them, with a note that they were issued by my orders," snapped Flachsenberg.

*   *   *

One final example of a similar nature; an extract from the war diary of *U.207*:

"18.30. Red light sighted to port. On closing it was found to be coming from two bright yellow rubber dinghies, one with four men in it and the other with two. The men waved to us. Circled round the boats. Occupants were the crew of a British aircraft.

"19.20. Survivors taken aboard as prisoners of war. Had I given them food and water and left them to their own devices, they would, in this fine weather, have stood a very good chance of being picked up by a flying-boat. On the other hand they would never by their own exertions have been able to reach the coast which was 440 miles away.

"The next day: wind force 6–7. Sea force 6. I took the rubber boats with me, in order to be able, should the need arise, to cast my prisoners adrift again."

There followed the names of two British officers, three NCO's and a seaman.

Entry by Doenitz, after *U.207* had returned to base:

"Action approved."

CHAPTER XVIII

THE EXPERIMENTS OF HELMUTH WALTER

Situation Report.

Attacks on convoys were becoming increasingly difficult, owing to the expanding number of escort vessels. For some little time past, destroyers and patrol craft had been stationed between the columns of merchantmen to counteract the German infiltration tactics. In addition, the British had now taken to stationing some of their new "killer groups" at considerable distances from the convoys, with the result that the U-boats were frequently discovered, attacked and driven off before they could close with their target. The radius of action of British aircraft was ever widening, and the vital area of the battle of the Atlantic was consequently extending further and further westwards. "Our only answer lies in U-boats which can travel far faster under water than those at present in service," declared Doenitz at a Fuehrer conference. Some hope seemed to be afforded by the plans of Helmuth Walter, an engineer of the Germania shipbuilding wharf. These plans had received Raeder's support but were maturing very slowly owing to lack of funds. The basis of Walter's plans and experiments was hydrogen-peroxide or perhydrol.

*　　　*　　　*

If you put your finger into a glass of concentrated hydrogen-peroxide (H_2O_2) you would at first feel nothing. But on taking it out of the glass you would find that the whole surface of the skin, up to the point of immersion, had been burnt and bleached. Later the pain would become maddening. One drop of this hydrogen-peroxide on a piece of wood, and it will immediately burst into flames which will spread at an amazing speed. Water is the only thing which can extinguish it. Neither sand nor the normal foam extinguishers are of the slightest use. There are only a very few substances—glass, certain types of rubber, burnished V2 and V4 steel—that do not act as catalysts in contact with hydrogen-peroxide.

When Walter submitted his plans to the German Navy in 1937,

191

he saw two possible ways in which use could be made of oxygen released by disintegration and of the high thermal energy of perhydrol resulting from it:—

A. He hoped to increase the performance of diesel engines without having to rely on oxygen from the atmosphere.

B. He foresaw even greater practical possibilities, if he could succeed in using the highly compressed gases enriched with oxygen as motive power for a turbine.

Raeder, however, was not in position to put at Walter's disposal the very considerable sum of money that would be required for expensive experiments, however much he himself was convinced that Walter's ideas would produce a revolution in submarine propulsion. But, as the air force had also begun to take an interest in Walter's research in connection with a beam-controlled fighter they had in mind, Walter received a very considerable subsidiary sum from the influential Goering.

It was, perhaps, due to the nature of the man that Walter's experiments were not conducted in a co-ordinated manner.

This restless—I had almost said unstable—scientific genius had no sooner launched one experimental project on its way than he would rush into the office with fresh plans. Had the navy been able to provide him with an adequate staff of scientists and technicians, Helmuth Walter's brilliant conceptions would have been followed up in a more orderly fashion and would have been brought to a swifter and more thorough conclusion.

Walter's band of collaborators was small and it remained small, even in 1940 after he had proved that the ideas he had evolved in 1934 and submitted to Doenitz in 1937 were now at last capable of realisation. In spite of the meagre funds and inadequate plant at his disposal, a few months after the outbreak of war, Walter succeeded in producing the first experimental turbine.

The equipment was just as primitive as it was uneconomic. It could not yet make use of the liberated oxygen, because it did not as yet have any supply of gas-oil. All it really did was to drive a turbine by means of the steam-oxygen mixture.

The apparatus consisted simply of a pump for the concentrated substance, a supply pipe for the perhydrol, a catalyst, bound with porous clay, a transmission valve for the steam-oxygen mixture and a turbine attached.

Right: The commander at the periscope. The torpedo has just been fired

Centre: Waiting for orders. Will depth charges follow?

Bottom left: Crash dive! The flooding valves are opened

Bottom right: Operating the hydrophones. Alert but calm

Depth charges. Gauges break. A pipe bursts. Without waiting for orders a man leaps forward and closes the valves

The restricted space of the compartment which houses a now lame Diesel

This worked quite simply. The perhydrol was pumped up out of the container and sprayed through very fine jets on to the catalyst. This caused disintegration. The water liberated by the disintegration was turned into steam at 485 degrees Centigrade by the generated heat quantity. This produced the vaporised steam-oxygen mixture already mentioned, and this in its turn was directed under high pressure into the turbine.

The first experimental model proved that the apparatus was capable of a very high performance and that with it great energy could be generated in a small space. The hopes cherished in the preliminary exploratory stage appeared to have been realised.

The experimental U-boat *V.80*, built in 1940, with "A-steam plant", as Walter named the plant without combustion chamber and supplementary fuel oil, was tested by the civil engineers of the Germania shipbuilding yards and proved a success.

The boat achieved an underwater speed of 26 knots as compared with the usual 9 knots. There were plenty of people in authority who did not believe these results and plenty more who regarded the whole experiment as a waste of time that was as costly and useless as it was dangerous.

The last part of this latter criticism was justified to a certain degree. It quickly became apparent that an escape of carbon dioxyde from the glands of the turbine was, technically speaking, inevitable. The constructors, however, had foreseen this danger and had counteracted it by putting in an armour-plated, gas-proof bulkhead.

In the meanwhile, on the experimental bench Walter had developed the final form of *V.300*, a double plant designed for a craft with twin propellers.

"But where," asked the High Command, "do you propose to put the perhydrol, if, as you say, you want 15 tons for one single hour's running?"

Walter was ready for that objection. Taking a pencil from his pocket he drew a circle on a bit of paper and below it he drew a second circle, this forming approximately a figure 8.

"The upper circle," he said, "is a cross-section of the normal pressure hull; the circle below represents a second pressure hull interlocked with the one above it."

It was in this lower half of the 8, Walter explained, that he proposed to carry the perhydrol. It would be large enough to hold sufficient perhydrol for at least five or six hours at maximum speed, enough, that is, to bring the U-boat, which would be equipped with both diesel and electric motors as well, swiftly up to any convoy and enable it to withdraw to safety with equal rapidity after the attack.

"But in what sort of container are you going to put this bloody stuff?" was another question, for it could not be put into any ordinary fuel tank in the same way as normal fuel oil; the tank would have to be lined either with glass, with pure aluminium, rubber or V2 or V4 steel. Even that, however, afforded no solution, for with the enormous rate of perhydrol consumption there arose the further problem of how to compensate for this swift loss of weight while the ship was travelling under water. With ordinary fuel oil this is the easiest thing in the world, because the oil is lighter than water; it is carried therefore in tanks that can be flooded from below, which means that the water entering through ducts in the bottom of the tank rises gradually as the oil is drawn off and used from the top.

Perhydrol, however, could not be allowed to come into contact with sea water, because it would at once mix with the water, and the requisite concentration would thus become diluted.

With the simplicity of genius Walter found the solution to this problem in milopan sacks which were to be hung in the tank and into which the perhydrol would be loaded. Milopan is an acid-proof type of synthetic rubber which does not act as a catalyst. With the perhydrol contained in these sacks (hanging within the tank itself) sea water could, with impunity, be allowed to flow in through valves at the bottom of the tank and thus compensate for the gradual loss of weight as the perhydrol was being consumed.

Raeder sanctioned the construction of four Type XVIIa Walter U-boats as experimental craft and for instructional purposes, two to be built by the Germania shipbuilding yard and two by Blohm and Voss of Hamburg.

With the new method of propulsion the principle which had hitherto held good, namely, that a U-boat travels more slowly submerged than on the surface, would now be reversed. The whole tactics of submarine warfare would be revolutionised. The

Walter U-boat would be able to overtake and attack any convoy submerged, undetected and unhampered by any aircraft. The Walter U-boat of the Type XVIIb, operational type, could travel submerged at an estimated maximum speed of 23 knots, enough, that is, to allow the boat to withdraw at high speed from the danger zone. In order to save the use of the Walter plant for the purely operational phase, these U-boats would be fitted with electric motors, in addition to their diesel motors.

In September 1942 Raeder spoke on the Walter U-boat at a Fuehrer Headquarters conference. He hoped, he said, to see his way clear within two months to give the order for the construction of the first twenty-four Type XVIIb operational craft. He had satisfied himself as to their potentialities. If the new U-boats proved to be a success, which he himself was convinced that they would be, he would at once give orders for their mass production, provided that he was granted the necessary funds.

"The U-boats play so decisive a role as regards the outcome of the war that the necessary action must be taken as a matter of highest priority," declared Hitler in support of Raeder.

Many months passed, however, before the situation clarified. In the meanwhile, Raeder had retired. Doenitz had assumed the office of Commander-in-Chief. The construction of the first four experimental U-boats was retarded in favour of new projects. . . .

Nothing further was taken until calamity had overtaken the Reich and by then it was too late. The alternative that had been under consideration was the construction of electric U-boats. It was Walter's figure of 8 that gave the idea its initial impetus. Instead of perhydrol it was proposed to use the lower half of the 8 to house the bigger electric batteries which would give the Type XXI and XIII U-boats an estimated underwater speed of 19 knots.

CHAPTER XIX

ANOTHER "PAUKENSCHLAG"—OFF CAPE TOWN

Situation Report—Autumn 1942.

In order to eliminate the time-consuming outward and inward passages through the Bay of Biscay—passages, incidentally, which were becoming ever more hazardous as the result of increased enemy air activity—the German Navy commissioned a number of supply U-boats. These craft were to supply the U-boats at sea with everything they required for the continuation and extension of their operational activities. They further allowed Doenitz to extend the sphere of his operations to include also the southernmost portions of the South Atlantic. Once again he succeeded in a "Paukenschlag" by sending a battle group into the very harbour of Cape Town itself. On the other hand, however, the enemy was inexplicably succeeding in attacking the secret supply rendezvous with increasing frequency. That he had broken the German secret cipher was out of the question.

*   *   *

It was August.

Emmermann was sitting, happy and in high spirits, at his own wedding breakfast, when he received a telegram—"Report forthwith for duty to U-boat HQ."

In the middle of the first night of his honeymoon Emmermann left his young wife and hastened to report to U-boat HQ. The senior naval staff officer handed him a sealed envelope.

"Read these through, please. They are your operational orders; and if you have any questions, please let me know at once."

"And is this what you've recalled me from leave for?"

"It happens sometimes, you know, Emmermann."

"I got married the day before yesterday."

"Oh! I wish we'd known that."

Emmermann slit open the envelope, not particularly eagerly, for all these damn operation orders, he knew, were much of a muchness.

"You will proceed through the Bay of Biscay to sector . . . Subsequent orders will be issued by U-boat HQ."

"This looks as though it might be something rather special."

"It is, old boy. You have a cup of tea and wait a bit. You'll be surprised!"

The objective was Cape Town. Emmermann and three other U-boats were to carry out a foray against it. The other commanders of the group were to be Merten, Witte and Poske.

"All contact with the enemy before reaching the objective will be avoided."

Zero hour for the attack itself was to be communicated later by signal. Arrangements for replenishment of supplies at sea had been made. Estimated length of operation—twenty weeks.

At brief intervals the four U-boats set forth. None was aware of the whereabouts of the others. Until the operational sector was reached, each commander was to act independently and had to ensure that he reached the South Atlantic unobserved. The days and weeks passed in monotonous rhythm. A gigantic turtle was the sole cause of excitement in Emmermann's boat. He was just north of the Azores at the time, a place where U-boats quite frequently came across these strange inhabitants of the sea. They are not easy to catch, and a special net is required for the purpose. But it is harder still to shoot them, for even machine-gun bullets will ricochet off the rounded armour-plating of the turtle.

But they got him, for all that; and the cook prepared a soup that would have been greeted with applause in the Great Eastern Hotel in Calcutta's Chowringhi Street.

They sighted a few steamers, but at once took evasive action.

At the end of five weeks Emmermann found himself to the south of St. Helena. A U-boat tanker, a "milch cow", was already waiting. Everything went splendidly. They took on fuel and stores.

A signal was received: "Provisional date of attack, 9 October, new moon."

A little later, to the north-west of their objective, Emmermann met Merten and drank coffee with him for a few hours. It was a heavenly day. The sea and deep blue cloudless sky were both like silk. The two U-boat crews entertained each other. Half of Merten's crew were invited to take coffee aboard Emmermann's boat, and half of his crew were guests aboard Merten's. The cooks competed eagerly to see who could produce the best cakes.

Although he was the senior of the two, Merten went over to Emmermann as his guest. Together they sat on the conning-tower and discussed the best way to find out where the enemy's main shipping lanes were.

This was not quite as easy as it sounded, because they knew that recently the German naval auxiliary, *Doggerbank*, which had swopped the flag of the mercantile marine for that of the navy, had laid mines off Cape Town and Cape Agulhas. Where exactly, were these mines, and whereabouts were the channels that the South Africans had cleared through them?

The two vessels separated. Emmermann was quite determined to thrust his way into the harbour of the capital itself. He held a brief council of war with his crew and told them bluntly what was afoot. It did not sound too promising. One could guard against attack by aircraft, against depth charges and against almost everything else, except mines.

The night of 6 October was dark. Coming from the north-west and trusting to his luck, Emmermann set course for Cape Town. At high tide he went in over the minefield. He ordered all those not on duty to remain on deck in their life jackets. He left only those few men whose presence was essential inside the boat. His intention was to try and find out what entrances and exits the British had cleared through the German minefield and, secondly, where they had placed their own minefield.

After some hours they caught a glimpse of the first lights. Very soon they were able to discern the dark outline of Table Mountain looming up behind the town. Cape Town itself was brilliantly lighted, as in peacetime. Emmermann pressed on deeper into the roadstead, at first on the surface and later submerged to avoid detection by the many freighters lying in the channel.

"Off life jackets!"

Emmermann let each man in turn have a look at Cape Town through the periscope, that harbour which, with Rio and Sydney, is regarded as one of the most beautiful in the world.

Behind the German minefield the South Africans appeared to feel quite happy and secure. There was nothing to indicate that they envisaged any intrusion by a German U-boat. Their experts were convinced that it would be quite impossible for any U-boat to operate in these far-distant waters of the southern hemisphere.

Emmermann bottomed in 250 feet of water. The powerful swell from the latitudes of the dreaded Roaring Forties, which swept right up to the harbour itself, was felt even at the considerable depth at which the U-boat was lying. The boat moved restlessly. She was constantly being lifted up, and sometimes dropped back so hard on to the rocky bottom that she creaked and groaned. In the afternoon Emmermann rose to periscope depth. Throughout the whole morning there had been a terrific noise up above of the grinding of ship's propellers, and Emmermann's heart beat a little faster as he blew his tanks to come up. He feared that at any moment he might collide with one of the scurrying tugs or one of the steamers sailing into or out of the harbour.

His first glance through the periscope was reassuring. There was no ship in the immediate vicinity. The sea, however, was so smooth that he could hardly raise his periscope more than a few inches without running a grave risk of discovery. Cape Town was bathed in brilliant sunshine. The houses, hotels and port installations could be clearly recognised. With his periscope camera Emmermann quickly took a couple of snaps of the town and the harbour.

"Otherwise no one will believe us afterwards," he said; and his snapshots were destined to become concrete proof of the fact.

Emmermann felt like a beggar without a penny in his pocket, gazing at the brightly lighted windows of some fabulous shop, full of wonderful treasures. The idea of being able to go for a walk in Cape Town, to sit on the terrace of one of its world-famous hotels drinking a cup of coffee or sipping a glass of the superb, dark blue Cape wine, was like a lovely dream.

A couple of hundred yards away Emmermann saw a small patrol craft, obviously guarding the direct line of entry into the harbour itself. Ships were constantly entering and leaving harbour. Many of them had two funnels and one, indeed, had three.

During the night Cape Town gave a firework display with searchlight exercises. Aircraft circling round, and the searchlights trying to pick them up. Every now and then a long finger of light would sparkle blindingly white as it caught some aircraft in its beam.

Throughout the next day Emmermann continued his observations, and it was not very long before he had plotted the exact course on which the ships were leaving the harbour. To make absolutely certain, a few hours before zero hour he followed a thousand yards behind a freighter proceeding to sea.

It was ten minutes to midnight . . . ten more minutes to 9 October. . . . Suddenly a ship loomed up, steaming unsuspectingly straight into Emmermann's line of fire—and what a ship!

Ten minutes before the specified zero hour the first torpedo leapt from its tube. It hit the great ship below the forecastle, and she plunged head over heels into the depths.

"Another!" shouted the look-out almost before the first ship had disappeared. This one was even bigger and it, too, had all its lights ablaze and did not seem to have noticed that the ship ahead had disappeared.

"Fire!"

"Well—that's a couple of them for breakfast," commented Emmermann.

The navigating lights had provided him with all the data he required, and his attacks had been executed with copy-book precision. Later in the night he added a third ship to his total.

The other U-boats also reported successes. During the first two nights a total of 200,000 tons was sent to the bottom. It was certainly a "Paukenschlag."

But these fireworks could not continue forever, of course. The South Africans had been jerked to their feet and they reacted swiftly, comprehensively and, indeed, damned unpleasantly. The very next day Emmermann was picked up by a search group in the "hide-out" of his own selection, and for twenty-eight hours his life was made a misery by an unceasing stream of depth charges. The next day, however, brought him handsome compensation. The 25,000-ton liner *Orcades*, which apparently had not been forewarned, ran straight into his arms and was struck by two torpedoes.

Emmerman saw the boats being lowered and observed that they were filled with troops. A transport, obviously. He could not fire again as he had to submerge to 120 feet to reload. And from down below they heard the grinding of screws as the transport got under way again.

After he had reloaded Emmermann was able to surface. For two hours Emmermann chased the giant liner at his best speed. At last he came up with her and attacked her with three torpedoes from the other side. In three minutes the colossus capsized.

For three further weeks Emmermann cruised off the city of his dreams. But he met with no further success.

*　　*　　*

On Friday 13 November Merten scored his greatest success. Between midnight and midnight he attacked six ships. All six sank, and among them had been a 19,500-ton merchantman and the armed passenger liner, *City of Cairo*. Her camouflage and the guns mounted on her forecastle and stern showed beyond any doubt that she was acting as a troop transport.

It was shortly after sunset that the look-out sighted a most peculiar cloud. The sea was as smooth as a mill-pond, and the sky as blue as Delft porcelain. The little cloud in the eastern sky looked like a giant mushroom that had been released from below the horizon. Merten turned his U-boat towards it, and then darkness fell. A silhouette emerged, a ship without lights coming towards them.

Merten had to make several attempts before he was able to reach a firing position. He fired and hit. The complicated technique involved in the firing of a torpedo came almost as second nature to him. In the same, almost automatic manner in which an experienced surgeon handles his knife, Merten calculated, assessed and . . . fired.

When the columns of water had subsided, he could see, by the flickering lights of lamps aboard the ship, that two boats had been lowered.

"Enemy is using his radio!" reported the operator.

Merten fired a second torpedo. This tore asunder the after part of the ship between mast and stern.

"Enemy has ceased signalling."

Merten rose to the surface.

*　　　*　　　*

In November 1942 160 U-boats were operating in the Atlantic, 26 in the Arctic, 19 in the Mediterranean and the first two special U-boats appeared in the Black Sea.

117 Allied ships were sunk in all areas by the U-boats alone. The losses in this single month amounted to 1,062,000 tons. A convincing, if dearly bought, success at the cost of 18 U-boats.

German losses in 1942 were heavy. In some months they were even gravely disturbing. But the successes achieved balanced the losses—and justified them.

In 1942 Germany lost 86 U-boats.

The total losses since the beginning of the war were now 149.

Part Five
1943

CHAPTER XX

THE BREAK-UP OF THE U-BOAT FORCE

Situation Report—Spring 1943.

During the spring of 1943 the U-boats persisted with their attacks and, in spite of fantastic hurricanes in the Atlantic, achieved resounding successes. In March alone 32 ships were sunk out of two convoys reported by the radio interception service and located by reconnaissance U-boats. Doenitz, who had assumed the post of Commander-in-Chief on the retirement of Raeder, contemplated scrapping all the heavy surface ships of the Navy. He urgently required their crews to man the new U-boats, the production of which now stood at 27 per month and was to be raised in the second half of the year to over 30. 1942 was regarded merely as a prologue. At first it appeared as though these prophecies would come true. The successes achieved were indeed staggering, and in their brilliance the disaster of Stalingrad became a pale shadow. "Thanks to our U-boats, we have at last gripped Britain by the throat," said Goebbels in April.

But the enemy, too, had not been idle. The Allies had now thrown 2,600 warships of all kinds into the fight with the grey wolves of the sea—more than half of the total war potential of the Western Powers. Most of the heavy bombers available were seeking their targets in the wide expanses of the Atlantic, and only a very few remained at their disposal for attacking land objectives.

In May a catastrophic disaster overtook the German U-boats. In complete secrecy the Allies developed a new radar device, the ASV (Air to Surface Vessel) Panorama, the 6-cm. waves of which could not be picked up by the German Metox.

Metox was now useless. Under cover of darkness the enemy bombers approached their target. Gliding in silently, they could not miss, and surprised, helpless and unable to put up a fight, the U-boat disappeared. What the Germans did not know was the fact that the ridiculously small number of twelve aircraft equipped with ASV

Panorama sufficed to command the whole coastal waters of France. Nor was that all. To the "killer groups" had now been added the "support groups", composed of an escort carrier and three destroyers. In May the ASV Panorama in the air and the "killer" and "support" groups at sea were thrown with great zest and energy into the battle of the Atlantic at its most decisive point.

During that month 45* German U-boats were destroyed. U-boat Headquarters was paralysed with horror. On 24 May Doenitz recalled all U-boats from the North and Central Atlantic. A few of them he transferred for duty to the south of the Azores. "We are facing the greatest crisis in the history of submarine warfare," declared the Commander-in-Chief at a Fuehrer conference held after this holocaust. "New radar apparatus has for the first time rendered it impossible for us to put up a fight."

The German experts were forced to admit that, for the time being at least, no counter measures seemed possible. For one thing, there was a dearth of magnetron valves, which up till now had been completely neglected. To mass produce them would require at least 15 to 20 months' preparation. It was a stroke of sheer luck that Telefunken had, anyway, one detector-receiver under development which was able to detect the approach of enemy magnetron-equipped aircraft at a range of 10 kilometres. The apparatus was given the code name "Naxos". But it, too, was not immediately available.

In the stress of war fifty years of normal development had been compressed into five years. Germany had been overtaken. And by now, when the danger had at last been realised, Britain's long lead could no longer be reduced.

The first blow struck Hamburg; and Hamburg became a third Stalingrad. Between the 25 and 30 July the Hansa city was attacked several times by a thousand and more bombers, and degenerated into a heap of dust and rubble. 41,000 of her citizens were killed, 600,000 remained without a roof over their heads, 35,719 dwelling houses were destroyed, many of the ship-building yards were severely damaged and ten ships, among them a new ship of 36,000 tons, were sunk.

In the countryside around Hamburg, strips of tinfoil were found scattered about the ground. Thirty of these strips tied in a bundle and dropped from the air sufficed to deceive the German "Freya" apparatus. As late as February the Hamburg A.A. defences were shooting down

---

* British sources quote 37.

20 per cent of the attacking aircraft. In this July week so fateful for the Hanseatic port it was a bare 2 per cent !
During the third week in May—after the withdrawal of the U-boats—the Allies did not lose a single ship on the North Atlantic convoy routes. In July the U-boats, all told, sank 96,000 tons. But meanwhile the Allies had extended their endeavours to other sea areas, to the Mediterranean, the Caribbean and the South Atlantic. Here, too, the grey wolves met with much sterner opposition. The following examples are typical of how the hazards had increased in every sea area.

*   *   *

The British destroyer *Harvester* sighted a U-boat which was following a ship and which, when it saw the destroyer, submerged. *Harvester* dropped depth charges and forced the U-boat, leaking badly, to surface. *U.444* defended herself with her gun and machine guns. But *Harvester*'s guns, too, were scoring hits. In the flurry of the action the captain of the British ship succeeded in manœuvring into a position from which he could ram. At a speed of 27 knots he crashed into the U-boat. The collision was so violent that the destroyer's sides, too, were torn open. The U-boat slid along the side of her assailant and became jammed under the destroyer's propeller shaft, where she stuck fast for a good ten minutes. In this situation the destroyer, of course, could drop no depth charges. Nor had she any means with which to engage the U-boat from her stern. *U.444*, commanded by Sub-Lieutenant Langfeldt, then slipped clear and disappeared into the night. The destroyer was forced to stop, because an explosion had put her other engine out of action. An hour later, the French corvette *Aconit*, cruising in the vicinity, picked up the German U-boat, sailing perforce at slow speed, in her searchlights. *U.444* had been severely damaged in her encounter with *Harvester* and was quite unable to evade the second attempt to ram her. The corvette ripped open her pressure hull and as she sank chased her with depth charges. Only five of the German crew were rescued.

Meanwhile, steaming at 11 knots, *Harvester* was trying to reach port. On the way, however, her propeller shaft broke, and she drifted, helpless and compelled to await a tow.

U.432 (Lieutenant Eckert) sighted the disabled destroyer and hit her with two torpedoes. *Harvester* broke in two and sank.

204

U.432, her commander and crew jubilant at their success, then submerged. In the meanwhile *Aconit* had returned. She located the U-boat and bombarded her with depth charges. *U.432* lost trim and was compelled to surface. Eckert was killed at once by the corvette's fire. Immediately afterwards his U-boat was rammed and·sunk.

*   *   *

While trying to attack a convoy to the south of the Equator, the new commander of *U.128*, a much-decorated but untrained officer but recently transferred from the Luftwaffe, fired off six torpedoes and missed with all of them—and was bombed by an aircraft for his pains while at periscope depth.

Young Steinert, the commander, gave the order to crash dive, and the boat sank like a stone. Under the pressure from the blast of exploding bombs every single fuse was blown.

Midshipman Ossadnik rushed to his action station; there he met the chief engine-room artificer, who was due for relief, and then he hastened back to the control-room to help in any way he could. The emergency lighting was not functioning, and in the beam of his torch he saw the depth-gauge needle creeping slowly deeper and deeper. It was already at 829 feet as the depth reached by the badly damaged U-boat. The chief engineer, a former chief petty officer, was a proven expert at his job, familiar with all the hazards and possibilities of submarine warfare; he was now a lieutenant and from the very beginning his relations with the rather cocksure young commander had been somewhat strained. On his own responsibility he now ordered the tanks to be blown in order to try and halt the downward plunge which would undoubtedly have been the end of the U-boat and her crew. His swift action saved the situation.

U.128 had not completely surfaced before the A.A. crew went hurrying to man their gun. The two aircraft, which were still circling round, tried to come in to the attack from different angles, but both were driven off.

While this was happening the chief engineer and his men had got down to the task of making the ship capable of submerging. But the damage that faced them required a great deal of time to repair, and meanwhile dead and wounded, casualties caused by the aircraft's fire, were lying on the bridge.

205

To crown it all, two destroyers now appeared which at once opened fire on *U.128*. Young Steinert, however, was in no mood to submit tamely. He hoped that at full speed on the surface he might be able to reach the shelter of the nearby neutral coast. On his orders the chief engineer fed the propellers with all the power, of both diesel and electric motors, at his disposal. *U.128* was making over 18 knots.

The destroyers pursued her, firing with everything they had. An unlucky shot hit the ammunition stacked in the conning-tower and exploded it.

Six hours after the bombs had dropped and compelled the U-boat to surface, Steinert at last gave the order to abandon the heavily damaged boat, which, in spite of all endeavours, was still not fit to dive. What with the hit on the conning-tower and the bad luck with the ammunition *U.128* was in grave danger of being swamped and of sinking of her own accord.

Ossadnik jumped into the water with Otto Reigert. Both were wearing their submerged escape apparatus. The rubber dinghies had been shot to hell and were of no use to anybody. While *U.128* was sinking the destroyers continued to fire, to the dire peril of the survivors.

"Bloody fine gentlemen—I don't think!" growled Reigert, shaking his fist.

"Steady," said Ossadnik. "That sort of thing won't help us. And, anyway, they probably think we're trying to submerge."

"Could be."

The most important thing at the moment was to keep the group of swimmers together, and Steinert, who was proving to be a stout fellow in a tight corner, was making sure that they did so.

Suddenly an aircraft came roaring towards them, and plunged straight at the nearest group of swimmers. The men yelled. Most of them dived, fearing they were about to be machine-gunned.

But the aircraft did not open fire. Instead, it dropped a collapsible rubber dinghy, in which some of the survivors might save themselves, and in which they put the badly wounded, among them the chief engineer.

It was not until six hours later that the destroyer came nearer, cautiously as though still wary of the U-boat that had vanished.

Ossadnik was among the first to clamber up the scrambling nets and on to the deck of the American destroyer.

One after the other the Germans were hauled safely aboard. The wounded at once received attention from a solicitous doctor, who spared no pains even over the most superficial of hurts and who gave particular attention to the chief engineer. The latter, in spite of everything that the American medical personnel most willingly did for him, had been fatally injured.

The destroyer put in to Pernambuco and saw to it that the survivors were decently housed in barracks. "This was the nicest time I had during the whole war. The Brazilians behaved splendidly and looked after our wants in a wonderful way. I wish I could say the same for the Germans settled here. They seemed to think it would be a good idea to insure themselves against future possibilities." Thus wrote young Ossadnik in his diary.

Later, the survivors of *U.128* were taken to the States in the cruiser *Milwaukee*. During the voyage they were interrogated, but in a decent and friendly manner; and later, on shore, they were put through the hoop pretty sharply for four days in an American camp.

U.591 was also lost south of the Equator. Her commander, Lieutenant Ziesmer, admitted that he too was surprised at the decent manner in which they were treated by the Americans:

"Our boat was well and truly hit and sank quickly. There was no time to think. We had no lifeboat. Only a few of the life-jackets remained serviceable, not enough to go round among the seven and twenty of us who were splashing about in the warm, tropical sea.

"Even so, we were only too thankful to have got clear. The empty sea poured over the spot where, but a few minutes ago, had floated the casket that contained all our precious little personal possessions, the photos of our wives and sweethearts, and that we had called our home.

"All faces were turned skywards. Less than two hundred feet up were roaring the aircraft that had destroyed our U-boat. As it passed over us a bright yellow packet fell from its silver belly and landed with a splash quite close to the struggling men. Heavens! A boat!

"It was, it is true, only a tiny, collapsible dinghy, but it was a symbol of hope, and the men all felt more stalwart-hearted at the sight of it. Two square yards was the size of the little yellow blob designed to carry two, or, at the most, three persons. We got five into it, three wounded and two non-swimmers who had up till now been laboriously held above water by their comrades. The rest of us took it in turn to hang on to its sides and take a breather.

"The aircraft disappeared.

"I do not know whether the others, who, unlike myself, had never before been in this southern hemisphere, gave any thought to the sharks. Sharks abounded in these waters, and I shuddered as I recalled the fact. I had once seen a man, who had been sitting on the edge of a raft, dragged by the leg into the sea by one of these monsters.

"Suddenly a frenzied shout arose from fifteen, twenty throats. The first shark, plainly recognisable from its sharp, pointed fins, was steering purposefully towards us. The dinghy capsized and until the panic subsided remained floating bottom upwards, with men clinging in a frightened cluster wherever a hand could get a grip. Swiftly I counted the heads. There were still twenty-seven of us. 'Thank God for that,' I thought. We very quickly righted the boat, and its five occupants were soon safely settled once more. The other twenty-two of us splashed about, pressed closely together, like chicks with a hen when danger threatens.

"Our hearts thumped painfully. This waiting seemed to tear at the fibres of the very being of each one of us, in the same way that a steel hawser suddenly snaps and exposes its black soul.

"Whom would it grab? Whom would it grab? Whom? . . .

"Suddenly the bulk of the beast, looking terrifyingly enormous in its proximity, rose close before me. I dived and for a moment found myself staring into the cold merciless eyes of the monster. Then I shut my eyes and shrieked with all the force of my lungs and with the final strength of utter desperation.

"The shark turned away.

"To this day I do not know whether I really gave a full-throated shriek or merely a water-quenched gurgle. Whatever it was, it caused the shark, that tiger among aquatic animals, to flee.

"Soon it returned. But at least it returned alone. Each time it allowed itself to be driven away by yells and noise, and we began to feel that we were once more masters of the situation.

Depth charges exploding, as seen by the enemy

Motor launches being used to combat U-boats

Even after being rammed by a tanker Kremer's U-boat, having suffered enormous damage to bows, conning tower and periscope, arrived safely home

As seen from a British destroyer, a sinking U-boat in a Norwegian fjord

"The shark, however, had by no means become bored with the proceedings, and the circle it wove round us became narrower and narrower.

"Suddenly someone spotted blood on its dorsal fins. One or two cried out in horror.

"Taking a closer look I realised that the 'blood' was the red label of a box of matches that had become impaled on the fin.

"Shortly before this, a second aircraft had flown over and had dropped a packet similar to that dropped by the first plane; but it had been carried away by the wind. In spite of my protests, two of my crew swam over to it to try and find the dinghy. They returned empty-handed. As far as I was concerned, I was only too pleased to see them return at all. In this second packet there must obviously have been matches and flares. The whole bundle had been meticulously gone over by our sinister companion, and during its search a box of matches had become impaled on its fin.

"The appearance of the second aircraft was proof that they were still looking for us, and that gave us a feeling of quiet hope. But the sun was sinking dangerously near the horizon. Not a few of the men were being seized with cramp after their long hours of exertion. The changing of places at the dinghy's side began to occur at ever briefer intervals. In our own minds we had a pretty good idea as to who among us would be the first to succumb.

"The sun set. The night shrouded us in the menacing, swiftly falling shadows of the tropics. In the last glimmer of light of this fateful day yet another aircraft appeared over the horizon. And then another. They were certainly doing their best to find us.

"From the way it was flying, I had the impression that the second aircraft was guiding some ship to the spot. Very soon no less than eight aircraft were circling above us, and finally we saw mastheads appearing over the horizon, a thin streak against the darkening sky.

"Within an hour the whole twenty-seven of us stood, stark naked, on the deck of an American mine-sweeper. With our pale, strained faces, our tangled beards and our staring eyes, we must have been a pitiable spectacle. Quickly we were given towels, shirts, trousers and canvas shoes. A bottle of gin passed from hand to hand, and there was a good swig for each of us.

" 'Is the skipper with you?' asked an American officer.

" 'I am the skipper,' I replied.

"I was then taken to the captain, a young man about my own age. He asked me my name, the number of survivors and how many men were missing. He promised to continue the search for these latter. He rose lithely, shook me by the hand and commiserated with me at the loss of my boat.

"I thanked him for having saved us.

" 'You're welcome,' he said, with a deprecatory wave of his hand."

* * *

The manner in which the 1,600-ton supply U-boat, *U.459* (Commander Wilamowitz-Moellendorf), was lost is almost incredible.

While on day patrol, the skipper of Wellington "Q" of 172 Squadron, W. T. H. Jennings, sighted the German U-boat. He turned his aircraft towards it, was met with heavy and well-directed fire and shot down. Jennings steered his falling aircraft direct at the U-boat and landed with a thundering crash upon its deck. Whether he had done this deliberately or whether it was sheer chance will never be known, for the British pilot was killed instantly in the smash. The aircraft had destroyed the guns on the U-boat's deck and had started a big fire. Most of the wreckage had slithered away into the sea on either side of the U-boat, and what remained on deck was quickly cleared away. But on the upper deck there remained two depth charges, which the crew rolled carefully into the water. The speed of the U-boat was not great enough, however, to take her beyond the reach of the effects of the resultant explosions, and she was so badly damaged aft that she was left incapable of diving and out of control.

Wilamowitz first fished the rear-gunner of the Wellington, who had survived the crash, out of the water. Then he received a report from his chief engineer that it would not be possible to get the U-boat under way again.

Seeing that another hostile aircraft was approaching, Wilamowitz blew up his own boat and sank her. The survivors were later picked up and taken prisoner. Wilamowitz was not among them. He had not been wounded or even hurt.

He had remained in his ship.

* * *

Something very similar happened to Liberator "D" of 200 Squadron, when her pilot sighted and attacked *U.468* (Lieutenant Schamong) on 11 August. In this case, too, the U-boat's A.A. gunners were successful. Firing coolly and deliberately they shot the aircraft down in flames.

The pilot of the Liberator was a New Zealander, Flying Officer L. A. Trigg. With a complete disregard of the flames that were enveloping his aircraft, Trigg turned directly towards the U-boat. The gunners, convinced that the attacker had had enough, ceased fire. But Trigg succeeded in manœuvring his aircraft into an attacking position. Before the flaming Liberator crashed into the sea, he released the depth charges he was carrying. They fell close beside the U-boat and ripped her pressure hull wide open. As it crashed into the sea, the Liberator exploded, and all her crew were killed instantly. *U.468*, too, failed to survive the battle and sank. By the tragic irony of a merciless fate the survivors of the U-boat saved themselves in a rubber dinghy salvaged from the wreckage of the Liberator.

*   *   *

"Aphrodite" was a sheet-anchor which raised the hopes of Germany in the murderous battle of U-boat versus radar.

It was night. A German U-boat was hastening at its best surface speed towards its sector of operations. Silhouettes loomed up over the horizon. Patrol craft.

"Away Aphrodite!" ordered the commander.

On deck there started a most ghostly performance. Some sort of rubber balloons with wires hanging from them were passed up through the hatch. On deck a man was engaged in blowing up one of these balloons with a small cylinder of compressed air. Two or three of his mates stood round him to help. "Stop! Too much!"

The balloon had got too fat. One of the men let some of the air out. "Stop! . . . Too little!" Once again the cylinder come into action. In the meanwhile the shadows had come appreciably closer.

There was a heavy sea running. The group of men working on the balloon required all their seamen's skill to avoid being hurled into a corner. At last they succeeded in getting the balloon blown up to the desired size.

With great care it was pushed overboard. It was just an ordinary rubber balloon, from which some metal strips were hanging; and, as it had been inflated to the correct extent very precisely computed by its inventor, it would hover just above the surface of the sea.

The commander was cursing like fury. This damn balloon game had gone on far too long for his fancy.

"Thought out by some blasted pen-pusher who obviously hasn't a notion of what seafaring in a U-boat means. I'd like to see him fix his own box of tricks himself . . . on a dark night . . . and with hostile patrol craft approaching . . . *and* with a sea and wind like this!"

There was no doubt about it, the commander was thoroughly wild. So, too, were his men. But he had been given strict orders to give Aphrodite a thorough test, and that was that.

The U-boat turned back. The patrol craft were put off the scent by the radar decoy—Aphrodite—which caused echoes on the enemy radar exactly like those reflected from a U-boat's conning-tower.

Aphrodite was but an improvisation and so it remained, a helpful expedient, but nothing more. The only real hope of a change of fortune lay in the new U-boats. For the time being "Do or Die" had to remain the U-boat's slogan.

This was the Knight's Cross spirit.

CHAPTER XXI

DYSENTERY ABOARD!

Situation Report—Autumn 1943.
The U-boat situation at this time is well illustrated by the experiences
of U.172, under the command of Carl Emmermann. The enemy
seemed to be finding out when and where the German U-boats would
be taking on supplies. The mystery was how they obtained such
information.

*   *   *

At the end of October, after a five-month trip, Commander Carl
Emmermann returned to his base in France.

"What news of the rest of the flotilla, Sir?" he asked his flotilla
commander. He mentioned some names . . . but all the answer
he got was a shrug of the shoulders. . . . After each name came this
silent yet all-revealing answer.

"You're lucky to be here, Emmermann; and we're only too
thankful to be able to welcome you and wish you luck."

Lucky? Emmermann felt his throat contract. He watched
Captain Kuhnke turn away and drum his knuckles on the window.
It was answer enough.

Emmermann's thoughts turned to the voyage he had just
completed. It had been a grim trip, a devilish exploit on which
U.172 had embarked the previous June.

His orders had been to operate in the South Atlantic. First of
all there had been the long underwater run to the south of the
Azores. Then he had received a signal. "Take on supplies from
supply ship, *U.118.*" Czygan had one of the Type IXd2 supply
U-boats. Emmermann had set course for the rendezvous. Some
hours before he reached it his operator reported underwater
explosions, followed by faint propeller noises.

Emmerman leapt to the hydrophones. His face was set and
grim.

"I'm afraid, Sir. . . ." began the operator, but Emmermann cut
him short with an abrupt gesture, and turned on his heel.

The rendezvous with *U.118*, he knew, would not take place.

Doenitz had then ordered Lange, whose ship was a IXc type operational craft, to meet Emmermann and act as his supply ship.

Lange was furious. "Bloody nonsense! It's enough to make a man spit blood! To come all the way through the Bay of Biscay harried to hell by aircraft, just to become a flaming milch cow!"

Emmermann took on supplies and later had a few successes. He was informed by signal that he had been awarded Oak Leaves to his Knight's Cross. That was something he had not expected. His chief engineer saw that he wasn't over-pleased about it . . . laurels issued in advance always sit uneasily on the brow. "We shall look pretty silly if, when we get home, we've got nothing more to chalk up on the tally board," said Emmermann. Nor did there seem to be much prospect of anything more.

As his area of operations Emmermann had been given the Brazilian coast from Natal to Rio—a gigantic area, bigger than the Mediterranean. In addition, Guggenberger and Kraus with Type IXd2's, Hoeltring and Mueller with old VIIc's and Maus with a IXc were operating in the same area.

"H'm," said Emmermann to himself. "What would you do if you were skipper of a British steamer? What course would you steer in order to avoid these damn U-boats?"

Having worked out an answer to his own satisfaction he began criss-crossing the probably shipping lane in wide, sweeping arcs.

At first he remained in the vicinity of Rio, cruising to and fro, searching. Once or twice they obtained faint echoes on the Metox. But that was all. By this time the enemy aircraft were only operating their radar intermittently and it could not therefore be located with any accuracy.

"I rather feel, too, that the Metox is giving us away," said Emmermann to his radio operator.

"Quite possible, Sir. Some of my pals in other U-boats have come to the same conclusion."

"It's always the same; when we go out on a long trip gadgets like that are apt to become obsolete. Technique runs ahead of time."

"Well—just take a look at our antiquated armament," intervened the first officer. "Other people already have the new quadruple guns, while we have to be content with a poor, old 2-cm. and an antiquated 10·5-cm."

"I know, but we must do the best we can with what we've got, and that's all there is to it."

"In that case, Sir," went on the first officer, "I suggest we stop using the Metox altogether, for it's pretty obvious that some new apparatus has been perfected—though we haven't got it, worse luck—that renders Metox useless."

"Right! Close the damn thing down!"

And, indeed, later it became known that the enemy had found that the Metox radiated a definite impulse on which it was easy to take a bearing.

A terse note was entered in the war-log.

Once again fuel was getting low, and, as Emmermann had feared, success had eluded him. Doenitz ordered him to obtain fuel from Guggenberger to keep him happy, and fixed a rendez-vous for the two U-boats.

But after a day or two more, nothing further was heard from either Guggenberger or Maus. They had recently both been off Rio, a little to the south of Emmermann. Then, according to the latest reports from U-boat Headquarters, they had been surprised by aircraft while charging batteries and had been sunk.

Then, one day, Emmermann sighted two steamships. For weeks they had not seen a thing, and now two of them had to come at the same time. As one was steaming north and the other south, Emmermann had no option but to let one go. Nor was he able to sink his chosen victim swiftly and silently. Rio was alerted by the SOS signals of the other ship. Emmermann accordingly left the area and made for Santos, and there he destroyed the fourth ship so far on this voyage.

"24,000 tons isn't a bad beginning these hard time," Emmermann said consolingly to his crew who hated the eternal monotony of cruising up and down, searching and searching.

That same day a signal came in from Hoeltring, who was operating south-west of Natal. "Badly damaged by aircraft and A/S patrols."

Then another signal:

"U-boat Headquarters to *U.172*. Proceed forthwith to Hoeltring's assistance." There followed precise details of the position, and the signal ended with the final sentence, "You will yourselves arrange rendezvous."

Emmermann had another word with his radio operator.

"Are you absolutely, one hundred per cent, sure that our cipher is safe?"

"Absolutely, Sir. It is unbreakable."

"Then how can you explain why the enemy always appears to know our rendezvous—no, damn it, always does know them?"

The operator shrugged his shoulders. "I'm certain he doesn't get his information unaided," he said.

Unaided! . . . The operator had confirmed what Emmermann himself had been fearfully suspecting for some time. The enemy Intelligence Service must be receiving accurate information from some official German source.

Emmermann wrapped up his signal in such a way that he felt sure that even if the enemy picked it up it would mean nothing to him, and that no one but U-boat HQ and Hoeltring himself would understand it. He referred to a position which had been fixed in a previous signal. All went well, and Emmermann met Hoeltring as planned. Hoeltring had had the utmost difficulty in evading the relentless pursuit of aircraft and a destroyer search group. His U-boat was incapable of submerging. Only his port electric motor was working and his hydroplanes had jammed.

"There's not much we can do about it, Hoeltring," said Emmermann.

"I'm afraid not. It's a dockyard job."

Hoeltring gazed out across the sea, a wonderful, shimmering deep-blue sea, rising and falling gently.

By this time Maus had also arrived, and the three commanders sat down to discuss ways and means.

"We shall have to scuttle your boat, Hoeltring. I'll take one half your crew, and Maus can take on the other half. It's the only thing we can do."

The other two agreed. During the last few days, en route for the rendezvous, Hoeltring had seen no sign of any aircraft, so Emmermann felt justified in risking the transfer of Hoeltring's fuel oil and stores as well.

Emmermann got his fresh supply of fuel after all, even though the circumstances which enabled him to do so were indeed tragic.

Stores were ferried from boat to boat in rubber dinghies. Tins of ham and every sort of foodstuff piled up on Emmermann's upper deck.

While all this was going on, none of the three commanders had given voice to the anxiety that was at the back of his mind. The fact that Hoeltring had not sighted an aircraft for two or three days was no proof that the enemy was inactive. Emmermann, Maus and Hoeltring had all been eyeing the gathering clouds with increasing misgiving. Without driving them unduly, they quietly urged their men to hurry.

Then it happened.

"Aircraft on port beam—range 2000!"

"Cast off! Full ahead!" shouted Emmermann.

A four-engined Liberator was flying at a height of 150 feet straight at Emmermann's U-boat.

Five bombs came hurtling down. The eight forward cannons of the Flying Fortress spewed their shells at the U-boats. The deadly chirrup of bullets whistled about the ears of the men on the bridge. Those on deck rushed to take cover behind the conning-tower. The bombs fell into the sea on the port beam, between Emmermann and Hoeltring. They exploded with ear-splitting roars and enveloped both boats in seething fountains of water which came crashing down on their decks.

Emmermann and those with him clung fast to the bridge coaming. He felt the boat sinking beneath him. "This is the end," he thought—and once more he took a snapshot. Then, however, he realised that she was rising again.

Black smoke emerged from the exhaust. At last! The chief had got his diesels running. The ship began to move forward. The Liberator flew ahead, turned and prepared to deliver a second attack. The two bombs fell left and right, a bare fifteen feet away.

"This time they've got us!" flashed through Emmermann's mind.

Each second seemed an eternity.

Were they duds? Why the hell didn't the damn things go off?

Yard by yard *U.172* went ahead. Emmermann felt as though he were dancing on a rumbling volcano. He looked at the pale faces of his men. Their gaze was fixed on the spot where the bombs had fallen into the sea.

Rrumm! Once . . . twice. Fifty yards astern the sea burst into two huge hillocks of water.

"Depth charges!"

"If those had been bombs. . . ."

If!

The diesels had now warmed up, and the speed increased.

Then came another nightmare.

"Rudder jammed to port."

"Both motors running full ahead," reported the helmsman.

"Bos'n! Man the 10·5. Pass up the ammunition!"

At a height of little more than fifty feet the aircraft was diving straight towards them. Petty Officer Schmidt had manned the 2·5-cm. Calmly he waited till the aircraft was all but on top of them. Then he let drive a murderous burst. Emmermann and the others saw the bullets ricochet harmlessly off the underbelly of the giant bird.

"The bloody thing's armoured!"

"Pass up armour-piercing ammunition!" yelled Schmidt.

The U-boats were threshing wildly this way and that. Maus crossed *U.172*'s bows. As he did so, Emmermann yelled to him through a megaphone.

"Rudder jammed!"

Maus raised a hand to signal that he had understood. Then he was gone.

Once again the aircraft turned towards the U-boats. Then *U.172*'s 2·5-cm. jammed. Beside the gun young Schiemann collapsed with a groan.

"Bring him up on the bridge!"

Below a few hands were outstretched. There was nothing more they could do.

"Jump to it! Up with him!" The willing hands of the gun crew got him up on to the conning-tower. Machine gun bullets had made a sorry mess of his chest and throat.

One of the engine-room hands who had also been shot in the chest was passed down through the conning-tower.

Orders and reports followed each other in rapid succession.

"Compass out of action!"

"Alarm!"

The aircraft, obviously, had emptied its bomb-rack. Emmermann crash dived to avoid the fire of its cannon and to set about repairing the damage underwater. Within twenty-four hours *U.172* was once more ready for action.

Outside, darkness had now fallen and Emmermann rose to the surface.

Most of the damage had already been repaired. Only the compass was beyond repair. The magnetic compass, too, was out of order. Only the stars remained to guide them.

A signal informed them that Maus had shot down the aircraft shortly after Emmermann had dived and had taken Hoeltring's crew aboard and scuttled his helpless and useless ship. The next day Emmermann and Maus met. As had been agreed, Emmermann took over half Hoeltring's crew. None of the U-boat's rubber dinghies was serviceable, and so the men had to swim across. Empty torpedo-pistol containers served as transport for their goods and chattels.

Emmermann now had ninety-five men aboard, and enough fuel oil and provisions to reach the Azores. Each man of his crew shared his quarters with his shipwrecked opposite number.

And so they set off for home. Maus quickly disappeared from sight. They did not wish to proceed in company, as both Emmermann and Maus feared that the presence of another U-boat might distract the attention of their look-outs.

As if they had not troubles enough, more came hurrying towards them.

One of the midshipmen was taken seriously ill. His temperature rose to over 100 degrees and he was attacked with shivering fits.

"I don't quite know what to make of it, but to me it looks to be a pretty grim business. Give me the first aid book."

Emmermann started to flick through the pages of the small medical handbook issued to U-boats. His eye was arrested by paragraph 15—Dysentery. Suddenly he brought his fist down with a crash on the small table.

"My God! Listen to this, chief—written by some idiot who doesn't know the difference between a U-boat and a sanatorium!"

"The patient should be placed in a cool and well-ventilated room," he read aloud. "He must be kept strictly isolated, as dysentery is highly contagious. The whole body should be wrapped in cloths soaked in warm water. . . ."

Emmermann pitched the book on to the table.

"Silly fool! . . . In a U-boat, with two small hand-pump closets for ninety-five men, and precious little fresh water to spare! Too easy, isn't it!"

The next day two more went down. They first complained of violent pains, then came the diarrhœa, then high fever, delirium.

The forward w.c. was at once reserved for the sick men. Emmermann at once reduced the day's water ration, in order to be able to give his patients, if not clean linen, at least sheets soaked in fresh water. "Half a glass of water per man per day."

The men accepted these restrictions with stoical fortitude. Each successive day two or three of them went down. That those who had first been struck down were already on the mend and fit for light duty aroused some hope that the disease would not strike the whole crew at the same time.

One evening Emmermann had turned in for a rest and was fast asleep in his bunk. In his subconscious mind he thought he heard muffled shouts and the noise of a scuffle.

"Hold him!" shouted someone. "Hold him!"

Emmermann leapt from his bunk and ran almost slap into the arms of Eberhardt, stark naked and waving a knife dripping with blood. There was a mad and feverish glint in his eyes. He glared at Emmermann, who stood motionless facing him. Then he seemed to recognise his commander, for he shouted:

"I've got him, Sir! He was after me the whole time! With a knife! With a knife like this! . . ." And he waved the blood-stained bread-knife in Emmermann's face.

"Good, Eberhardt! I'm glad you got him all right," said Emmermann quietly. "If you've done him in, you won't want that knife any more, will you? . . . Come on, give it to me like a good chap."

Before the young seaman had time to think Emmermann stepped unhurriedly forward and took the knife from his hand.

"Now—come along, lad!" Emmermann seized him by the shoulders, turned him round and pushed him firmly past the first officer and the chief petty officer who were standing behind him. Then his friends took him over and led him back to the forecastle.

It was only then that Emmermann had time to find out what had happened.

The seaman had indeed attacked another man with the bread-knife and had tried to murder him. In his delirium he had hurled himself on the chief engineer and had stabbed him. The knife had pierced Frowein's arm, and before he and the others who rushed to his assistance could seize him, Eberhardt had leapt through the bulkhead.

Towards evening the chief petty officer reported to the commander:

"Eberhardt's better, Sir," he said. "He's in his right senses, anyway."

"I hope you haven't told him what happened?"

"Well—we did, Sir. But I don't think it makes any odds. He just won't believe a word we say."

"Pity—you shouldn't have said anything. Of course, he doesn't remember a thing of what he did in his delirium." Emmermann stalked off to visit the sick man.

"Well, you wild and woolly ruffian!"

"Sir—I didn't mean it, really I didn't! I—I—don't rightly know what I did do! I . . ."

"That's all right, Eberhardt. Nobody's blaming you. Even the chief bears no hard feelings. The great thing is to get fit again. So forget all about it. The chief only wanted to help, you know. But then you started seeing ghosts. You recognised me all right, though, didn't you? Now—have a good sleep and forget the whole thing."

From that moment Emmermann put a guard on the sick men.

It was a bit of luck that he had half Hoeltring's crew aboard. Some of them had gone down with the dysentery, but the presence of the rest made all the difference to the running of the ship.

The epidemic ceased as suddenly as it had started. In the vicinity of the Cape Verde Islands Emmermann was forced to dive by a high-flying aircraft; and as there was nothing he could do about it, they settled down to a game of cards. Suddenly they were disturbed by distant explosions, bombs, perhaps eight or ten miles away. They all thought the same thing . . . Maus!

Emmermann looked at the anxious face of Hoeltring's chief engineer, Lieutenant Jürgens, who was sitting opposite him. His commander and half the crew were aboard Maus's ship. Carefully Jürgens laid his cards on the table. Some of them slipped to the floor. Jürgens bent to retrieve them. He remained bent for quite a long time—an understandably long time.

The next day there were no signals from Maus.

Later, they heard that most of the ship's company had been saved. Hoeltring, who had been wounded, could not be persuaded to leave his command. He had gone down with her.

Two days later, Emmermann met Commander Kuppisch's U-boat, from which he was to obtain supplies, particularly water. Kuppisch's boat was one of the new big IXd2 U-boats. He himself was an old salt, a member of the Monsoon Group, which was under orders for Japan. He had been one of the most successful of the U-boat commanders in the early stages of the war, but had then been given a shore appointment and had not been to sea for a very long while. As a result he was inclined to take the very real danger from the air a little too light-heartedly.

When he met *U.172* in the early hours of the morning he was astonished to see that six look-outs had been posted, that the 2-cm. light automatics were manned and that the 10·5 was loaded and ready for action.

"Emmermann! Is this a private war or . . . ? You look devilish pugnacious, old boy."

"Better safe than sorry!"

Kuppisch laughed and waved an airy hand. "I've been here a fortnight," he said, "and I haven't even heard an aircraft."

Through a megaphone Emmermann told him of the experiences of the last two days. "We're not on our own here," he concluded. "Believe me, not a square yard round here is safe from aircraft."

"H'm," replied Kuppisch, thoughtfully. "That sounds damn serious. If anyone else down at the base had pitched me that yarn, I'd . . . But coming from you—that's very different. I bow to superior knowledge." He cleared his A.A. guns for action and sent everyone below except those actually required on deck.

The work of transferring stores proceeded at pace. Hoffmann, the first officer, took charge of the food side of the operation, and within two hours *U.172* had obtained all that she required.

Her crew gave three cheers for Kuppisch and wished him luck on the big adventure that lay before him. Then Emmermann departed at his best speed. Kuppisch's boat became smaller and smaller, a little dark speck, and finally passed from view.

Emmermann then decided to travel submerged. It was admittedly slower, but it was far safer.

A bare twenty minutes had passed when once again they heard that hateful rumbling and grumbling of explosions. Emmermann rushed to the listening-room. Between the explosion of bombs he could hear the threshing of propellers. Then there was silence.

"Operator, can you still hear anything?"

"No, Sir, nothing."

And Kuppisch, indeed it had been, as Emmermann learnt later. He had been surprised and sunk by aircraft from a carrier.

"That's the third U-boat whose destruction we've had to sit and listen to," said Emmermann bitterly.

"Yes—and the seventh that has gone down near us during this voyage," added Hoffmann.

Emmermann said nothing. He disappeared into the tiny compartment that was graced with the title of cabin.

Close in under the Spanish coast, he proceeded at speed through the night towards his base. It was a night of rare beauty at sea. Left, right and ahead bobbed Spanish fishing smacks, their lights shining brightly and peacefully, and he had no difficulty in avoiding them.

Unheralded he ran into harbour. Among others on deck stood the lad who had been wounded in the chest. Only a bit of sticking-plaster now marked the spot.

Later, Emmermann had a word with the senior medical officer of the flotilla about the dysentery epidemic.

"Your crew had become very vulnerable to illness, Emmermann. Nervous strain—It's only the fact that your lads were so fighting fit and had such implicit faith that saved you from real disaster. Five unbroken months of operations in a U-boat is just too long. An Everest expedition is a week-end picnic in comparison."

CHAPTER XXII

"DR. FUG"—DR. CAUER, PROFESSOR OF CHEMISTRY

Situation Report.

Death stalked the U-boats in all the seven seas of the world. Carriers with thirty and forty aircraft aboard were now protecting the convoys. The U-boat commander who valued his ship, his life and the lives of his men had now to remain underwater. But as the whale must come up to breathe, so the U-boat had to surface in order to recharge her batteries. The U-boat, admittedly, was not quite defenceless when she surfaced; but she was certainly insufficiently armed. The German armament industry, reeling under the hail of bombs that poured down on it, could not produce enough to arm all U-boats with effective weapons of defence. But more and more aircraft filled the skies, and the U-boats inevitably fell victims in the end to this endless array.

In June seventeen U-boats were sunk—eleven by aircraft. In July thirty-seven were lost—thirty of them due to aircraft attack.

In July a conference was held at the Walter Works in Kiel, attended by fifty gentlemen from the shipbuilding and armament industries and in the presence of the new flag officer of U-boats, Admiral von Friedeburg. The subject under review was the Walter U-boat. As a result an order was given to the Howaldt shipbuilding yard to construct a new and smaller type of the Walter U-boat, known as the Gabler Boat, for operation in coastal waters. The company proposed to present the first boat of this type to the Naval High Command as a Christmas present and then, if the craft proved a success, to lay down one hundred more of them. Twenty-four of the larger high-seas craft, the Walter Type XVIIb, were also to be constructed forthwith. The experimental and instructional version of the same craft, the Type XVIIa, were never commissioned at all. But the results that had been obtained with the first experimental U-boat, the V.80, were regarded as being so satisfactory that it was thought unnecessary to waste a lot of time in trials with the standard type. Within six weeks, the ribs of the first Gabler Boat were being fashioned. Suddenly, however, the whole project was dropped, supposedly in favour of another programme. The same thing happened with the XVIIb's.

The "other" programme was concerned with Electro U-boats.

The first essential was to find some temporary expedient for use in the boats already in service, if these latter were not to be withdrawn altogether. The answer was furnished by the Snort, a ventilating mast that could be raised when the U-boat was submerged to ventilate the boat and thus allow the diesels to be used when submerged. The Snort was also a blessing for the Walter U-boats, since it permitted them to proceed submerged the whole way to their operations area on their electric or, alternatively, their diesel motors, and thus save their turbines exclusively for the attack itself.

The net result was that the Walter Boats could always get away from the majority of the pursuers, whereas the Electric U-boats, to which Doenitz had given preference, with their maximum underwater speed of 19 knots, were just those few but so decisive knots too slow.

The first few craft of the old types were very quickly provided with Snorts. But one day a whole crew was knocked out and all but poisoned by the influx of fumes, because, for the purpose of ventilation, all bulkheads had to be left open. . . .

*   *   *

As it was, the fug in a U-boat was just as thick as an ordinary, healthy man could stand. But now, with the advent of the Snort, ordinary fug could become positively dangerous. The idea went round that prolonged use of the Snort was very harmful to health.

As a matter of extreme urgency, Dr. Cauer, an expert on clinical climatology, was instructed to make an examination of atmospheric conditions inside a U-boat when travelling on the surface and submerged. Cauer was told that the results of his investigations were to be kept strictly secret.

One fine day the crews of the first Snort-fitted U-boats saw a civilian, accompanied by Admiral Thidsen and followed by a whole gang of people carrying weird and wonderful-looking apparatus, step aboard *U.237.*

The innumerable gold rings with which he was surrounded abashed Dr. Cauer not a whit. He chatted away as gaily as he would have done with his own people or with the modest seamen themselves. On the other hand, he exhibited a quite astonishing energy and physical agility, such as they were not accustomed to see in civilians.

Like a seasoned mariner he leapt on to the bridge and disappeared in a trice down the conning-tower. The Admiral and the other gentlemen followed him more slowly. Cauer shook hands with the commander and the chief engineer and overwhelmed them with a torrent of questions, first about all the apparatus in the control-room, then about the ventilation of the ship and the fug and what they thought could be done about it?

Meanwhile all his weird-looking gadgets were being handed down into the ship.

"And now, may I please say a few words to the crew?"

"Please do!" said the commander with a little bow and a sly smile. "I'm afraid I didn't quite catch your name, Doctor . . . er Doctor Fug!" The Admiral frowned. The crew were shaken with silent laughter. "Dr. Fug! First class, my dear fellow!" Cauer laughed boisterously. "If you can't remember my real name, I couldn't ask for a better!"

U.237 cast off, put to sea and submerged to periscope depth.

The sea was calm, and the exercises could be carried out in peace and quiet.

The experiment began. As soon as the Snort was cut out, the diesel tore the air out of the ship. Cauer was conscious of a maddening pain in his ears and a frightful pressure behind his eyes. He staggered. The motor stuttered . . . stopped . . . was restarted.

Cauer was standing at the end of the starboard diesel, which was labouring ponderously. He saw fumes rising like grey-black ghosts and filling the boat. "Good God!" the thought flashed through his mind. "That must be pure formaldehyde." Still he refrained from giving the agreed signal. He wanted to see exactly where the fumes and smoke would flow and find out for himself exactly what would happen next. The man in charge of the diesel collapsed beside him. Cauer decided that the moment to give the signal had come. Suddenly he was seized with a feeling of cramp in his jaws, and barely had he drawn two or three gasps of breath than he felt the cramp spreading to his arms. His hands clenched and his arms twisted involuntarily. He realised that he was about to lose consciousness. He pressed his mouth closed again and tried to stagger away from the diesel.

The outlines of the two diesel monsters seemed to be whirling wildly round his head. His knees began to totter. He was about to sink to the deck when suddenly a hand wrenched him roughly away from the motors. In the adjacent space the air was a little better. But the semi-conscious professor was still staggering and helpless. He groped for something to hold on to, and his right hand landed in a boiling hot brew. He withdrew it quickly and, hazy and nebulous as his mind was, he was conscious that his hand, as he wrung it in pain, landed on something soft and then slid down some sort of corrugated metal surface. Then he collapsed.

At last he began to recover, and the mists around him began to take shape. One of them, straight in front of him, was the admiral himself, who was gazing at the scientist with grave concern.

The admiral broke the silence.

"That, my dear Cauer, is the way you thanked us for yanking you out of the engine-room," he said, smilingly.

Cauer's right hand, as he groped and wrung it in pain, had landed on the admiral's face, and the rough, metallic surface which he had noticed had been the epaulettes of that distinguished officer!

A relieved giggle ran through the ship. The admiral, then, was human after all.

Up came the commander to enquire anxiously how he felt— and at the same time to hand him a generously-filled glass.

"You know, Dr. Fug," he began, with one eye askance on the admiral, "when you came aboard we thought—here's another of those land-lubbers who has sat down in his nice, dry, comfortable room and worked out the ideal way to run a U-boat. But, by God, we can all make mistakes sometimes!"

"That's true—and it goes for all of us!" replied Cauer with a laugh and turned to start picking bits of peas out of the admiral's epaulettes, apologising profusely as he did so. Then he rushed off and set to work with all his gadgets.

Three times that day Cauer had the experiment repeated, and by the time $U.237$ ran in to Kiel harbour again it was already dark.

Working day and night, Cauer produced 1,413 chemical formulae, 1,321 sets of physical calculations. To his wife he said: "They're grand fellows, and there's nothing I wouldn't do for them."

The results of his research were of the greatest value for the later development of new types of U-boat fitted with Snort.

*　　　*　　　*

CHAPTER XXIII

HOW BRANDI, THE CRUISER KING,
LOST HIS U-BOAT

Situation Report.

A new torpedo had been developed. It was given the name of Zaunkoenig (Wren) and was intended primarily for use against destroyers. A highly sensitive accoustic instrument had been built into the torpedo head, which picked up the noise of a propeller and "homed" the torpedo automatically to it. The Zaunkoenig was first tested during an attack on two convoys, both strongly escorted. The two outward bound convoys, one consisting of twenty-seven and the other of forty-one ships, were 90 miles apart and 650 miles from their starting points when the fifteen U-boats delivered their attack. The British combined the two convoys into one, in order to be able to concentrate the available escort forces. But the attack continued, and with the new torpedo the U-boats sank twelve destroyers and six merchantmen. During the action the radio interception service deciphered a signal from the frigate, H.M.S. Itchin, which had picked up the crews of the sunken destroyer St. Croix and corvette Polyanthus. This ran: "A remarkable and disturbing feature is the fact that all ships have been hit in the vicinity of the propellers." Later H.M.S. Itchen herself was sunk, as she was in the act of signalling that she had sighted a U-boat ahead of her. Of the three crews aboard her only three men were picked up by the S.S. James Smith.

The Allies made the most strenuous endeavours to counteract this new weapon. U-boat commanders returning from subsequent operations reported that destroyers were now stopping when they sighted a U-boat. From this it was obvious that the enemy had found out about the principles on which the new torpedo worked; and eventually, though not for some considerable time, they found a counter-measure, in the shape of an acoustic buoy which was towed behind the ship.

One of the commanders who was later to score a great success with the new torpedo was Albrecht Brandi, who lost his first U-boat in

1943 off the African coast in the Mediterranean, survived the sinking of two further boats and is now an architect.

*   *   *

"Two British aircraft-carriers, three cruisers and some twenty destroyers and corvettes are at present carrying out manœuvres off Gibraltar."

So ran a message received towards the end of August from Naval Intelligence.

The water of the Mediterranean is crystal clear and as transparent as glass. It is often as smooth as a duck pond, too. Even a slightly protruding periscope in these waters leaves behind it a long trail of foam. This is visible to an aircraft from a long way away and could well betray the U-boat. Indeed, it often did so. A permanent British air reconnaissance now covered the Mediterranean like a closely woven net. It made things very difficult indeed for the U-boats.

On 28 August, 1943 Brandi was ready to sail. Here is his report:

"I put to sea in great haste. First I went with the speed of a cyclist—on the surface; and the rest of the way I went on foot, as it were, submerged. Very cautiously I nosed my way towards the enemy formation. The destroyers had formed two protective rings round the two aircraft carriers and the cruisers.

"I dived under the outer ring of destroyers and slipped, at silent running speed, nearer to the big ships. I raised my periscope for a few seconds at a time.

"According to my calculations the capital ships should now have been in range. Steady, I thought to myself. Just a little closer still and, for heaven's sake keep calm!

"Very soon the aircraft-carriers were in my sights, looking huge and massive. . . . And, at that moment, just as I was about to give the warning order for a salvo, the ships altered course, as though they were manœuvring to get out of the line of fire of an attacking U-boat. And to practise the manœuvre was, of course, very probably the object of the exercise they were conducting. I held my fire. The chances of hitting were too slender and the risk of losing my boat proportionally great.

"I spent the whole day manœuvring and turning, trying to get into position for a shot, but without success. A nerve-racking day.

"Over our heads and all round us we could hear the high note of the British destroyers and corvettes—a repulsive sound. At any moment, I felt, they must locate us. But the British evidently felt so secure that they were neglecting to use their hydrophones. Otherwise they could not have failed to pick us up.

"The fact that I had succeeded in making contact with the enemy and that he had already been exercising for some days led me to hope that I might yet get a good opportunity. Even so, it was enough to make me weep to have aircraft-carriers of the size of the *Formidable* and the *Illustrious* so close to my sights. I knew them because I had seen pictures of them on our recognition charts.

"On the second day, too, I had no luck. On the third day I could not even get near the ships.

"In the end, after these long and fruitless days, I was determined to have something in the bag to go home with. I got two destroyers. Two destroyers with a left and right—two torpedoes each from a salvo of four.

"This effort resulted in a hell of a hullaballoo among the A/S defences and patrols in Gibraltar. We had been so close when I fired that we had actually been able to see quite a lot of what was going on on the Rock.

"Underwater I made for the protection of the African coast. Destroyers were rushing about in all directions above our heads. Depth charges were being fired by the score! but all of them missing us by a mile. The men grinned broadly—for the first time on this operation.

"As the tropical night fell over North Africa and the narrow strip of the Straits I surfaced. Our batteries needed charging, but above all we needed some fresh air.

"It was a lovely, starlit night. All around us was peace, and nowhere was there even a shadow to be seen, nor even the rumble of a single aircraft. I handed over the watch to Count Arco, told him to set course for Mellile on the African coast and turned in. At the moment, so it seemed to me, our radar was of more importance than look-outs. Suddenly two terrific explosions rent the silence of the night. The U-boat staggered violently. I sprang up.

"Then came a third explosion, which caused the boat to rear

like a bucking horse. There was a crashing and splintering of glass and then the lights went out. An indescribable pandemonium reigned and there was complete chaos. Pipes were bursting everywhere. The floor plates were flung out of their sockets, and as I rushed to the control-room my foot got caught between two pipes which had been uncovered. The harder I tried to free my foot the tighter it seemed to jam. The men who had been in the bow compartment were rushing, as I had been, towards the control-room. They banged and buffeted and trod on me as they tried to squeeze past or climb over me. And the more they did so, the more thoroughly I got jammed. In the dark, of course, they could not even see I was there at all, much less who I was. Desperate situations demand desperate remedies, and I used pretty rough methods to free myself from the embraces of my good and zealous friends. Nor did my tongue fail to make most adequate contribution as I told them exactly what I thought of them and pointed out that I, too, had a job of work to do.

"At last some order was restored, and at last, with some assistance, I got my foot free. I groped my way into the control-room. From there I rushed to the bridge.

"As I reached the bridge I was greeted with a truly hellish bellow. For all I know, the bridge watch may well have been cheering. Count Arco pointed excitedly over the port bow, and I was just in time to see a hostile 'plane sinking below the waves.

"While we had thought the boat to be sinking the bridge watch had shot down the aircraft. The men had seen the merest silhouette, fired at it and hit it!

" 'All hands on deck!' I yelled. We had been damaged all right. Even the diesels had broken down, and the boat was all but a total wreck. Then I heard what had happened.

"The third bomb must have missed the side of the U-boat by a whisker and had then exploded at a depth of fifty or sixty feet directly beneath us; none of us below, I think, had noticed very much the way the bomb explosion had lifted the boat; but when she plunged down again—and as she did so, a solid stream of water from the descending columns thrown up by the bomb had come crashing down into the ship—all I remember thinking is: "We've had it! So this is what it feels like to be drowned!'

"With one lame diesel we tried to continue our way to the coast.

I hoped we should be able to lay the boat close in to the cliff and camouflage her with a few tarpaulins and some rocks.

" 'If that chap didn't use his radio, Sir, there's a chance that they won't send another 'plane.'

" 'Oh yes, they will! That fellow couldn't have gone on cruising around for ever, remember; and when he's overdue, the squadron will send someone to find out what's happened to him.'

"And sure enough, the second aircraft duly appeared . . . and pretty quick, too. Obviously, the first pilot had sent a signal before he had attacked. The second 'plane cruised round us in a circle at a very respectful distance.

"The water we had shipped had got at the batteries, and chlorine gas was forming rapidly. With the exception of those, clad in special masks, whose presence down below was essential, the whole of my crew were now on the upper deck. The helmsman, too, was below, steering by hand—the other steering having given out—and I yelled my orders to him down the conning-tower. This worked quite well, and better than I had expected. Even so, it was a weird and wonderfully curly course we weaved.

"The aircraft, too, had no intention of remaining a passive spectator. Every now and then came a burst of fire. My chaps crawled behind the conning-tower for cover, round and round and round. When the aircraft came up on the port side, they skipped over to starboard, then back again and so on. I could hardly believe my ears! My rascals had begun to sing . . . a song about two people in love, if you please! Both the title and the words were appropriate, since it described the lovers going round on a merry-go-round: 'round and round'.

"So did the crew! Port side . . . starboard . . . for'ard . . . aft . . . round the tower and off again! Even those louts who had got wind up were singing—probably louder than anybody else. But it was a healthy sign, and as long as they sang, I didn't give a damn what (or how) they sang.

"We were making straight for the high cliffs ashore, at the foot of which the sea lay in deep shadow. If we could get into those shadows, I felt we might be a little safer. And at last we got there, at last we were out of sight of that beastly, brass-coloured watcher in the sky.

"What a hope! They discharged flares, exactly over the spot

we had reached. To evade further observation seemed to be quite impossible. We ran along the shore for about a quarter of a mile. There was still a good hour before dawn. One hour—and in that hour something had to happen. As soon as it was light more aircraft, and probably surface vessels as well, were bound to put in an appearance and, crippled as we were, blow us to bits.

"In the meanwhile the chief engineer had checked up on the damage. He could not possibly carry out the repairs. If we could have kept close inshore and camouflaged for a few days, we might have been able to do something. As it was. . . .

"We were spared the trouble of any further study of the problem. While we were discussing it, the U-boat, at half speed on her solitary diesel, ran on to a submerged reef and stuck there, in spite of all our endeavours to move her.

"To abandon my *U.617* was one of the hardest decisions I have ever had to take in life. She was a grand and gallant craft. But there was no way out.

"My first step was to send all superfluous men ashore; and as the task of preparing the boat for demolition and firing the charge seemed to me to be one that I as commander and I alone should undertake, I told the whole lot to get out. There were many protests. Some asked to remain aboard, others volunteered, and there was no lack of these, to do the job for me, and in the end I was obliged to give the formal order to abandon ship. Only my first officer and the senior chief petty officer disobeyed.

" 'You can't manage it alone, Sir,' they insisted. 'You'll have to let us give you a hand.'

"They helped me to prepare the torpedo and to lay the fuse. We had to work dressed in our life-saving gear in the dark, and it wasn't easy to co-ordinate our actions. We removed the 'pistol' from the stern torpedo and put a detonator in its place.

" 'Now,' I said, 'now comes the tricky part. We must remain aboard. You understand that, you fellows, we must stay aboard while the torpedo goes up. In no circumstances whatever must anyone be in the water when the ship blows up. That would be certain death.

"Beside the torpedo we stacked a few subsidiary charges. And then came the fatal moment. The fuse started to splutter and burn; it would go on doing so for nine minutes.

"Those were the longest minutes of my life. No one spoke a word. Every now and then we glanced at each other. The two others stood holding fast with both hands to the stanchions. I myself leant up against the conning-tower, not pressed too close to it, but rather lounging against it. At the same time I held on to the lower guard rail that runs round the conning-tower. Our knees knocked a bit! Six minutes . . . seven . . . eight . . . 21, 22, 23, 24 seconds. . . .

"A column of flame leapt out of the U-boat and at the same time there was a nerve-shattering roar. I felt as though I had been hurtled straight to heaven. In actual fact the 500-ton ship only rose a few inches. We were all completely deafened. As though we were watching a silent film, we saw bits of the after-part of the boat fly through the air, and then we felt her begin to sink, at first slowly and then with ever-gathering speed. Then we were all three in the water, swimming through thick oil, for the fuel tanks had burst. Once I glanced over my shoulder. We had done a good job.

"In silence we swam towards the shore. I gave a hail . . . then another . . . no reply.

" 'Where the devil have those fatheads got to?' I asked angrily. 'Have they gone to ground or have they been taken prisoner or what?'

"At last somebody answered, and as we made our way ashore some of the men behaved in a most unseemly and unseamanlike manner. They rushed at us, flung their arms round us and hailed us as heroes.

" 'Why the hell didn't you blackguards answer my hail?' I asked with feigned anger.

"There was a moment of silence.

" 'We—didn't think it was you calling, Sir,' stammered some-one at last.

" 'Eh?'

" 'We thought it must be somebody else, Sir. We didn't want to give ourselves away, Sir, so we took cover.'

" 'We didn't see how you could still be alive, Sir,' added another in cheerful amplification.

"Dawn was now approaching. The rising sun disclosed a land-scape of cliff and rock which would have pleased the heart of a photographer, but was of poor comfort to us.

" 'What now, Sir?'

" 'First of all, destroy all the secret matter—war diary, W/T log and all the rest of it.'

"That was easier said than done. Till you've had a try, you've no idea how hard it is to burn thick books until there is nothing left of them. Some went ahead with this job in a hollow between the rocks while others went off to spy out the land. Suddenly one of the look-outs who had been posted came running back, panting excitedly.

" 'They're coming!'

" 'Who?'

" 'The British! Three corvettes, aircraft.' . . . As he spoke we heard the throb of aircraft in the air. Like lightning we took cover in the hollows and shelters the crew had scraped out earlier in the morning. Then we peeped round the edges of the rocks to see what would happen. The aircraft dropped their bombs on the wrecked U-boat. The corvettes—they were, as we later established—the destroyers *Hyacinth* and *Harlem*, and the corvette *Wolonging*—arranged a nice little practice shoot. Presumably they thought we were still on board. Some of the ricochets came flying over our heads.

"In the British communiqué these fireworks were celebrated as a sinking. Apparently all the bangs and noise had woken up the coastguards, for when all was quiet again and the British had departed, a Moroccan in Spanish uniform came trotting up. In his hand he brandished a long, fearsome-looking flintlock, and from his gestures you would have thought he was at the head of a whole army.

"We were his prisoners, he shouted, and he fiddled about with his old blunderbuss to such purpose that we really began to get quite nervous.

" 'Take the popgun away from the excited gentleman!'

"In a moment it was done. Our Moroccan dithered and cursed in his own, unintelligible language, and what he was trying to say was obvious to us all. In the end, to obviate any unfortunate accident, we had to tie him up. We now began a hard and dreary march through this stony, trackless land of rock. Many of the crew had no shoes and had to tear strips from their shirts and bind their feet with them. After three continuous weeks in our steel cylinder we emerged jaundiced and yellowy-green of face, into the full glare of the African sun.

"A few hours later a Spanish officer appeared on the scene, and in French, of a sort, we were able to make ourselves understood. He invited us with great politeness to follow him to the fort. And there is no gainsaying that that was just what we wanted to do, for we didn't want to die of thirst, and if we were to get home at all, the first stop, obviously, was his fort. The Spanish officer even promised to provide me with a fresh-water bath, for I was filthy and covered from head to foot in oil. In the heat of the sun the biting, caustic diesel oil had fairly burnt my skin, and it was only the thought of that bath that kept me going through the trials of that weary march.

"We were all completely exhausted. Some of the men had to be carried.

"But even the longest march must come to an end some time, and at long last we reached a more or less mediaeval fort, and I got my promised bath.

"I had been dreaming of a lovely, shining bath of porcelain and a sparkling, refreshing shower, and I could hardly believe my eyes when I was led to a little hut, which was like those particular little huts one sees in the country. Only the little heart-shaped 'window' was missing. On the other hand, I caught sight of a large funnel on the roof and a ladder leading up to it.

" 'So that's the "bath",' I thought. 'I'm glad I didn't know while we were foot-slogging it.'

"We were given half a bucket of water per man! Half a bucket!

"And even that was poured down the funnel on to us as slowly as if it had been the most costly of olive oils. My salient memory of this period of temporary internment remains, however, that of Spanish chivalry."

CHAPTER XXIV

U-BOATS IN FAR EASTERN WATERS

Situation Report.

As early as 1941 closer co-operation with the Japanese authorities was widely advocated in Germany. In the autumn of 1942 the desire to co-ordinate the war effort became even stronger. The German Supreme Command, with a fine disregard for the gradual diminution of our own forces, was actually contemplating, in addition to action in the Middle East, the extension of similar operations against India. This, in any case, would have required the co-ordination of German and Japanese interests. A request that the new German U-cruisers of the Type IXd2 should be allowed to operate in the Persian Gulf in conjunction with Japanese submarines was at first met with stiff and very precise reserve, albeit expressed in terms of truly Oriental politeness. The Japanese may well have been overconfident, particularly as their success over the major portions of the enemy forces in the Far East had been achieved with little cost to themselves.

In the Spring of 1943, however, this victory psychosis gave place to considerations of a more realistic nature. It was appreciated that German U-boat activities in the Indian Ocean would also serve Japanese interests, particularly as the main forces of the Japanese fleet had now had to be concentrated in the Pacific to oppose the increased strength of the United States.

In addition, owing to shortage of raw materials and the blockade of the enemy it was thought that essential raw materials might be transported by U-boats on their return to base after the accomplishment of the operational tasks that had been allotted to them. The Japanese agreed. In the Spring of 1943 German bases were established in Singapore and Batavia for the clearance of blockade-runners, and Penang for the supply and maintenance of U-boats.

At the beginning of July the first Monsoon Group sailed from French and Norwegian bases. Out of a total of eleven U-boats, only five reached the Indian Ocean and were detailed for operations in the area between India and the Gulf of Suez. At the end of 1943 the second

Monsoon Group set out. Only one U-boat reached the operational area. Later, in the next Spring, the U-boats proceeded singly to Japanese waters. Of the sixteen U-boats that did so, only six succeeded in reaching their Asiatic bases. The remainder, like those of the Monsoon Groups, were destroyed en route, mostly in the Atlantic. The senior naval officer, Southern Area, was Commander Wilhelm Dommes, who reached Penang after 156 continuous days at sea, including operations in the Indian Ocean. The difficulties which he had to face were enormous.

*　　*　　*

Wilhelm Dommes, a captain of the Merchant Navy and still a lieutenant-commander when he reached his Far Eastern base, was the only U-boat specialist among the commanders of the various bases, and he was pushed from pillar to post whenever and wherever an opinion or advice was required. The distances separating the various bases cannot be measured by European standards. The distance between the two extreme points of the Southern Area system of bases was more than twelve hundred miles, as far as from Koenigsberg to Madrid.

Dommes, it is true, had two Arado float-planes which had originally belonged to an auxiliary cruiser. But he was casting longing eyes on another, Japanese, boat, if only for the spare parts with which it could supply him. On his own responsibility, taking full advantage of the intense curiosity that the Japanese displayed for anything new in the technical sphere, he struck an excellent and quite grotesque bargain with them.

The Japanese had evinced burning interest in "Bachstelze" (sea-stilts). This was the name given to a sort of kite which had been developed for use with the big U-cruisers, and was designed to give the ship a wider field of observation. The kite, to which a bos'n's chair for the observer or lookout was attached, could be sent up when a U-boat was under way.

In practice, Bachstelze proved a failure owing to the danger from surprise air attacks.

Dommes struck a bargain with the Japs. He exchanged a sea-stilt for a Reichiki, a Japanese flying-boat which was a thousand times more valuable. And thus he at least became a little more mobile.

Amenities and facilities offered by the Far Eastern bases were makeshift in comparison with the European ones to which the U-boats were accustomed. Means of communication, however, were good. Each base possessed an adequate radio station, the equipment for which had been obtained, for the most part, from Japan. All these W/T stations were in constant communication with the German Admiral's Headquarters in Tokyo. Direct communication by radio with Germany was also possible but problematical, dependent as it was on the season of the year and the time of day.

Between Penang and Singapore there was even a telephone service. But it functioned very badly and was overloaded most of the time with Japanese official business.

The personnel establishment, too, was extremely unsatisfactory. Each of the bases could muster no more than about fifty German service personnel, and these were nearly all required for office work, administration and communications.

Within the limits of the means available the Japanese authorities gave the Germans every assistance in their endeavour to fit out these bases on a European standard and in a manner that met local service requirements. Every German base was allotted an adequate number of bungalows as offices and living quarters. In spite of increasing shortages, ample rations were always readily available.

The Japanese helped, too, to organise swimming and shooting facilities, golf, tennis and other games. They responded wholeheartedly to the German request for adequate convalescent quarters for the submariners, who frequented health centres such as Penang Hill, Frazer Hill and the Cameron Highlands in Malaya, and Selapentanta and Chikopo in Java.

*   *   *

The main problem, however, remained the overhaul of the technically highly complicated U-boats, the maintenance of which called for technicians of the highest possible skill. In East Asia, however, there were at the outset not even any experienced submariners available, to say nothing of technical specialists. It was only when a Type IXc U-boat was handed over to the Japanese Navy as a model for their own constructors that its crew became free to form the nucleus of a repair and maintenance group. But for incoming U-boats they could never do more than render assistance; they could not supply a temporary harbour crew, even though the incoming crew, after one hundred and fifty and sometimes two hundred days at sea and on operations, were in desperate need of change and rest.

So, the U-boat crews were compelled often to take a hand themselves if they were to maintain their schedule.

The general standard of health at that time caused much anxiety. The inadequate means available for combating malaria led to widespread infection. Very often as many as twenty-five per cent of a crew would succumb to malaria and various skin diseases. Only the essential minimum of convalescence could be allowed to the patients. First and foremost came the U-boats and their jobs. Even so, the crews never grumbled. They carried out their arduous duties without a murmur, for they knew that their very lives depended on the seaworthiness of their ship and—they were also eager for success. The net result of all this was that the health of a crew was worse when they set out again from their base than when they had returned to rest and re-fit.

Japanese labour, too, was not of much value.

Simple jobs, such as painting, re-caulking, repair and maintenance of the less complicated components, could safely be left in the hands of the dockyards themselves; but all the difficult and intricate work had to be done by the crew themselves with the help of the German repair groups.

Most of this work was done in the early morning or late evening to avoid the excessive midday heat.

Spares and replacements, etc., arrived regularly.

Initially, two German tankers, *Brake* (10,000 tons) and the *Charlotte Schliemann* (7,000 tons), were available for the operations in the Indian Ocean. It was the *Charlotte Schliemann* that acted as supply ship for a group of six U-boats, including Hartmann's which had operated to the south-east of Madagascar. In September 1943 *Brake* carried out the first replenishment of the Monsoon Group without untoward incident. For a time all went well, but only for a time. Very soon the enemy was to extend the scope of his intensive air reconnaissance to include these waters as well.

The German authorities also had three Italian U-boats at their disposal. These had escaped to Japan on the fall of Eritrea. They were of no fighting value and were used chiefly as transports between the various bases and the Japanese mainland.

The wide expanses of the Indian Ocean, and the enemy's custom of using his fastest ships sailing independently in these waters, accounted for the fact that German successes, numerically, were comparatively small and not very convincing. The average tonnage sunk per U-boat was about 25,000 tons.

On the other hand, the ships that were sunk were all carrying valuable cargoes, which could only be replaced with great difficulty. All the hard work and effort that had been put into the execution of these operations was therefore fully justified. In addition, the activities of these U-boats compelled the enemy to divert aircraft and A/S vessels from other operational areas.

*　　*　　*

U.553 was one of the first U-boats to fall victim to an attack from the air after replenishing from the *Brake*. It was on a Sunday, 17 October 1943, that *U.553*, which had just sunk a merchantman in the narrows separating the Persian Gulf from the Gulf of Oman, was attacked. Lieutenant Hennig thought that a crash dive would get him out of trouble, but the bombs damaged the pressure hull, and Hennig was unable to bring his boat to the surface again.

At that moment there were two men in the control room beneath the conning-tower, the first officer, Sub-Lieutenant Paaschen and Seaman Guenther Schmidt. Water was pouring into the U-boat at a great rate, and the two men quickly realised that she was sinking with increasing speed.

"Out!" shouted Paaschen, with the water already gurgling around his feet. He clambered up the ladder and tried to open the conning-tower hatch, on which the pressure of water was already considerable. As the water in the ship was also rising very swiftly the two men, the only two in the control-room, hoped that their strength would suffice to push the hatch open.

Paaschen and Schmidt had both put on their submerged escape gear. The hatch would not budge. The seconds ticked by, and it was only a matter of seconds before the ship plunged to the bottom. And each second seemed like an eternity to the trapped men. . . . At last, suddenly, the hatch moved, with a last effort the men opened it and air from within burst gurgling upwards. The hatch flew back. Paaschen and Schmidt clung on desperately to avoid being sucked out with the escaping air. Gradually, however, the violence of its movement subsided. The hatch lay supine and open. The conning-tower was full of water. The pressure had stabilised.

Paaschen motioned Schmidt to go ahead, though he had to use force before the seaman would obey him. It is the custom of the service, when life is at stake, that the men come first, then the officers and lastly the commander.

Schmidt was whirled upwards. When he reached the surface his senses were reeling. He waited and watched for the appearance of his officer. A few second later Paaschen appeared not far away. Schmidt called to him. No answer.

"Sir! . . . Sir! It's Schmidt! Are you all right?"

Paaschen remained inert and motionless, his head drooping loosely into the water. Schmidt swam across and shook him. Was he merely unconscious?

For half an hour Schmidt held up the sagging form of his officer before he was at last convinced that Paaschen was no longer alive. His lungs had burst.

Overhead the aircraft that had dropped the fatal bombs circled round and flew away, and Schmidt, the sole survivor from *U.533*, was left struggling in the water alone. Night was falling swiftly. It had been pure luck that he had happened to glance at the chart just before the disaster had occurred. The setting sun gave him his bearings. He struck out in an attempt to reach the shore which was not too far distant. How far it was, Schmidt did not know, nor could he see it.

Darkness came. Schmidt made a silent, friendly pact with the stars. The Southern Cross that shone above him pointed the way he should go. Would the light of dawn give him his first glimpse of land? At times his arms felt like lead, and cramp threatened to creep up his legs and paralyse them. But his life-belt stood him in good stead and held him above water, water which gleamed fluorescently with every movement that he made.

As the sky began to lighten and a wave lifted him, Schmidt thought he could see a grey shadow in the distance, far, far ahead of him. Some hours later he was sure; it was land. But evening was already falling before he crawled up the steep foreshore of the

Arabian coast after a battle with the waves that had lasted for eight and twenty hours. He slipped through the mass of rocks into which the swell had flung him and then he collapsed.

When he came to his senses again he found himself surrounded by a group of excitedly chattering natives who had carried him further up the foreshore.

When the Arabs realised that the stranger was alive, they were delighted, and doubly so when they found out that he was an "Allemanno". They carried Schmidt into a miserable little hut and pressed upon him all the modest food and drink they had to offer. They rushed off to fetch the children and all their relations. to gaze in wonder with them at this marvel of marvels, a German submariner.

Schmidt tried to make the Arabs understand that he could not remain where he was. Shaking their heads mournfully, but willingly, the sons of the desert trotted off to get help from the British.

A few days later Schmidt was picked up by a British patrol and taken to Basra. From there he was taken by air to Cairo. As he looked back at the glistening sea that seemed to melt into the horizon far behind him, Schmidt's thoughts turned once again to his ship. Far away there, to the south, she lay in her grave.

CHAPTER XXV

U-792, THE WONDER U-BOAT

Situation Report.

In the spring of 1943, one month before the German U-boats met their Stalingrad, Lieutenant Heller was appointed to take charge of the Trials of the new Walter U-boat, the type XVIIa. Without any reflection on Heller, it did seem a little odd that the trials of a new weapon which would revolutionise submarine warfare should be in charge of a mere lieutenant. Or, should I say, could have revolutionised, if only. . . .

The Walter team now included Heep (engine construction) and Gabler (ship construction). The whole team was now under the direction of Dr. Fischer, the Director of Shipbuilding, and Moeller, the naval architect, acted as construction supervisor.

Heller's duties included the supervision of all trials and tests, the training of the technical personnel and, later, the duties of U-boat Headquarters representative on the Acceptance Board.

*   *   *

From the beginning of July Heller was in charge of the first courses of instruction for special technical personnel detailed for duty in the envisaged operational craft, Types XVIIb and XXVI. He was a first-class instructor with an easy conversational way of leading his pupils through the most intricate of mechanical theses. He cracked plenty of jokes, and his metaphors were apt and vivid.

After the July conference, at which fifty senior officers, inventors and industrialists had participated, Heller was waiting from day to day for the delivery of the first two experimental craft. But it was the end of November before they were ready; on 1 December the first two arrived in Hela, *U.792* (Blohm and Voss) and *U.794* (Germania Shipbuilding Yards).

Heller wasted no time and before Christmas he had completed his first tentative runs with *U.792*. There were minor failures and breakdowns in plenty. But they were all ironed out by the Walter people, all enthusiastic technicians of the highest order.

*   *   *

Captain Sachs, submariner and holder of the Meritorious Service Gold Cross in the First World War, was by nature a suspicious fellow. When Heller told him that *U.792* had in fact achieved a speed of 25 knots submerged, he replied that he would like to see her do it himself and asked that she should run over the measured mile in his presence.

"That won't be too easy, Sir," said Heller.

"To put a fast one across me, you mean!"

"No, Sir," replied Heller quietly. "What I mean is that it won't be too easy to arrange for you to be able to see for yourself that the boat actually does what I've promised you she does. At full speed we can't, of course, raise the periscope. It would break off like a carrot. So we must find some other way. My idea was to fix two head-lamps for'ard on the conning-tower. You'll be able to see the light underwater, Sir, and if you follow us in a motor torpedo boat you'll have plenty of speed. I suggest I do a first run at the minimum speed with the Walter turbine—13 knots, then a second run at 16 knots, and finally a last run at full-speed, 25 knots. We'll keep in touch by underwater signalling."

"Could you get all that fixed up by tomorrow evening?"

"Yes, certainly, Sir."

"Fine—and see that the whole area is cleared and kept clear. Right! I'll see you at 20.00 to-morrow."

"Very good, Sir."

In command of *U.792*'s trial run was Lieutenant Heitz. The MTB was commanded by Papa Sachs in person.

The next evening everything was set and ready. Heller and Sachs went briefly over the arrangements made, and then *U.792* with Heller aboard dived and disappeared.

The head-lamps were switched on, and the U-boat did its first run at the agreed 13 knots. Papa Sachs in his MTB kept just ahead of her. He could see the electric light of the U-boat that was surging along behind him and he was well content. There's something in this damn contraption after all, he thought. The first run, then, went without a hitch. Papa Sachs made a signal to that effect, and Heller replied: "Signal understood."

The two vessels then swung round in a circle preparatory to the second run. Papa Sachs, of course, was still on the surface and Heller below it. As the latter approached the beginning of the measured mile he worked up to the agreed 16 knots, gave the arranged signal.

"Well—no reply yet from the MTB?" asked Heller.

"No reply, Sir," answered the operator.

"Never mind, we'll carry on."

U.792 duly completed her second run, and still there was no signal.

"Well, he must have been able to see us anyway. Put about and prepare for the final run at 25 knots."

At her full speed *U.792* completed the course, turned and repeated the performance.

Still not a whisper from the MTB.

Heller surfaced.

For some strange reason the MTB was two miles away.

"What the hell do you think you're playing at?" roared Papa Sachs as soon as the two vessels were within hailing distance. "I don't advise you to try any monkey tricks, young man!"

"No, Sir! May I suggest we repeat the runs?"

"Very well! Carry on!"

But the repeat performance was equally unsuccessful. This time, too, all that Captain Sachs had been able to observe had been the first run. On the next two he had seen nothing. And for security reasons he was not allowed to call on other observers for assistance (not, in any case, that he had the least desire to do so).

Once again the two craft were lying alongside each other. Papa Sachs was as red as a turkey cock, he was bubbling with indignation and seemed on the point of exploding.

"This is a bit over the odds, Heller! It's a bare-faced swindle! You and your blasted tub did one run and then, I suppose, lay doggo on the bottom. And then you come along and tell me you've done 25 knots! It won't go down, young man, not with me!"

"May I suggest, Sir, that we go ashore and talk it over and try and find where and how the thing went wrong?"

"We certainly will! I want to clear this matter up. And let me tell you this—if anyone made a mistake, it was you! Either that, or you tried to make a fool of me. You're a fool or worse, Sir—and you can take your choice!"

Heller was the first ashore. He knew a small place where they ran a nice line in cognac, and he hastily sent for a bottle. Old Papa Sachs was in a hell of temper; but a drop of decent cognac would probably mellow the old boy.

The subsequent "inquest" went very smoothly. Sachs liked this young fellow whose very persistence made him inclined to believe him. He was still mad that the show had gone all wrong; but at least they'd found out why.

They now realised that the U-boat had a turning circle of about 150 yards, whereas that of the MTB was over 400 yards. They hadn't allowed for that one. It had thus come about that Heller was in position for the next run while the MTB was still far away, completing her turn. The underwater signalling had failed, they presumed, simply because the angle had been too acute.

There was, then, nothing for it but to devise some other method of timing the ship over the measured mile. To make sure this time, they positioned a U-boat at each end of the measured mile. In addition to Sachs' observing the lights, these U-boats were to follow *U.792*'s course with their hydrophones. For security reasons, only the commanders were to be allowed on deck. All was soon ready. Captain Sachs stepped once more aboard his MTB. This time, surely, nothing could go wrong.

It did, though; for with the greatest skill in the world you can't run exactly two set miles one immediately after the other in opposite directions.

The first run was observed as before. It was also picked up by the hydrophones. The other two runs could not be checked, for the light was not observed until after the U-boat had run through the check-point and had started to slow down. There had been no clear hydrophone effect and no sound of propellers.

A personal knowledge of Captain Sachs is really necessary to enable the reader to appreciate what happened next. Not for nothing was he known throughout the navy as "Papa" Sachs, and when anything went wrong he could be as high-handed as any father with his erring son.

247

But Heller did not wilt under the storm. He waited quietly until it had blown itself out, before coming forward with new suggestions.

"It's no use our going on like this, Sir. To do the thing properly will cost a bit of money, and we must find it. The only thing to do is to lay shore-fed electric cables transversely along the measured mile, fix a loop or coil round the conning-tower and instal electrical measuring instruments inside the boat.'

"Now you're talking!" cried Sachs, and he very quickly found both the requisite money and the cable-layers.

The final result of the third and last trial showed *U.742* to have covered the mile at a speed of exactly 25 knots, or just over 30 miles an hour. This had now been established technically beyond doubt. What, however, still remained a mystery, and a rather disturbing one at that, was why no echoes had been picked up on the hydrophones.

For the time being they thought that a blind spot must have been responsible. At that time they had no idea that it was something quite different which had eradicated the echoes.

CHAPTER XXVI

A SOMBRE PROSPECT

Situation Report—1943.

At last we had succeeded in picking up the deadly centimetre wavelengths of the enemy's radar. In the summer came the Haganuk wavelength indicator, "Wanze". This was followed by the small and even better detector, "Borkum". It was thanks to this latter that the truly catastrophic rate of losses in the spring did not continue. In August the total number of U-boats lost was still as high as twenty-five. In September, the month in which the "Zaunkoenig" torpedo was taken into use, our losses were only ten. In October they rose steeply again to twenty-six. In November the number was nineteen; in December only eight. This last low figure was admittedly due in part to the fact that during this month most of the operational U-boats were withdrawn to be fitted with Snorts and trained in the use of them.

The Special Communiqués—paeans of glorious success—still echoed in the ears of the German people; the last of them had been issued in March, during which month U-boats sank 108 ships, a total of 700,000 tons. After that the grey wolves were mentioned no more. In September, with the introduction of the "Zaunkoenig" success rose somewhat. In October it was down again to thirteen ships and 97,000 tons. In November the total fell below even that of the opening months of the war. In December another thirteen ships, 87,000 tons were sunk. By far the greater number of these ships were sunk in the South Atlantic and the Indian Ocean, the operational area of the Monsoon Groups. In December, too, the battleship Scharnhorst, *was lost. Like the other heavy ships,* Scharnhorst *had not, after all, been withdrawn from service, since Doenitz had realised that he had been wrong and that he could not afford to dispense with these capital ships.*

The total losses in U-boats in 1943 amounted to 237—a total which could still be made good by new construction. But "The European Stronghold" was tottering. In the east the vast Russian steam-roller of men and material was slowly pushing the German armies back. In the

Pacific the Japanese took one beating after another. Portugal had given the U.S.A. bases in the Azores. Italy was out. After the fall of North Africa, German U-boat operations in the Mediterranean became more hazardous than ever. One of the U-boats lost there was U.593 (Commander Kelbing). He lost his boat on his fifteenth operational voyage, a fact that was mentioned by the British radio as proof that even the best and most experienced U-boat commanders were now falling victims to the new, improved and increased A/S measures being taken by the Allies. The commentator made a particular point of the fact that throughout all his fifteen operations Kelbing had not once had occasion to award any punishment to any member of his crew. . . .

*   *   *

It was on 10 December that *U.593* set out from Toulon on her fifteenth operation. On 11 December Kelbing was off the African coast. Before first light on 12 December *U.593* submerged in order not to expose herself to the risk of unpleasant surprises. The noise of destroyer propellers could be heard on the hydrophones. Kelbing rose to periscope depth and in the twilight he could discern a faint silhouette. He decided to have a shot with a "Zaunkoenig", and notwithstanding his very scanty preliminary calculations, he scored a hit. The destroyer turned out to be H.M.S. *Tynedale*. *U.593* at once withdrew further out to sea. They could hear the explosions of single depth charges, a long way away. Another quick look through the periscope revealed a typical, cloudless Mediterranean sky. There was not a puff of wind. The sea was as smooth as a billiard table, and when the periscope was raised it left a long, broad trail behind it that no aircraft could have failed to see.

Kelbing knew that the sinking of the destroyer would bring out all the Allied A/S forces and aircraft. Moreover, with a full moon shining in a clear sky he could hardly expect to be able to get away during the night.

He had 36 hours in which to act, for his supply of oxygen would last for just that time.

About midday another destroyer approached and was so placed that Kelbing could not possibly miss her. H.M.S. *Holcome* was hit amidships and broke in half.

"So far so good," thought *U.593*'s commander. "But how I'm

going to get out of this witches' cauldron, I don't quite know."

There was no need for him to say much to his crew. They had been long enough in the Mediterranean to realise that their chances of getting away were pretty poor.

By evasive action and numerous course alternatives, *U.593* tried to shake off her pursuers.

"There's only one thing to be done," said Kelbing. "When night falls, as soon as the hydrophones give us a reasonably clear chance, we must surface and try and get away as fast as we can."

Shortly after midnight conditions seemed to be favourable. *U.593* surfaced, and Kelbing hastened on the bridge. Here he got a bit of a shock. The moon stood high above the boat and it was as light as day. The machine guns were all manned, and the chief engineer quickly worked up his diesels to their maximum speed. There was nothing in sight. Their luck seemed to be in.

A few short minutes later, however, the look-out reported the approach of a Wellington. It was approaching from starboard and flying straight at the U-boat. Kelbing knew from the navigation lights of the aircraft that it was not alone; but judging from its movements it did not appear to have spotted the U-boat.

"Damnation! We're dished up to him on a silver salver," cursed Kelbing, realising that even a crash dive wouldn't help matters very much. The range to the on-coming Wellington was 1,500 yards when the U-boats' guns opened fire. From six 2-cm. barrels tracer tore through the sky towards the bomber. The pilot rose and turned sharply away and in doing so exposed the broad under-belly of the aircraft to the German gunners. Kelbing could see the bright flashes as bullets struck home.

"Good shooting, lads! Give her all you've got!"

The gunners did their utmost. They compelled the hard-hit aircraft to turn away out of action and jettison its bombs. They fell a long way away from the U-boat, and behind the columns of their explosions the attacker disappeared.

"The rest won't be long in coming after all this display of fireworks," shouted the officer on watch to the commander.

Kelbing submerged. While the U-boat was going slowly down, they heard the noise of destroyers. Then a patrol vessel passed directly over them. But no depth charges were dropped.

Now Kelbing was faced with other, equally pressing worries.

The few minutes on the surface had not been sufficient either to top up the compressed air or to charge the batteries. To surface again would be suicidal. The chief engineer reduced current consumption to a minimum. The commander nodded approvingly.

"With a bit of luck we may be able to hang on till evening," he said. And the operative word, undoubtedly was—"may".

"Tomorrow night, Sir, we'll have a reprieve of about three quarters of an hour," said the navigator, who had worked out that there would be about forty-five minutes between nightfall and moonrise. It might just give them a chance of getting away.

Overhead the destroyers were still continuing the search, and the high note of their propellers sounded like the baying of a pack of hounds.

Kelbing gazed with unseeing eyes at his companions. "What a sublime faith these fellows have," he thought, "and what a fine example of calm and self-control they give; and they're none of them raw recruits and they know as well as I do that it's neck or nothing now."

The operator kept continual watch on the hydrophones. With great caution *U.593* slipped this way and that out of the immediate danger zone. Suddenly, however, the operator reported propeller echoes rapidly increasing in strength. Very soon the dreaded sound was clearly audible to everyone. But in it Kelbing detected a new note, like the shrill scream of a circular saw, that drowned the normal threshing sound of propellers. He was, unfortunately, not destined to get home and report upon this new experience and upon the new instrument which was to render the "Zaunkoenig" useless and which the enemy was testing for the first time in the Mediterranean.

Down came the depth charges. In their mind's eye, the crew could see these sinister cylinders sinking slowly downwards, nearer and ever nearer to the U-boat. And then the crashing explosions started. The din was indescribable; the men felt as though they were cowering in some tin can upon which a colossus was raining blows with a giant hammer. The damage caused by the nearest of the charges was appalling.

The electric bulbs burst throughout the boat. Lockers and shelves came tumbling down. The steering gear was put out of action. Both electric motors stopped. The ship dipped violently by the bows.

"All hands aft!"

Those who had been asleep leapt from their bunks at the roar of the first explosions—not from fear, but in order to be ready for any emergency. The men clattered and crawled on all fours over the floor plates to increase the weight in the stern and thus restore the ship to an even keel. The stern dipped with the suddenness of a seesaw.

"All hands for'ard!"

Once again came the hectic scramble—in the reverse direction.

There are no adequate words to describe what happened next. a film, possibly, might have given some idea of it. In these seconds of deadly danger, the fate of each man would require a chapter to itself. Mortal fear gripped the whole crew. But not one of them gave any sign of the fact. Rudderless, the boat hung poised at a depth of some 350 feet. Then she began slowly to sink—deeper . . . and deeper.

"Second series!"

Once again there was an infernal din.

The boat continued its downward plunge. At 680 feet Kelbing held her. Over the inter-com came the report:—"There's a leak in the diesel room!"

"How much?"

"Two pints a minute!"

"Well—that's not serious, thank goodness," said Kelbing to the chief engineer in a relieved tone of voice. The latter was doing all he knew to restore the trim of the boat. She started to rise, and to rise quickly, and Kelbing realised that even if she were shipping water, it was only a few pints, and at all costs he must prevent her from breaking surface. If only they could get the motors running again! . . . He opened the air vents a little, to prevent the boat from going right to the surface.

At once she started to sink—not slowly, but at a frightening speed.

The chief engineer came hastening with another report:

"They made a mistake, Sir! It's much more than two pints!"

Nothing could halt her now.

"Very well—up we go! Surface!" There was no hint of excite-

253

ment in Kelbing's voice. He gave the order calmly, as though the U-boat were on peacetime manœuvres, not on the way to certain captivity if not to death itself.

Petty Officer Uberschär swiftly opened the blowing valve. A hissing stream of air poured into the diving tanks. But so much air had been used when they were at 600 feet that the hissing became less and less violent, petered and then stopped altogether. For a moment the men's hearts stopped, too. The compressed air bottles were empty. But the boat still hung poised at a depth of nearly 350 feet—and with her stern down at an angle of 40 degrees.

Supporting himself at a queer angle in the control-room was Kelbing's chief engineer, Lieutenant Liebe. Even now in this desperate situation, with his hand, as it were, already on the side of his coffin, he was the personification of unshakable composure. He tapped the face of the depth gauge with an exploratory knuckle. But the needle gave no response. If only those motors would get going again.

Kelbing crept aft. But in the diesel compartment the men were already knee-deep in water, working desperately to get their motors started.

The ship was very quiet. Not a soul shouted, not a soul groaned. They were all panting a little, but the air supply was running short, and the men's gasps had nothing to do with fear. Those who were not busy with repairs remained squatting quietly, as though nothing had happened. Only the threatening splash of water and the rhythmic tapping on the depth gauge broke the silence.

Suddenly the revolution indicator of the starboard motor flickered to and fro, mounted to half speed.

How the mechanics got that half-submerged electric motor to function again is something which Kelbing cannot understand to this very day.

The depth gauge, too, now showed signs of life. It rose slowly but steadily, and then as the boat started to level out the crew knew that U.593 had reached the surface.

Kelbing tore open the conning tower hatch. U.593 was lying, bathed in bright sunshine, between two destroyers which were firing with all they had got at the target between them, a target they could not miss. It was a hellish nightmare. Shells and mach-ine-gun bullets hurtled and whistled, bursting and screaming all round the U-boat. Even to try and offer resistance would have been madness.

"All hands on deck!"

Kelbing hoped that when the enemy saw all the crew clambering out on to the deck he would cease fire. As the first men emerged from the conning tower he seized them by the arm.

"Lend a hand here! Help the others out!"

Together the commander and his men helped to pull their shipmates, already exhausted by the foul air and impeded by their life jackets, through the hatch. Meanwhile the tornado of fire from the two destroyers continued, unabated. There was nothing else for it—as each man emerged he dived straight into the sea. Still the destroyers continued to fire. It was only after twenty men were already swimming about in the water that they ceased fire. Kelbing was now able to get the rest of his crew out of the shattered and wrecked shell that had once been his ship. He was relieved to see that the destroyers were already picking up the men struggling in the water.

The last to emerge through the conning-tower hatch were Liebe, the chief engineer, and Hühnert, the torpedo petty officer. *U.593*'s stern was already under water, but she refused to sink any further, although the chief engineer had opened all the flooding-valves.

As they emerged Kelbing saw that a motor boat had been launched from one of the destroyers. He had but a matter of minutes to prevent his ship, and with her the secret codes, from falling into the hands of the enemy.

Two demolition charges had, in addition, been clamped to the U-boat's side, and the fuses were burning steadily. But would they detonate the charges? Had they been properly laid? At all costs, she must not be allowed to fall into the hands of the enemy.

Before Kelbing himself could do anything, the portly Hühnert had swung himself like a weasel down through the hatch.

"I'll go for'ard, Sir, and see if I can't find something else to open!" he shouted from below. He had realised that the ship was being kept afloat by air that had collected in the bow compartment. One of the flooding-valves, too, might have jammed. *U.593* was liable to sink at any moment.

Kelbing clattered down after his petty officer, calling to him to

255

come back. But as he reached the foot of the conning-tower, Hühnert's grinning face appeared from the direction of the bow compartment.

"Up you go Sir—quick! I've opened the torpedo hatch!"

The two men clambered out and ran towards the forecastle which was just sticking out of the water. With a combined effort they tore open the torpedo hatch, the clips of which Hühnert had already unscrewed from inside the boat.

Water was now pouring into the forecastle with every sea that broke over the U-boat. The enemy could not possibly get into her. As he stood up again he saw a motor boat flying the American flag coming alongside. Light machine-guns kept Kelbing and Hühnert covered.

"My God! If the fellow's nippy and knows his way about a U-boat he might still slip down the hatch, grab the ciphers and come out again!" The disturbing thought flashed through Kelbing's mind.

A lieutenant sprang aboard. "Where is the commander?" he asked. Kelbing went slowly, very slowly towards him. Every second gained was of importance.

"Keep off, the torpedoes will blow up in a few seconds," he told the young American officer, speaking slowly, almost benignly.

The lie did the trick. The American hastily pushed Kelbing and his petty officer into the motor boat and withdrew at full speed. A few moments later *U.593*'s bows dipped and, as though she were doing an ordinary dive, she plunged down into the depths forever.

Those who were still swimming about raised a cheer.

The submariners were received aboard the American destroyer with cigarettes and then pushed down to the boiler room for a wash. Kelbing himself was immediately conducted to the captain's cabin where water and clean clothing awaited him. The American captain came in and greeted Kelbing with a handshake, like an old friend.

"Hallo! Glad to know you! You've had bad luck. . . . Take it easy!"

Over a cup of coffee Kelbing thanked the American captain for having stopped the tornado of fire that had been directed at the U-boat. As a result, the whole crew had been rescued.

The American captain was a little apologetic. "I guess we

The first Walter U-boat. The experimental *V.80* in the Baltic

The control room of *V.80* with its dual steering, as seen from the turbine compartment

A British
aerial photo-
graph of a
convoy in the
North Atlantic

A tanker
blows up

The next
morning burn-
ing wrecks mark
the passage of
the convoy

thought your guys were trying to man the machine-guns," he said.

"Yes—it looked like it. Actually they were only trying to get at the collapsible dinghy stowed under the machine-guns."

"Well—at this distance, we couldn't see that, you know."

There ₁ as a slight pause, then the American officer stood up.

"I hope you'll consider yourself my guest aboard this ship," he said. "I'll see to it that your men don't lack for anything. We're all one here—seamen among seamen."

Later Kelbing and his chief engineer were invited to dinner. Here, too, they were treated as guests and not as prisoners. After dinner the captain disappeared on to the bridge. With some good Canadian Club circulating, conversation in the wardroom soon became animated. Talk ranged over every possible subject except —war. Only once did an officer even mention it.

"Say, Captain," he drawled, "haven't your torpedoes improved quite a lot recently?"

A brother officer intervened quickly:

"Cut it out!" he said tersely.

There was a frank and friendly spirit abroad, that spirit, based on decency and mutual respect which always binds fighting men —on both sides; and it was not long before Kelbing was quite convinced that his foes had continued to fire on him under a perfectly sincere misapprehension.

Part Six

1944

CHAPTER XXVII

DOENITZ AND THE WALTER U-BOATS

Situation Report.

The New Year heralded the start of a race with time. Somehow or other time had to be gained, until the new electric U-boats could be put into commission.

The production programme was running at full pressure. Throughout northern Germany, the component sections were being constructed, hurried to the yards on the coast and there assembled with the least possible delay. Admiral Time was now also Admiral Commanding the Dockyards.

"The day will come when I shall confront Churchill with a new and revolutionary form of submarine warfare. The U-boat arm has not collapsed under the blows of 1943. On the contrary, it is now stronger than ever before. 1944 will be a hard year, but a year destined to be crowned with success," declared Doenitz at a conference in Stettin. Hans Fritsche, the radio commentator, told the German people that at long last real, total war under the sea was at hand. This was to be waged with completely new types of U-boats, against which the enemy counter-measures would be powerless.

To this the Allied answer was massed air raids on the Siemens and Schuckert Works, in which the electric motors for the new U-boats were being built. The great workshops disintegrated into a heap of twisted metal and rubble. At the Berghof, Doenitz had to face Hitler and revise his confident prophecy that the new electro boats would bring about a decisive turn of the tide in the battle of the Atlantic.

Meanwhile, the Zeiss works, which made the periscope lenses also suffered heavy air raids.

In the Atlantic the old, out-dated types still carried on the unequal fight. Only a minute number of them were fitted with Snort. Why, then, did not Doenitz withdraw these boats from an Atlantic in which the enemy was now so overwhelmingly superior? Why did he not bring them home and concentrate all the available forces that would thus have been freed on the construction of the new types? His argument was that, by remaining where they were, these U-boats were tying down vast enemy forces at sea and, in particular, in the air. Moreover, the U-boat Command was most anxious not to lose direct contact with all the various anti-submarine measures and devices which the enemy was constantly developing.

The spectre of imminent invasion dominated the thoughts of the staffs of all three services. Doenitz had given orders for the development of midget submarines with which, in conjunction with the larger U-boats, he proposed to attack the invasion fleet, when it came. These midgets were one-man or two-men craft; their crews were all volunteers and were formed into small commando units raised by the German Navy towards the end of the war. Many of these men had absolutely no experience of the sea.

Opinions upon the armament with which the A/A U-boats should be equipped varied very considerably, and in order to settle the issue, the commander-in-chief declared that he would himself inspect one of these boats and then make a decision. In March six of these A/A U-boats lay in the Walter yards at Hela awaiting inspection. Beyond them the Walter U-boat, U.792, lay moored.

*   *   *

Having completed his inspection, the commander-in-chief asked Heller to show him over *U.792.* In the turbine-room he sat on the thrust block and asked Heller to explain everything.

"Heller, we're on our own here. Tell me honestly what you think of this whole box of tricks. I'm no technician at all. All I see is a mass of metal. Is this thing any good as a U-boat or not?"

"It certainly is, Sir. It's much more than that—it's the perfect means of submerged propulsion, a complete revolution."

Heller made a great impression on Doenitz. His subsequent report was clear, terse and wholly convincing.

"Well, Heller, if that is so, then we must build these ships as quickly as possible. I'll tell you what—I'd like to come on a trial run with you. Could you fix that some time?"

"Tomorrow would be a good time, Sir. Tomorrow *U.795* will

be available, a Blohm and Voss built boat, better constructed than this one, which was built by the Germania Company."

"Fine! Tomorrow it is, then, Heller."

Doenitz and his staff went ashore in the tender *Hela*. Her captain was Commander Neumann, an old friend of Heller's, and as the two men had not seen each other for some time, their meeting later in Neumann's cabin was a joyous one. Neumann raised his glass, congratulated his old friend on his success and wished him luck. For he, too, had heard how enthusiastic Doenitz had been about the Walter U-boat and Heller's description of it.

But in the navy things seldom turn out as expected. . . .

Just as he was finishing lunch, Doenitz received a telephone call, summoning him to an urgent conference. He was determined, however, not to abandon his trial run in the Walter U-boat, and decided to hold it then and there.

"Fix it up for me, Thedsen, will you?" he said to the vice-admiral.

But Heller was nowhere to be found. Despatch riders sought him everywhere, phone calls were put through to every conceivable office: "Heller to report at once to Admiral Thedsen."

At last he was found, and half an hour after Doenitz had given the order he was reporting to the vice-admiral.

"Sir, *U.793* only came in half an hour ago from a training run. She'll have to take on fuel first."

"The C-in-C can't wait for that. Can't you take the other U-boat, Heller?"

"I'd rather not, Sir."

"I quite appreciate your point, but I think you must."

Aboard *U.795* stepped, in addition to Doenitz, the Admiral Commanding U-boats, Admiral Hans Heinz Friedeburg, Admiral Köhler from the Naval High Command and Vice-Admiral Godt from the U-boat Operations Command.

Thedsen was a little anxious. He had always been a keen supporter of the Walter U-boat, but he knew that the boats built by the Germania Company were not always one hundred per cent.

Heller put the U-boat, which still had no Snort, through all its paces, explaining everything as he went along. He executed the various emergency manoeuvres. He switched frequently from the electric motor to the Walter turbine, and every now and then raised his periscope to permit his distinguished guests to take a look around. Doenitz himself was here, there and everywhere. He stuck close to Heller's side. No action of the crew escaped his eager eye. During the trial not very much was said. But Heller could see for himself that the C.-in-C. and the officers with him, all of whom had come aboard perhaps a little sceptical, were first surprised, then astonished and finally full of enthusiasm.

When U.795 came alongside after a trip devoid of any vestige of untoward incident, Doenitz shook hands warmly with Heller.

"You're quite right, Heller. Not only can we use this invention, but it is, as you said, a complete revolution in underwater propulsion. How long, exactly, have we known about it?"

"Theoretically, since 1937, Sir. In practice, since 1940."

In the wardroom of the *Swakopmund* Doenitz made a short speech. "The Walter U-boat," he said, "has far exceeded my highest expectations. I intend to advise that the construction of this type of U-boat should be given the utmost priority."

The workmen at Blohm and Voss, who about this time had been taken off work on the construction of Walter U-boats, were put back on the job. Once again they got down to the building of the operational type, Type XVIIb, which had originally been ordered by Raeder.

A few weeks after Doenitz's visit, Reichsminister Speer arrived. He was responsible for the allocation of the new fuel, the electrolytic manufacture of which could be undertaken by two factories only—one near Springe and the other in Bad Lauterberg in the Harz. The supply of this fuel was limited, not only by this factor, but also because it was required by the Air Force for its jet aircraft. Heller was therefore not surprised when he saw that the officer accompanying Speer was Field Marshal Milch of the Air Force.

Heller picked up his visitors at Gotenhafen and put U.793 through her paces over the measured mile.

Speer remained silent. Throughout the trial he did not utter one word. Milch on the other hand was most enthusiastic. "This is a first class show, Heller!" he cried. "If only the navy can get their hooks on to it quickly enough, we'll still save something from the wreck."

Speer looked at Milch in astonishment. He stood up and with

nothing more than a curt "Thank you, Herr Heller," stalked off.

This visit brought no grist to the navy's mill. Speer refused to support priority construction of the new U-boats.

A little later the men on the construction of the Walter U-boats at Blohm and Voss were once more laid off. Doenitz then had a personal interview with Speer. Work on the U-boats was once more resumed. And once more precious time had been wasted. For six whole weeks the men on the construction of U-boats which might have changed the whole course of the battle of the Atlantic had remained idle.

In April 1944 Doenitz spoke again at Fuehrer Headquarters of his endeavours to concentrate construction solely on the Walter U-boats. He described the bottle-necks encountered, the most serious of which was to be found in the construction of the pressure hulls.

The navy, he said, had unfortunately once again been compelled to cede priority to the air force, with the result that the construction of the electric U-boats of the Type XXI had fallen still further behind schedule.

That Doenitz was working at a great disadvantage Hitler readily conceded. But he made the point that the situation had to be regarded as a whole and from a wider viewpoint. It would then be realised, he said, that Air Force Fighter Command must have everything for which it asked, if it were to be in a position to prevent even more widespread destruction of industry. Therefore the U-boat arm would still have to be patient and tag along a little behind. In other words, the cat, obviously, was biting its own tail.

CHAPTER XXVIII

EMERGENCY IN THE INDIAN OCEAN, TOO

Situation Report—Spring 1944.
The efforts made by the Naval High Command to concentrate U-boats in the Atlantic, with the object of pinning down large enemy forces, led to very severe losses and appallingly little success. In January nineteen U-boats and the lives of nine hundred all but irreplaceable specialists was the price paid for the sinking of eighteen Allied ships. Nor did this shattering ratio change in the next month. Then came the month of May which shed a glare of gruesome reality on the state of the battle of the Atlantic. As opposed to the sinking of four Allied merchantmen of a total tonnage of about 24,000 tons, Doenitz had to write off twenty-five U-boats! Nor was all this to be ascribed wholly to the activities of the enemy. In anticipation of an invasion, Doenitz had stationed a large proportion of the U-boats available, not only in the bases in western France but also in Norwegian ports; for the commander-in-chief thought it quite possible that some flanking operation might be staged before the actual invasion itself.
Nearly half of the ships lost by the Allies fell victims to the Monsoon Groups, a fact which gives an even less favourable appearance to events in the Atlantic, which hitherto had been so happy a hunting-ground for the U-boats. But now, in the Indian Ocean, in the Bay of Bengal, in the Persian Gulf, the Java Sea and even off Australia, the enemy's anti-submarine forces, at sea and in the air, grew stronger and stronger, week by week.

*   *   *

At the end of February the supply ship *Brake*, fully laden, lay waiting at the secret rendezvous in the Indian Ocean. The ship was in radio communication with the German U-boat base in Penang, via which Lieutenant Pich, *U.168* had reported that he had engine trouble and would be reaching the rendezvous a day later than had been arranged. *Brake* acknowledged the signal and waited. Some other U-boats, among them one or two based on home ports and operating in the Madagascar—Cape Town area, had announced their intention of coming to pick up supplies.

The next day was a Sunday, the Sunday which was dedicated to the memory of fallen soldiers. Captain Koelschenbach mustered *Brake*'s crew to a memorial service for the dead of both wars. About midday a loud yell shattered the Sabbath tranquility of the ship.

The look-out insisted that he had sighted an aircraft.

"The chap's barmy!" growled Koelschenbach to himself, as he hurried on to the bridge. "It's probably a seagull. How could an aircraft get to this out-of-the-way spot?"

When the warning shout had been given, the crews had manned their A.A. guns, and Captain Koelschenbach, on the bridge quickly realised that the look-out had not been wrong, after all. An aircraft was circling round and round the rendezvous, beyond the range of the German guns. It was obvious to Koelschenbach that the 'plane could only have come from a carrier, and his conviction was very soon confirmed.

Mast-heads were visible coming fast over the horizon, followed swiftly by the unmistakable silhouettes of two destroyers racing at high speed towards *Brake*. And, for good measure, a cruiser was following close behind them.

Koelschenbach stood like a rock in a seething sea of excitement and disorder. What could he hope to do with a poor old 10·5-cm. against this well-armed enemy formation?

"Lower the boats!" he roared.

The end was inevitable. The destroyers fired the usual salvo across *Brake*'s bows.

"If only Pich were here!" muttered Thomson, the chief quartermaster, furiously.

"Well, he's not!" retorted Koelschenbach tersely, and urged the men to greater speed. The ship was abandoned so swiftly that when the demolition charges went up three men were found to be missing. No one had any idea where they had got to.

The supply ship sank. The British withdrew.

The aircraft, too, disappeared. But within an hour they were back again. It became quite obvious that they were expecting the arrival of U-boats at the rendezvous. How had they found out about the rendezvous?

The aircraft turned and vanished again. Scarcely had they done so than the conning-tower of a U-boat rose like a foam-enveloped monster of the deep. *Brake*'s lifeboats were packed closely together, and Pich was barely a hundred yards away from them. He could see for himself that the men in the boats must belong to *Brake*. When he appeared in person on the conning-tower, he was greeted with loud shouts and urgently, if not joyfully, waving hands.

"*Brake?*" he asked, suspiciously.

"*Brake!*" went back the reply, and the man who was standing precariously on the thwart, supported by his friends, clenched his fist and pointed downwards with his thumb. "Aircraft!" he yelled.

Lieutenant Pich gave a sign to denote that he had understood and manœuvred his U-boat up to the lifeboats. At the moment, with aircraft in the offing, the great thing was to disappear quickly.

As the last man clambered up on to the conning-tower the port look-out sighted aircraft approaching.

Pich dived as quickly as he possibly could. The chief engineer had allowed for the weight of the eighty survivors taken aboard, and, though the ship sank swiftly, he was able to control her at 250 feet.

"Where are the bombs?" thought Pich.

While the U-boat had been submerging, some of the men had heard a scratching noise, which might have been something hitting the outer hull. But nothing further had been heard.

"Captain Koelschenbach! Tell your men that I'll have the hide off anyone who speaks or makes a noise, if I have to wait till I get to Heaven to do it!"

For three hours the survivors did not dare to lift a finger.

At night-fall, after ten hours, Pich surfaced.

The operator at once heard echoes on the hydrophones. The aircraft, then, were still hanging about, and the echoes were so strong that they couldn't be very far off. Down went Pich again.

The chief engineer was compelled to release some oxygen into the ship, for, as a result of the eighty extra men aboard the carbon dioxide content had already exceeded the safety limit. But the fug had again become intolerable very quickly. The men began to breathe in short gasps.

At last night came once again, and for the second time Pich surfaced. He opened the hatch. The sky was clear. The aircraft had gone. The U-boat could now proceed on the surface in the direction of Java. His destination was Batavia.

The chief engineer seemed to have one or two little worries which he was discussing quietly with the Commander. Nor were they so very little, either.... For one thing, the fuel was running low.

Fifty miles away from Batavia the motors started to pack up. The chief engineer whipped up every drop of oil he could find. With infinite caution he nursed the boat on, mile by mile. The drinking water had also given out. With literally the last cough of his motors, Pich reached Tanjok Priok, the port of Batavia.

It was only later that they discovered a great dent in the outer hull, the explanation of the metallic bump they had heard as the ship dived. The bomb had landed and slid off ... without exploding. ...

*   *   *

A few weeks later the Italian submarine *It.23* was expected in Penang. But in vain.

It all happened shortly after eight o'clock in the morning, just after the watch had been relieved.

Most of the crew, plus a few men seconded for duty from *Brake* and some survivors from the German auxiliary cruiser, *Michel*, which had been sunk by a U-boat in Japanese waters, were lounging on the upper deck, admiring the exotic tropical coast.

Suddenly there was the roar of a terrific explosion. The U-boat disappeared in a huge column of water and sank like a stone. She had been hit by a torpedo just forward of the conning-tower.

Those who but a few moments before had been taking their ease on the sunlit deck were now struggling for their lives in the water. Thick, dark brown oil rose to the surface, smearing the men all over and making their eyes burn most painfully. They were admittedly not very far from the shore. But there were currents, strong currents.

In the meanwhile the commander of the base in Penang, uneasy at the ship's non-arrival, had sent out an Arado 196 on reconnaissance. The aircraft had no difficulty in locating the survivors. But in the float-plane itself there was, of course, no room for them, and the only thing the pilot could do was to lash as many as he could—five and no more—securely to the floats. The rest would have to wait their turn. The attempt proved a success. All the survivors were thus safely rescued.

Thus, what aircraft were accomplishing over the exits from the Bay of Biscay the American submarines were accomplishing off the south-east coasts of Asia.

And very soon this underwater front collapsed, too.

CHAPTER XXIX

ESCAPE FROM 200 FEET BELOW THE SURFACE

U.763 IN PORTSMOUTH HARBOUR

Situation Report—June 1944.

On the 6 June the world witnessed the greatest landing in history. On this day one hundred and nine U-boats were engaged in the battle of the Atlantic, and seventy of them were actually at sea on operations. Of the twelve Snort-equipped U-boats which were operating in the Channel during June and July, six were lost. But before they perished they sank eleven Allied destroyers and twelve transports.

A few days before the invasion we had succeeded in introducing the first of the one-man torpedoes into the Channel. Of the first twenty-seven only four were destroyed by the enemy, while they themselves accounted for a few merchantmen and one Canadian mine-sweeper. A few days later, however, came the counterblow. The weapon which had scored a success in its first surprise attack had now to be written off as useless. Greater prospects of success were afforded by the midget sub-marines, but these were not yet ready for action.

The production figures for the new electric U-boats, too, made depressing reading.

U.269 was one of the U-boats that was lost during the first weeks of the invasion. When the news of the Normandy landings came through, this boat was in dock at St. Nazaire after completion of her Snort trials. Never was a U-boat so swiftly provisioned and made ready for sea.

*   *   *

That very evening they set forth. The new commander was Lieutenant Uhl, an officer of the Administrative Branch who had recently completed his training and who now had to find his feet as commander of a U-boat. As his chief quartermaster Uhl had Gustav Krieg, who was not only an old and experienced submariner but also a bit of a character. In the U-boat service he was known as "Pressure-proof Gustav".

This is how he got the nickname.

One dark night, when the U-boat had been forced to crash-dive, Gustav had a bit of bad luck. Try as he would, he had not been able to detach himself from the guardrail to which he had been lashed as a precaution against the rough seas. There he had stuck, unnoticed by the others who slipped with the agility of foxes down the conning-tower. They disappeared and closed the hatch with a crash. It was only after they had submerged that the chief quartermaster had been missed. Above their heads they could hear the grinding propellers of the destroyers. And somewhere out there poor old Gustav was hanging like a fish on a hook.

They surfaced, the semi-conscious man was cut free in a trice, and bundled down below; the hatch was slammed to and in a matter of moments the boat had rocketed downwards to safety.

Gustav had to go to hospital. The wonder, indeed, was that he had survived at all. From that day onwards his nickname had stuck. To return, however, to *U.269*.

While operating off Plymouth, Uhl received an order to proceed at once to Cherbourg and not to attack anything en route.

At 03.30 hours on 25 June the radio operator reported the noise of electric motors on a bearing of 156 degrees. At that moment *U.269* was at a depth of some 60 feet.

"Must be one of ours," said Uhl.

"I'm not so sure, Sir," replied old Pressure-proof, frowning rather perplexedly. "It certainly sounds like it. . . . On the other hand, it might be a destroyer that has stopped, but still has her motor generator running."

Uhl waved the suggestion aside. The chief engineer, too, thought it must be a German U-boat. "We'd better make our presence known," he said, "or before we know where we are we'll have a collision."

"Leave it to me, Sir," said the chief engineer. By flooding and pumping out his tanks he then emitted typical U-boat noises.

There was a pause, and then the quiet was shattered by the noise of the turbines of a destroyer approaching at speed.

Uhl did not go down any deeper. He put his money on a Zaunkoenig which he loosed off, into the blue.

The threshing of the destroyer's propellers became louder and stronger. Then suddenly other noises intervened, shrieking like a circular saw and drowning the high-pitched note of the propellers.

"Aha!" murmured Krieg, with an upward jerk of his thumb. Then he waved his hand through the air, as much as to say: "The Zaunkoenig is a wash-out." He knew that the enemy had actuated a buoy the destroyer was towing, the noise of which would attract the Zaunkoenig to itself.

And sure enough the torpedo turned straight at the buoy. But the latter was too small to operate the detonator; in a trice the first depth charges went splashing into the sea. A hurricane of roaring, tearing, crashing explosions followed.

The U-boat's lights went out and she was left in the semi-darkness of her emergency lighting.

A second pattern of charges splashed into the sea.

In the diesel-room water started to pour in just where the propeller shafts pass through the pressure hull. The packing had given way, blown out by the force of pressure from the explosions.

Third pattern!

This lot burst over and all round the U-boat. Bright blue sparks flashed from the switchboard. Oil squirted everywhere, thrust inwards by the frightful pressure on the fuel tanks.

"Surface!" yelled Uhl.

The chief engineer injected compressed air into all the tanks. The crew, pale as corpses, stood transfixed.

Then they heard a voice, the commander's voice.

"Hell-fire and damnation! Abandon ship when you're told, all of you!"

More depth charges began to drop. The destroyer had been quite unprepared for this sudden emergence of the U-boat and had dropped her fourth series. She was only a hundred yards away. The men who were already swimming in the water were caught in the pressure waves of the exploding charges. A few of them raised despairing arms.

Suddenly the noise of firing was heard. Willi Bender, the cook, had got behind the 3·7-cm. and was cracking away at the destroyer. Abandon ship or not. Willi was determined to defend her.

The shots flashed brightly from the gun's muzzle. The flickering light revealed a grim, determined but quite calm face behind the gun. And the destroyer, too, was now being hit. Then she began to fire back. Without a sound Willi Bender collapsed beside his gun. He had been shot through the head.

Hans Albert, a midshipman, tried to inflate his life jacket in the usual way from the bottle of compressed air. But his jacket had been torn to shreds by splinters. Well—he'd been lucky, even if his jacket had had it.

Behind him a few more of the crew had come hurtling out of the boat. But Albert still hesitated. His chief, the chief engineer, was still missing. Albert had seen him a moment before, down below. The chief petty officer from the control-room had also not yet appeared. Did the chief engineer fear that the U-boat might still remain afloat and fall into the enemy's hands?

The water was already lapping over the platform aft of the conning-tower, and a few seconds later the conning-tower platform itself was under water, and the sea started to pour into the still open hatch.

"She's sinking!" yelled Albert down the hatch. "Come up, Sir!"

There was no answer.

With great presence of mind Albert closed the hatch with his foot. There was no further need for him to dive overboard. *U.269* was diving for the last time. The chief engineer and Chief Petty Officer Jaburek had remained aboard.

Albert felt himself being drawn downwards by suction as the U-boat sank. But he did not go very deep and was soon on the surface again. A horrible din was throbbing through his head. Through a haze he dimly saw a rubber dinghy, and he heard voices calling. "Here! . . . Albert! . . . Here!"

Instinctively he struck out towards the raft, to which seven of his comrades were hanging. On it lay the severely injured torpedo officer, who had been badly crushed between two torpedoes.

The British destroyer had stopped quite close to the survivors. Those in the water could see the British seamen on the upper deck waving to them and could hear them calling.

"Let's beat it," said the voice of one of the men hanging on to the raft. "I'm damned if I'm going to be taken prisoner!"

"There are other U-boats about," added another. "They might see us and pick us up. I'd rather swim for it."

They set to and tried to paddle the raft away from the destroyer. "Mad," thought Albert, "stark, staring mad! We've just escaped by the skin of our teeth, and here we are, with but a single thought—to avoid being taken prisoner, to beat it, in the vague hope that perhaps we'll be picked up by a U-boat. And for what? To go out again in another U-boat . . . or perhaps to drown miserably when our strength gives out and no U-boat has turned up."

From under the stern of the destroyer there came a loud shout. Someone else was swimming to the rescue with every ounce of strength that he possessed towards the destroyer's stern, shouting, yelling as he went: "Sir! Lieutenant Uhl . . . Sir!"

They realised that the man who had shrieked, the man who had flung up his arms had been Uhl . . . their commander. And then they saw the man who had been swimming so frantically fish a cap out of the water. A white cap. A commander's cap. Uhl himself was hacked to pieces by the destroyer's propellers.

By this time the destroyer was close beside the raft. Scrambling nets were hanging down her sides. All the men had to do was to catch hold and clamber up. When it came to his turn Albert found he could not do it. He gripped the net, but all the strength had gone from his arms; his nerveless hands began to lose their hold, he was falling. . . .

Suddenly he felt a hand roughly grip the back of his neck. A British sailor had jumped down and grabbed him. He was hauled up safely.

Albert found himself standing on the deck of one of His Majesty's destroyers. But the faces surrounding him were not at all hostile. One of the British sailors, a fellow as solid and massive as the Eddystone Lighthouse itself, leapt towards him. In his hand he was holding a knife, and with one deft stroke he slit open Albert's wet uniform and tore it off him. Another British sailor was hastening forward. Over his arm hung towels. He gave Albert one and pressed a cake of soap into his hand, while another took him by the arm and pushed him gently along the deck.

It was only then that Albert realised that he had been swimming through a mass of oily water and was covered from head to foot with thick, dark brown oil. His hair was full of it, his eyes hurt and his skin felt as though he were afire. A wash under the warm douche was wonderful. When he emerged a smiling and sympathetic British sailor with deep blue, friendly eyes handed him a canvas kitbag. He murmured something and clapped Albert on the shoulder.

Albert unpacked his canvas bag. In it was everything that a

shipwrecked sailor could want; underclothes made in Australia, a pair of flannel trousers with a U.S.A. tab on them, a fine pullover, which had certainly been knitted by some English lady as her contribution to the war effort, a smart and simple navy-blue scarf, a few handkerchiefs stiffly laundered, a leather belt and the regulation pair of canvas shoes.

Albert and his companions seemed to be somewhat taken aback as they stepped into their clean clothes. This was something they had not expected.

Meanwhile, more and more of their shipmates were being hauled aboard. Among them was an engine-room hand, the man who had retrieved the commander's hat and was now wearing it.

As soon as he clambered on to the deck he was separated from the others and taken into a spare cabin. Gradually it dawned on him that he had been mistaken for the commander. He spoke no English, and his attempts at explanation met with no success. Rather the contrary, for the British immediately jumped to the conclusion that this commander had his own reasons for pretending to be an ordinary seaman.

"Ich," he said, tapping himself on the chest with an oil-smeared finger, "no Kommandant! Ich machine man!"

The British captain who had greeted him with some reserve not unmingled with esteem, smiled rather knowingly.

"O.K.," he said, and told someone to take a whisky and soda to the cabin.

They had nearly reached port before the misunderstanding was finally cleared up.

A little later, a joyous piece of news reached the German prisoners. Lieutenant Mürb and Petty Officer Jaburek had been saved after all! They had managed to escape from the sunken U-boat and were alive and well. Later they gave details of their escape:

Mürb and Jaburek had deliberately remained on board. It was their duty to blow up the boat and they proceeded accordingly, as a matter of course. Together they pulled aside the demolition charges that had previously been distributed through the ship and opened the air escape valves of the diving tanks. They thought they would still have time to get out before the demolition charges blew up. But there had been much more water in the boat than they had anticipated. It was not only the packing round the propellor

Bombproof pens in St. Nazaire harbour

A pen in Heligoland in which U-boats could be
repaired and refitted

THE END

U-boats found
by the Allies in
the German
shipbuilding
yards

British troops
clambering over
U-boats of the
Type XXI in
the Blohm &
Voss yards

Surrendered U-boats on Loch Ryan

shafts that had given way. The pressure hull itself had been ripped in several places.

Jaburek hastened ahead to climb out of the U-boat which had now began to sink rapidly. Mürb followed close at his heels and had reached the second rung of the ladder when he was overwhelmed by an inrush of water. The cascade was so strong that it swept both men back into the control-room. Mürb felt the boat sinking really fast and noticed quite distinctly when she hit bottom, not with a crash, but quite gently.

Then, quite suddenly, they realised that the inrush of water through the conning-tower had ceased. In amazement Mürb and Jaburek looked up. They could hardly realise that fate had given them a chance, a slender chance, of survival. The pressure of the water had closed the hatch tight. . . .

Another astonishing thing was that, with the gentle bump as the ship hit the bottom, all the lights in the control-room and the forward part of the ship had sprung to life again. Mürb glanced at the depth gauges one showed 90 feet and the other only 65. But the indicator used for greater depths stood at nearly 200 feet. Which was right?

To escape from a depth of 200 feet was an undertaking fraught with the most dangerous possible consequences, even with escape gear.

Mürb went swiftly into the officers' mess, for the charges in the control-room were liable to go up at any moment. "Now—why did I do that, I wonder?" he asked himself.

Was it courage that now made Mürb determined to await the inevitable with calm resignation?

He could hear Jaburek's voice coming from the upper part of the conning-tower. Jaburek was worried about his chief, and Mürb felt he could not leave his companion alone at a time like this. Swiftly he returned to the control-room and clambered up into the conning-tower. Together they closed the bulkhead between the upper conning-tower and the control-room, to protect them against the blast of the detonations.

The charges exploded, with a sharp, rending sound.

They re-opened the bulkhead. Water was streaming fast into the boat, and the air was being rapidly compressed by the onrush. Their ears began to hurt. They held their noses tight, in an effort to relieve the pressure on their ear-drums.

The water had now reached the batteries which began to give off volumes of poisonous gas. Mürb and Jaburek felt their throats contract. They could no longer speak, no longer take council together except by signs. But now both men were inbued with an indomitable will to live. There was still one way in which they might escape through the conning-tower.

But it required nerve. They would have to remain cool and calm, as cool as the water that was now lapping gently, almost caressingly, round them.

Jaburek had gone up to the top rung of the conning-tower ladder. He was holding the hand-wheel of the hatch in a firm grip. He had unscrewed it and was now waiting for the internal and external pressure to equalise and enable him to open the hatch.

Mürb waited in the conning-tower below him.

Quite clearly he heard Jaburek succeed in moving and then in opening the hatch. He heard the air escaping and the hatch then slam closed again. The same thing happened again, and then again. And then all was still.

He hoped that Jaburek had not been drawn upwards by the rush of air, as the hatch had opened and closed, and that he had not been caught and jammed in the hatch.

Then he thought he heard Jaburek getting out. Mürb straightened himself, held his breath and propelled himself upwards and out through the hatch.

Shooting up to the surface with the speed of an express lift, he lost consciousness. He was dimly aware of surrounding mist and a delightful feeling of being as light and free as air. Death, then, could not after all be such a grim customer if he approached so tenderly and carefully. . . .

When he fully regained his senses, Mürb found himself being held in the supporting arms of Jaburek. A British destroyer rescued them.

No one could believe that they had come up, alive, from a depth of 200 feet without escape gear.

On board the British destroyer the desperately wounded torpedo petty officer and another man were breathing their last. Mürb and Jaburek were hastened to the sick bay and they recovered from their terrifying experience without any ill effects.

The British buried the two dead men with full honours. As the two bodies, sewn in sailcloth and draped in the flag of the German Navy, slipped over the destroyer's side and down to their wet grave, the destroyer dipped ensign.

At the ship's side the British captain stood for a moment at the salute. Then he turned sharply about.

"Hoist the flag!"

The life and death struggle was once more under way.

*   *   *

"Hydrophone effects from every direction, Sir. The strongest are on the port bow," reported *U.763*'s operator to the commander, Lieutenant Cordes.

Cordes put on the earphones, while the operator continued to manipulate the controls. He gave a sign with his hand—carry on . . . carry on . . . Stop! Then he pushed back the earphones. "Sounds to me like a convoy," he said.

The slow thud of merchantmen and the high-pitched tone of destroyer propellers had been clearly audible.

"Ah well! Let's try our luck!" said Cordes with a smile and set course on the strongest of the echoes.

The U-boat was using Snort for the first time.

Cordes had crept into the conning-tower and glued himself to the periscope. "Up . . . Down . . . Up . . . Action stations! Jump to it, men!"

Cordes fired five torpedoes. When the sound of the explosions had died away and the operator had picked up the typical noises of sinking ships, Cordes raised his periscope for an instant.

"Three freighters and one destroyer," he told the crew.

U.763 submerged. "Dive deep!" Cordes ordered.

"I like the word 'deep,' said the chief engineer ironically. "We've just about 150 feet of water here."

But they had to go somewhere, and everyone knew that when the boat was close to the bottom the Asdic echoes were, fortunately, less accurate and reliable. She slipped her way over rocks and sand.

Without waiting for orders the torpedo men had, in the meanwhile, reloaded the tubes. They were working clad only in trousers and shoes, and in the great heat sweat poured off their backs as though they had been standing under a shower. "In with it, lads!" Rudolf Wieser encouraged his grunting shipmates as with a united heave they prepared to push the last torpedo into the gaping hole of the torpedo-tube. Then came the ping . . . ping of Asdic echoes . . . faintly close, but . . . Wieser's thoughts went no further, for at that moment down came the depth charges with a thunderous crash. With the noise of the explosions thundering in their ears they closed the valve. The torpedo hung suspended like a long, sleek, dimly shining fish in front of the tube.

"Absolute quiet!" ordered Cordes. Not that any order was necessary—the men were as quiet as mice.

For eight hours depth charges continued to come down. Some were near, some wide, while others were a long way off.

Twelve hours passed. Bombs, bombs, bombs.

Sixteen hours. Bombs . . . twenty-four hours . . . more bombs . . . . thirty . . . thirty-two . . . thirty-six hours—a whole day and a half!

The air was getting scarcer. Cordes ordered oxygen to be released. But the relief it gave did not last very long. More oxygen . . . and another brief respite. And then once more limbs began to grow heavy. Wieser felt a great weariness come over him, a pleasant feeling of lassitude. The coughing, the gasping of his shipmates receded into the distance.

Somebody was speaking. . . . The commander, wasn't it? . . . What was he talking about? Something about not going to sleep. . . . Pull yourself together. Ah yes, of course—pull yourself together. . . . "Rudi! Rudi! Wake up!" Someone shook Wieser violently by the shoulder.

"Wake up, Wieser! Don't go to sleep! If you do—you'll never wake up again."

Wieser pulled himself up with a confused start. "Sorry, Sir!"

"Sorry be damned! It's not only your life—it's the lives of all of us! And we've all got a job to do—still."

Cordes and his officers kept quietly walking about the boat, making sure that no man had given in to sleep. The board on which the depth charges had been chalked up was one mass of strokes. In orderly groups of five, one after another, 100, 200, 250 . . . 296! Two hundred and ninety-six! More than had been dropped in a whole year—in two years—in the bygone days.

The chief engineer was keeping a constant eye on the trim of the ship. The electric motors were humming at slow speed, and *U.763* crept slowly like a crab along the bottom. Gradually she was succeeding in wriggling her way out of the danger area.

A blessed peace now reigned both within the U-boat itself and on the surface above her. The depth charges had ceased to come down. Cordes went up to periscope depth to have a look round.

"It might be Christmas Eve, lads. The air is sweet and clear; there's peace on earth, and the stars are shining like candles on a Christmas tree. Off we go! Prepare to run on Snort."

With the first stream of air that swept through the ship Wieser leapt back to his torpedoes. The last of them was swiftly loaded. With the Snort in action the batteries, too, were beginning to recharge. Now that there was work to be done, the tense hours that had passed were swiftly forgotten.

Thiel, the first officer, took over the periscope. After a brief look he spoke into the intercom:

"To commander—lights on the port side. To navigator—check up on the chart."

Cortes and the navigator studied the chart together, and examined the tide tables, to try and get some idea of where they were.

"Lights to starboard as well," said the voice of the first officer.

"Hm—I think I'll go and have a look for myself," said Cordes. He made his way to the periscope.

"I rather think those must be lights from the invasion fleet," said Cordes. His first officer nodded. But neither of them seemed very sure.

"We'd better steer clear of those fellows. A westerly course should take us out into the open Channel, I think."

For a few minutes they proceeded on the new course without further interruption. But it did not last long.

"Lights ahead!"

"! ! ! !"

Cordes surfaced. He hoped that on the surface he would be able to break through the ring of encircling ships. Suddenly a destroyer loomed up, her foaming bow wave visible proof of the speed at which she was steaming.

"Hard aport! Crash dive!"

At 60 feet there was a resounding bump. *U.763* had hit the bottom with a bang.

"Damn it! This is the bloody limit! All we need now is a few depth charges; then we can make our wills."

But no depth charges came down, and *U.763*, slithering forward, slipped to the bottom of a deeper recess. She settled herself snugly into this narrow channel, 80 feet deep.

"And here we'll wait till morning," said Cordes. He detailed the watch, and then flung himself on his bunk and went to sleep.

At first light he was awakened. He went straight to the periscope. What met his astonished eyes made him wonder whether he was still dreaming. Ahead was land. To the left was land; to the right, more land. Houses were dotted about. Ships were lying at anchor, and behind it all he could see high chimneys and slipways. . . .

Then his eye picked out one or two lighthouses and other landmarks, and with the help of the navigator he hastily consulted his charts and handbooks.

"There! this is a hell of a joke—or is it? D'you know where we are?—In Portsmouth Roads!—and that's Portsmouth harbour!"

For a moment there was a stunned silence in the U-boat, broken by the first officer.

"A little while ago, Sir, that would have meant another gong on your chest," he said.

"And today it means the inside of a P. of W. camp, if we're lucky. If we're not, then the next world will receive us as poor, drowned sailors! Get the scuttling charges ready! Fix hand grenades to all the secret stuff! Then we must just wait and see what happens. The one thing we can't do is to surface."

Cordes waited till night fell. The operator reported a dull threshing of propellers.

"Convoy!" said Cordes after having taken over the hydrophones himself.

Suddenly a broad, satisfied grin spread over his face. "It's a chance" . . . he muttered to himself. "It's quite a chance!"

Hanging on to the rear of the outward bound convoy, they got out much more easily than the conflicting currents had let them get in.

And to crown all, as they were getting clear they received a signal:

"Proceed to Brest."

CHAPTER XXX

A LAME U-BOAT FLEES FROM BORDEAUX

Situation Report—Summer 1944.
In August Doenitz gave the order that all U-boats were to withdraw from the bases in Brest, Lorient and La Pallice, which had been turned into army strong-points. Some of the U-boats were ordered to ports that were still free on the Bay of Biscay and others to south Norway. The majority were still in the process of being fitted with Snorts. When, a little later, the U-boats based on the Bay of Biscay were sent to Norway and Germany for the same purpose, one of the greatest of all convoys ploughed its way through the Atlantic without once being attacked. Under the protection of one frigate and six corvettes, a mammoth convoy of 167 ships crossed the Atlantic at a speed of eight knots.
The British had developed a new type of mortar, which they had named Squid and with which they were now able to discharge depth charges ahead over the bows.
The situation in France was hopeless. However, in the ports and U-boat bases, the enemy came up against stubborn resistance. On 20 August, Bordeaux, which was less a U-boat base than a repair and maintenance dockyard, was also declared to be a fortress to be defended to the last.

      *****   *****   *****

Like a pack of hounds round a fox-hole, Allied destroyers, corvettes, frigates, A/S vessels and sloops formed a wide ring across the estuary of the Gironde, waiting for those U-boats which had remained in Bordeaux. In the air were dozens of aircraft from Coastal Command. Their crews were composed of the best A/S specialists the enemy possessed. There was not one square inch of water beyond the Gironde estuary that was not under the precise scrutiny of radar, hydrophones and Asdic.

Among the U-boats which these powerful forces were waiting so eagerly to destroy was *U.534*, a large, Type IXc boat, built at Finkenwärder. Here is her story.

On 12 August, after four months at sea, *U.534* returned safely to base. Home leave was out of the question. The Allied forces were already fighting in the outskirts of Paris, and in southern France the fanatical Maquis were waging war against the Germans and any of their allies who passed through the country.

Four months' home mail lay waiting in Lorient, which was *U.534*'s real base. But Lorient was cut off, and there was no way in which the men could get news either to or from home. At the same time reports of heavy air raids were continually pouring in.

It seemed to be becoming increasingly clear that Bordeaux was destined to be the grave of *U.534*, which, in any case, was no longer fit for operations. But her chief engineer, Lieutenant Schlumberger, had ideas of his own on the subject.

"Abandon our ship? Not on your life!"

"You're right, Schlumberger. That's one of the things that's just not done. It'd be a breach of faith to let the grand old tub down," agreed Lieutenant Willem Brinkmann, formerly of the merchant navy and now first officer aboard *U.534*.

"If we refuse to take 'no' as an answer, we'll get this ship ready for sea, somehow or other," declared the chief engineer. And between them, he and the first officer did, indeed, succeed in goading the dispirited workshops into continuing work on *U.534*.

In spite of all alarms the German U-boat crews remained undismayed by any feeling that their world was falling to pieces about their ears. Not for a moment did they seek refuge in the idea. "We've had it, anyway, so what's the use of anything?"

Formations of hostile aircraft filled the sky, day and night, unopposed, as though they were carrying out a peacetime exercise. The districts in the vicinity of the harbour resembled some bizarre, lunar landscape. But the U-boat crews carried on the work on the U-boat in the shelter of their concrete pens which were still proof against any bomb.

The commander of *U.534* was very sceptical.

"I'm not at all sure that it wouldn't be better to leave the boat alone, to pack up and beat it back home."

Brinkmann and Schlumberger did not agree and strongly defended their point of view. The air of confidence which these two experienced officers displayed went far to restoring the young commander's confidence. Even so. . . .

"But damn it, Schlumberger, the U-boat's a wreck. I'm no technical expert, but even I can see that. And the repairs which we ourselves have been able to do are nothing more than a temporary improvisation.

"There've been plenty of other wrecks out there, Sir, and their crews have still managed to get 'em home. The least we can do is to have a shot at it."

"You're right. I agree and—I'm grateful, Schlumberger. You're the senior and most experienced submariner of us all, and we'll do as you say and have a crack at it."

That afternoon thirty pigs were slaughtered, and the mess tables in *U.534* groaned under the weight of freshly boiled pork and succulent sauces. But the crew did little justice to the feast.

The admiral in charge of the dockyard was also very worried.

"It's plain, foolhardy madness, Schlumberger," he grunted.

Schlumberger smiled. "Just give me a chance, Sir." He and his men had, in the meanwhile, succeeded in rigging the Snort. Admittedly it had to remain fixed in position, for the components necessary to render it collapsible were lacking. Even so, it was a Snort, though how the damn thing worked the crew had no idea. Oh yes, they'd heard of it, of course.

At last the day when they were to put to sea arrived. Every single man in the base had something or other he wanted to send home. Even those whose gloomy forebodings had but yesterday been a source of such worry to the crew now began to see a glimmer of hope.

"This way with things you want to send home!" laughed the chief engineer and waved encouragingly to a couple of men who were approaching, somewhat hesitantly, with a small case of wine. "Fetch it here, lads. We'll stow it away somewhere!" he added.

In spite of all their splendid endeavour *U.534* could not in any sense be regarded as operationally fit for service, and "Little Karl" Doenitz would certainly, in the circumstances, turn a blind eye to the carrying of such somewhat unusual cargo.

As *U.534* went astern out of the concrete pen, sailors were still running beside her, pitching parcels and letters across for the "home mail".

The three cheers that re-echoed from the dripping concrete walls were not merely for the crew of the gallant wreck; they were also greetings home from those who remained behind, the last they could send before their bitter fate overtook them.

The chances that *U.534* would get home were slim enough, in all conscience. Within the ship there was complete confusion. But Schlumberger, as chief engineer responsible for the trim, swiftly set about restoring order.

"Don't touch the parcels and packages of the lads ashore," he said, "but all that muck from the magazine can go overboard."

Quite a lot of things went flying into the sea; and although the chief could still not trim the U-boat with accuracy, the crew could at least go about their lawful occasions unimpeded.

Schlumberger would have liked to try out the Snort; but *U.534* could not make a trial dive in the shallow waters.

The first enemy fighter-bombers now appeared in the sky. During the previous night other aircraft had scattered acoustic mines in the Gironde. The Allies, who had been warned by the French Resistance Movement that *U.534* intended to try and break out, were determined to spare no pains to destroy the solitary U-boat.

The German minesweeping had stopped some days previously, and commanders were already prepared to scuttle their ships.

"Not the most pleasant of prospects," murmured the U-boat commander, referring to the mine-strewn Gironde ahead. But his crew had regained their confidence—in themselves and in him. The technical personnel had accomplished what the dockyard had declared to be impossible. Their U-boat was afloat, and not only afloat but at sea and on the first leg of the way home.

As a precautionary measure the commander had the collapsible rubber dinghies brought on to the upper deck and inflated. He saw to it that they were stocked with food, water and arms. "Noise-buoys" were streamed on either side of the U-boat to counteract the acoustic mines and ensure that they exploded at a safe distance. By this means fourteen mines were exploded on the way down river—some of them close and some devilish close. Rumph! A great column of water on the beam! Rumph! Another column astern. The U-boat shivered and shook. The men on the conning-tower went paler than they had been when they had returned from their last long operational voyage.

"O.K., chaps!" called Brinkmann through the hatch. "It's only mines!"

"I like the 'only', blast you!" the chief engineer called back. But his equanimity soon made the others forget the danger.

"Chief engineer to commander—May we do a trial dive and adjust trim?"

"Yes, carry on, chief." The commander swept the horizon with his glasses. Far away he spotted an aircraft, but it was flying towards the coast. Then away over the starboard bow he spotted some tiny specks in the sky—more aircraft.

"Brinkmann, d'you think it might be a good idea to bottom and lie doggo till evening? I'm still a bit nervous about bombing, and you can bet your life the French have told them we've left."

"Good idea, Sir! There's one thing, though—part of the conning-tower will probably remain above the surface, and the Snort will certainly stick out yards."

"So what? We'll simply look like a sunken wreck—there are plenty about—and no one'll give us a thought."

"Hm! We'll only know that when evening comes—if we're still alive. But we might camouflage the conning tower and the Snort a bit, with some of those small trees there," replied Brinkmann, pointing to the river bank.

They cut off the leafy branches of a birch and tied them to the top of the Snort mast. They draped a few camouflage nets over the portion of the conning-tower which they thought might remain exposed. Then they submerged.

At last the chief engineer had leisure in which to adjust the trim of the U-boat. The commander remained at the periscope. Every now and then he allowed Brinkmann to relieve him for a while. With beating hearts they watched the fighter-bombers flying past and the great concourse of heavy bombers heading for France.

When dusk arrived at last, and the commander gave the order to surface, the crew breathed a sigh of relief.

Schuback, ex-pilot on the Elbe and now working as a naval pilot in Royan, was quite confident that he could bring the ship through to the open sea. He had no lights ashore or other navigation aids to help him; but he had confidence in his own eyes, and those of the look-outs, to spot each fairway buoy. Apart from that he now knew the river like the back of his hand. Even so, it was a crazy journey.

The "noise-buoys" kept up their eternal racket, mines went off with a roar to left and right and every now and then large formations of bombers droned over their heads. Between Le Verdon and Royan the stars overhead suddenly disappeared.

Clouds? No! Aircraft! Aircraft! Aircraft!

A gigantic formation swept through the sky, turned sharply towards Royan. In a moment the night was rent with the flashes and mighty roars of the explosions. Royan burst into flames.

"Your pilot station has probably been blown to hell, Herr Schuback."

"Probably? The whole place has been blown to hell! There doesn't seem much point in my going back after I pilot you out."

"You certainly won't be needed as a Gironde pilot. But you could be damn useful at home."

"Would you, in the circumstances, let me stay aboard, Sir?"

"Of course—if you prefer our leap into the unknown to solid earth beneath your feet." Schuback said he did.

The journey down the Gironde had brought the men to the limits of their endurance. Their nerves, it seemed, could stand no more. Their faces spoke volumes. They now moved and acted instinctively, spurred on by the animal urge for self-preservation. Each one of them knew what was at stake, and each one did his best to retain that last vestige of self-control which alone would enable him to play his part when sure and lightning-swift action was called for to save the ship.

At long last the open sea lay before them.

"Echo bearing 030 degrees—destroyer, Sir," whispered the operator to Brinkmann. "Aircraft, bearing 060 degrees," he continued, "echoes growing stronger . . . destroyer echoes, bearing 340."

Then everything seemed to happen at once.

"Aircraft to port . . . to starboard . . . all round the ship!"

At any moment a searchlight was bound to pierce the darkness. The A.A. gun crews closed up.

"From commander—report soundings."

"120 feet."

"Thank you. Carry on reporting."

"141 feet . . . 144 feet."

The commander had previously laid down that they would not submerge in less than 250 feet of water because of the mines. But to remain on the surface now would have been sheer madness.

"Better to risk bumping a mine down below than remain here and be blown to bits for a cert," muttered the commander; and then, after a slight pause: "A.A. gun crews below!"

The men tumbled swiftly through the hatch, while the radar operator continued his unceasing stream of reports. Suddenly, from ahead a searchlight leapt into life. The chalky white finger of light wavered inquisitively across the mouth of the Gironde. The moment the searchlight picked up *U.534*, the first salvoes would follow instantly. He sounded the alarm.

In a matter of seconds the bridge was clear.

As a destroyer was running into the estuary, *U.534* went to silent running speed. The close proximity of the river bank was a slice of luck. A few depth charges were exploding but they were far away; and the destroyer could not venture too close inshore.

U.534 was now at a depth of a bare 180 feet. But the proximity of the bank probably prevented the British from taking any accurate hydrophone bearing.

"Whatever happens," said the commander, "we've got to get clear of the estuary tonight."

"If we don't, they'll certainly have us in the morning," confirmed Brinkmann.

With the utmost caution the commander brought his U-boat up to periscope depth. Now and again a destroyer came closer than was comfortable.

"We must come up and make a bolt for it on the surface."

"H'm, and when he sees we've overcalled our hand, he'll double," said the chief engineer.

"It's the only chance, Schlumberger."

"I know. But if we lose this hand, it's game and rubber! However, I'm on; and it's your lead."

"Here goes then!"

U.534 surfaced and slipped along as close as she could to the bank, which formed a dark, shadowy strip on her starboard side.

"Not too close," warned the pilot. "You don't have to spit ashore! This part is full of reefs and shallows—and we've no charts."

The shadowy outline of the Verdon lighthouse, not lighted, of course, fortunately afforded them a reliable bearing; and by the time it had receded, the echoes on the hydrophones had also ceased. *U.534* could now afford to back her luck. With both diesels full ahead she steered south-west into the Bay of Biscay.

For half an hour she proceeded unmolested. Then the sound of approaching aircraft compelled her to dive swiftly. After half an hour she surfaced again. More echoes from approaching aircraft, and down she went once again, this time really deep. When all was quiet again, the commander rose to periscope depth.

"What about having a crack with the Snort?" suggested the chief engineer.

"Why, of course! I'd forgotten all about the darn thing! D'you think you can work it, Schlumberger? We don't know a darn thing about it."

"I'll have a try, Sir."

No Snort handbook was available on board, and in any case they were by no means certain that their improvisation would function.

"Right! When I raise my hand—switch on the diesels."

The chief engineer raised his hand. The two diesels sprang to life and—promptly choked. Exhaust gases streamed into the ship. Before ever they could lay hand on their escape gear, the mechanics in the diesel compartment fell like flies. The petty officer in charge just managed to close the valve and he, too, then crashed to the deck. In the control-room more men collapsed. The radio operator swayed in his seat and tumbled on to the floor plates. He twisted in agony and vomited. The chief engineer and two others managed to get their masks on just in time. "Blow tanks! Surface!"

U.534 emerged. But the conning-tower hatch refused to open. Brinkmann tore like a madman at the iron spindle.

"Leave it, Sir," called up the chief quartermaster. "I'll have a try through the cookhouse hatch."

With feverish activity the boat was ventilated. No sooner had the radio operator come to and regained his post than he at once picked up echoes. But for once in a way they faded, instead of growing stronger, and finally disappeared altogether.

"Whatever happens, we must get fresh air right through the boat before we submerge again," said the commander, and ordered the A.A. gun crews to take post, in order to be ready for any eventuality. The U-boat had just got under way again when she was suddenly illuminated in a bright shaft of light.

For a second Brinkmann was too astonished to move. The searchlight seemed very close and up in the air. At any second the bombs would inevitably come crashing down.

"Fire!" yelled Brinkmann. "Fire at the centre of the light and shoot like hell!"

Simultaneously the A.A. guns opened and the bombs dropped with a screeching roar; the last one fell close to the stern. The U-boat bucked violently, but nothing more happened. The pressure hull seemed to be intact. Close ahead the attacking aircraft exploded and crashed, a roaring ball of flame, into the sea. Before he died, however, its pilot had time to drop a flare; and *U.534* waited for the next onslaught.

"We may just get away before the others come. Crash dive! Hard a-starboard!"

While the boat described a semi-circle the A.A. gunners clambered in, and *U.534* dived at full speed, to get really deep as quickly as possible. All seemed to be going well. The U-boat was sharply down by the bows and was diving at tremendous speed. Scarcely was she well and truly underwater, however, before reports of leaks reached the commander from all sides.

It was impossible to say exactly what damage had been done. But water was pouring in. "This time we've had it," was the thought that flashed through all their minds.

Suddenly the inrush of water ceased. Without waiting for orders Schlumberger blew the diving tanks, hoping against hope that he had enough compressed air.

All around him the commander saw men standing transfixed, their eyes glued to the depth gauge. "All hands aft!"

Very, very slowly the bows began to rise. But the boat continued her downward course. The hiss of the compressed air still continued, and by now *U.534* had reached the maximum depth for which she had been designed. But on she went, deeper and deeper. How could she possibly withstand the pressure?

At last she was on an even keel, then her stern sank a little, and, with the help of her electric motors, *U.534* slowly began to rise. No one dared to say a word. They were still at a depth which, on paper, was synonymous with a swift end. Nor did they dare to surface completely, for day was already dawning. The chief engineer set the bilge pumps to work. He estimated that they had shipped at least twenty-five tons of water.

A sigh of intense relief swept through the ship. The depth gauge stood at 465 feet. At last they were out of the danger zone.

The commander was utterly exhausted. So, were many others, bathed in sweat and breathing with difficulty. Their shipmates who had been overcome by poisonous fumes lay gasping on their bunks. The navigator was giving each of them a little tinned milk to drink.

Meanwhile, the chief engineer found out the cause of the sudden inrush of water and what made it cease with equal suddenness.

During the wild burst of firing from the bridge and the roar of dropping bombs, a man on duty in the control-room had collapsed, and when the alarm sounded he was lying unconscious and unable to close the air supply valve. This it had been, then, that had caused the inrush; and it was stopped by two other men, who by their united efforts had succeeded in screwing the hand-wheel tight inch by inch, just in time.

U.534 stole along under the Spanish coast and the next afternoon she surfaced in the midst of a Spanish fishing fleet. It was high time to re-fill the compressed air cylinders and re-charge the batteries.

In the meanwhile, Schlumberger and his men had turned their attention to the caprices of the Snort. After one or two attempts, and taking every possible precaution, they succeeded in running on one diesel with the Snort in operation. *U.534* proceeded far out into the Atlantic and for a few days sent no signals. Then she sent a signal giving her position.

"Can you take over as weather-ship?" came back the answer from U-boat Headquarters, where no one, of course, had any idea of the deplorable state of *U.534*.

"Yes," flashed back the terse reply.

For four weeks *U.534* sent in meteorological reports from the sector allotted to her, and then, at last, set course for Rosengarten.

During the last few days before she reached port radio communication was impossible. Heavy storms raged over the North Atlantic, and the chief engineer needed all his skill to keep the ship at Snort depth.

On the pier to greet them stood the chief engineer of the flotilla from Bordeaux, Lieutenant Brinker, who had led 200 of the 600 submariners stationed in Bordeaux through the encircling enemy and back home overland.

"Didn't expect to see you fellows again! We'd written you off!" were his first words of greeting.

From Doenitz came a signal:

"Please express to all ranks my appreciation and admiration of unique feat of seamanship and technical ability."

CHAPTER XXXI

A PETTY OFFICER SAVES *U.178*

Situation Report.
Of the eighteen U-boats lost during August, no less than eight were
lost in the Indian Ocean. Some of these were used as transport U-boats.
Their cargo was loaded for the most part in the bow and stern
compartments and in the empty torpedo tubes. But the heavy and bulky
cargo could be carried only at the expense of sacrificing a certain
amount of fuel oil. It also called for the sacrifice of a considerable
portion of the U-boat's armament, so that she could not undertake any
operations during the homeward journey.
The U-boat transports which Doenitz had envisaged and which
were to carry 800 tons of freight, were still in the blue-print stage.
U.178 was one of the first of the U-boats that had to remain in the
Far East to be used for the transportation of raw materials to the
tottering power in Europe.

*　　　*　　　*

U.178 was commanded by Lieutenant Spahr, with Lieutenant
Wiebe as his chief engineer.

It was during Spahr's journey back from the Far East to
Europe. . . .

U.178 had been ordered to meet an Italian submarine somewhere in the south Indian Ocean. She had already been at sea in
the tropics for a long time, and this had had its effect on her
engines. The cylinder-liners of the diesels were worn in places,
with the result that cooling water seeped through into the lubricating oil in the sump; and that was something that even the best
diesel could not tolerate. The chief engine-room artificer had no
option but to dismantle the engine and replace the worn cylinder-
liner. Even in dock this is a hell of a job.

At last the operation was completed. But the piston was still
swaying gently in the chains of the lifting tackle.

Two mechanics, stripped to the waist, bathed in sweat and

smeared with dirt and oil, grabbed it firmly, to prevent it from damaging the conduits or the nearby fuel-oil tanks as the boat rolled gently in the swell.

And at that moment, of course, the air alarm had to sound. The U-boat had to submerge and submerge quickly. As she dived steeply the two men wedged themselves between the hanging piston and the fuel-oil tank, making a protective cushion of their bodies. By great good fortune the one bomb dropped by the aircraft fell very wide of its mark.

Wiebe's action station when the U-boat had to crash dive was in the control-room. As soon as the danger had passed and quiet was restored, he hastened off to look after his own men. The two mechanics, horribly torn, crushed and bleeding profusely, were dragged out from behind the piston.

"My God! You're in a pretty mess! Who the hell told you to do that?" roared Wiebe, gazing in consternation at the unfortunate mechanics.

"That's all right, Sir. Main thing is—no harm's been done to the boat!"

There is no doubt that the presence of mind of those two mechanics saved the U-boat from damage, and some pretty considerable damage at that, since she had submerged at speed at an angle of forty-five degrees.

When he reached the spot where he was to meet the Italian submarine, all Spahr found was a gigantic oil patch. This, then, must have been the place where the aircraft had dropped its other bombs. And how strange it was that in this case, too, the enemy must obviously have known when and where the two U-boats were to meet. The Italian submarine must have been hit as she was in the act of surfacing; Spahr could find no trace of any survivors. *U.178* accordingly set course for home.

Things aboard Spahr's U-boat followed their inevitable course. After the first worn cylinder-liner came a second and a third, a fourth, a fifth, a sixth and a seventh. There were no more replacements.

"We've got to do something about it," said Wiebe, in consultation with the commander. They were only just off Cape Town, and before them stretched the long, long way back to Europe.

"It's a hopeless proposition to set out on a journey like this on one lone diesel, to say nothing of having to pass through the most rigorously patrolled area in the world."

"What about trying to mount sheet metal, with rubber packing and jointing over the broken parts of the cylinder liner, Sir?" interposed an engine-room artificer, addressing himself to Wiebe. "In theory it ought to do the trick."

"Theoretically, my dear fellow, yes, but. . . . By God, man! That's a brain-wave if ever there was one!" exclaimed Wiebe, leaping excitedly to his feet.

The diesel compartment of *U.178* was quickly transformed into a workshop. Sweat poured in streams off the dirty, oil-besmeared bodies of the men. Officers, mechanics, petty officers, humble greasers were indistinguishable. They all worked with an invincible zeal, and it was fascinating to watch them cope with the restricted narrowness of their surroundings, twisting, turning sinuously, writhing hither and thither like snakes.

Had this handful of half-naked men been shown in a film working in the labyrinth of tubes, pipes and pistons the man in the stalls would undoubtedly have said comfortably: "All right on the screen, of course. But I'd like to see 'em do that in real life!"

But in real life they did just that—and a good deal more besides.

Thanks to their determination and ingenuity they did a job for which the people in the dockyards at home would have been awarded a Meritorious Service Cross.

Wiebe sat down wearily on the base of the diesel. He gazed sadly at the chaotic confusion of the dismantled motor and played idly with the useless taps which had foiled his plan. It was not the hard work he had done which had left him thus exhausted, but his thoughts and the shattering of all his hopes. The situation had now become critical in the extreme. Wiebe went off dejectedly to report to the commander.

"Cheer up, Wiebe! P'raps our luck will turn. We've got to meet a U-boat off the Ascension Islands to take over some secret stuff. Perhaps they'll be able to help us out with some taps."

A few days later they met the other U-boat. Aboard her were many old friends. No words were needed to persuade them to help in any way they could.

Wiebe went off at once to try the new taps. They were certainly of better material than the old ones. The other U-boat was anxious to stand by until the repairs had been completed, but Wiebe would not hear of it.

Wiebe and his men plunged into the gigantic task before them; and, working day and night, with scarce a wink of sleep, they did it.

In his diary the chief engineer wrote:

"Although the senior man has to make the ultimate decision when it comes to the question of how damage can best be repaired, it is, I must say, a grand experience to see even the most junior rating thinking the problem over and doing his best to help.

"What is important is that the 'little man' should have the courage to stand up and say his piece, when he thinks he has something to contribute."

U.178 reached Bordeaux safely, running on a diesel the cylinder-liners of which had been repaired with strips of sheet metal and rubber packing.

In a word, a petty officer had saved the U-boat.

CHAPTER XXXII

ALONGSIDE A BRITISH DESTROYER IN THE ARCTIC

Situation Report.

In the midst of the general collapse, in the midst of the orgy of destruction which had overtaken it on all fronts, the U-boat Arm re-equipped and re-armed itself with a superhuman effort. In September the first fourteen of the new U-boats were commissioned; they were followed by thirty-two in October and sixty-five in November. These figures represented the highest production figures for the whole war; against that must be set the fact that sinkings in October—7,000 tons—were the lowest ever, and were achieved for a loss of four U-boats. For this latter fact, of course, the withdrawal of most of the old type U-boats was primarily responsible.

The new types represented the last hope of stemming the stream of men and material across the Atlantic and relieving the pressure on the Western Front, and also of stopping the flood of succour to the East. These U-boats, which, among other innovations, had an automatic torpedo reloading device and additional quick-diving tanks which enabled them to submerge to over 450 feet in thirty seconds and thence to attain depths at which all currently known A/S weapons were innocuous, were due to begin operations in November. But this deadline could not be maintained. To ensure the safety of the crews and to avoid any jeopardisation of the very great hopes of success that had been pinned upon them, it was considered that they could not become operational until the spring of 1945. Further difficulties arose when the Finnish front collapsed and the Russian submarines were then free to menace the German training groups.

The Walter U-boat's method of propulsion would have been the ideal solution for all new U-boats. The first Type XVIIb was at long last commissioned. But now there was a shortage of perhydrol. The amount required by the air force and for the V-weapons had risen to astronomical proportions, and the only two factories which produced perhydrol could not meet the demand. If the competent authorities had attached greater importance to the production of perhydrol at the beginning of the war, the situation would have been very different. The midget U-boats, too, were suffering from growing pains, and did not achieve anything like the success that had been expected of them. The period allotted for the training of the crews of these midgets also proved to be too short.

The majority of the old type operational U-boats, part of which were now equipped with Snort, were transferred to bases in Norway.

* * *

The U-boats of the Norway flotilla had gained contact with yet another Russian convoy, and this time they felt they must succeed.

U.1163 (Balduhn), a Type VIIc, not yet equipped with a Snort, had also gained contact with the convoy but had then been driven off in bad weather by escorting aircraft. She then turned on to a reciprocal course towards the Russian coast. A Russian patrol vessel crossed her bows and opened fire with her guns. *U.1163* put an end to the fight with a "Zaunkoenig" and the Russian destroyer sank.

About midnight, Balduhn, who had submerged after sinking the Russian, surfaced again to recharge his batteries. He was just about to submerge again—all hands were at their action stations—when a British destroyer suddenly appeared out of the mist, not more than 250 yards away on the starboard side.

The enemy at once opened fire, and one of his first shells crashed into the sea thirty feet in front of *U.1163*'s bows. For a moment the crew stood transfixed with astonishment, but Balduhn's rapid orders brought them to their senses.

"Full ahead! No. 5 tube, stand by! . . . hard a-port!"

"No. 5 tube ready!"

By now, however, the U-boat and the destroyer, which had been preparing to ram, were so close to each other that a torpedo stood no chance of success. By a swift course alteration Balduhn just managed to avoid being rammed, and the destroyer hurtled past at twenty-five knots some fifty yards astern. She then turned hard to starboard, obviously with the intention of ramming the U-boat at right angles on the port side.

With the help of his experienced crew, the commander succeeded—if not in completely avoiding the collision, at least in lessening the consequences. Balduhn turned away to starboard, and the destroyer struck the portside of the outer hull at an acute angle. The pressure hull was undamaged. With a crashing, rending noise the side of the destroyer scraped along the whole length of the U-boat. The three minutes which had already passed since the destroyer had first appeared were beautifully peaceful in comparison with the minute which now followed.

For a whole minute destroyer and U-boat remained locked together side by side and going at full speed. Every movement of the British guncrews could be seen, and from the starboard wing of the bridge came a stream of orders from the British commander. Depth charges poured over her stern in endless array, causing the U-boat to leap high out of the water and her guns continued to blaze away frantically and quite uselessly.

Cowering, *U.1163* shook and shivered.

Under the violent blow of the collision she had developed a list of 30 degrees to starboard. Then she had gradually straightened again, bringing Britons and Germans even closer together. From the bridge of the U-boat they could have grasped the destroyer's guardrail.

The sea was pounding tumultuously. The diesels were roaring. Wild shouts, pistol shots, yelled orders and clouds of black and white smoke added to an indescribable inferno.

It was lucky for her that the U-boat lay so much deeper in the water than the destroyer and that therefore the British guns could not be brought to bear. But somewhat elevated, on the destroyer's forecastle stood a 2-cm. gun with its barrel pointing at the bridge of the U-boat.

The commander of the destroyer urged the gun crew to action. But for some reason or other the gun jammed. Equally Balduhn, whose gunners had just before shot down an aircraft, could not bring his A.A. weapons into action, because the U-boat had been on the point of submerging when the destroyer had appeared. The gun-shields had been down, the guns secured and the ammunition replaced in the watertight containers.

For a few moments, German and British sailors glared at each other at a range of a few yards.

At last the two ships separated, for the destroyer had stopped and then gone full astern, preparatory to a fresh attempt to ram.

Once again Balduhn succeeded in turning to port in good time, and the destroyer flashed past the stern of the U-boat. At once the destroyer switched on her searchlights and opened fire with every gun she could bring to bear. Rapidly a gap of 150 yards opened between the two ships, and Balduhn was quick to seize the chance afforded to him. At an angle of 45 degrees he plunged into the depths. The technical personnel had had no time to make a precise check of the damage incurred. The chief engineer was by no means certain that the boat was in a fit state to submerge.

All eyes were turned towards the depth gauge—270 feet, 300, 330, 360. Meanwhile the destroyer was doing her utmost with depth-charges. To increase the weight forward, all hands, with the exception of those on watch, had been sent into the bow compartment. Everything went like clockwork, and soon the British pursuer was shaken off.

Apart from the damage to her external fuel tanks, enemy shots had penetrated aft and also holed one of the diving tanks of *U.1163*.

She was well down by the stern. For five days she had to battle her way through heavy seas. For several days on end, in order to be prepared to submerge instantly, they had to put up with a permanent list of 30 degrees and more. Hot meals were out of the question and the men got precious little sleep. Cold, heavy seas, coming broadside on, swept over the bridge, and the men on watch, securely lashed though they were, had to be relieved at frequent intervals. But *U.1163* got home.

* * *

1944 was a quiet year for the U-boats, a year of reorganisation and rearmament, of frustration and of hope renewed. The Snort, although installed with much hesitant delay, had amply proved its value; and as the crews gained experience and passed on to each other all they had learnt, the major difficulties were speedily overcome.

Snort-fitted U-boats had once again penetrated into the English Channel from which they had been completely excluded during the past two years. The area was literally teeming with A/S forces of every kind, both at sea and in the air. Yet in spite of it all, those U-boats which had penetrated into the Channel and which the enemy Asdic failed to locate, sank five merchantmen and a frigate in the second half of December.

*   *   *

At a conference at Fuehrer Headquarters in December 1944, Lieutenant Nollemann, reporting on his experiences, declared that the introduction of the Snort had fully restored to the U-boats all their old effectiveness.

But the number of U-boats equipped with Snort was far too small. Further, the speed of the U-boats, which were now proceeding only submerged, was reduced, by the introduction of the Snort, to a maximum of six knots. At any higher speed the vibration would have been so violent that there would have been a grave danger of the Snort breaking.

In December the number of ships sunk rose again.

Figures and statistics can very often be misleading, of course, but it was a fact that at the end of 1944 losses had decreased and the Snort seemed to have proved its value.

Part Seven

1945

CHAPTER XXXIII

NEW EQUIPMENT FOR OLD AND NEW U-BOATS

Situation Report.

At the turn of the year, when it had become obvious that the new U-boat would not be ready to operate for some time to come, Doenitz tried another, a last and desperate, way of driving off the convoy air escorts with the old, normal type of U-boats available. Most of the U-boats now at sea had at last been equipped with exceptionally powerful and modern A.A. armament. Proceeding in groups on the surface their task was to drive away the escorting aircraft with the massed fire of their quadruple A.A. guns, or to keep them circling until their fuel was low and they were compelled to return to base. One or two and sometimes more of the aircraft were shot down. But the success was of little avail. Fresh aircraft at once appeared in the sky. But Doenitz had to abandon these tactics and with them his last hope of bringing relief to the land fronts and accelerating the employment of the new U-boats. The current situation and the prospects for the future were both equally hopeless.

The few U-boats of the old types that were equipped with Snort and experienced in its operation were now remaining thirty, forty and fifty days submerged. Very often they had to remain for lengthy periods at good depths. And this brought up a new and all too human problem.

*   *   *

The scene—*U.1206*, a Snort-fitted U-boat in the North Sea off Peterhead.

The commander disappeared into the little compartment that was no bigger than a small cupboard. The red light flashed on— "Occupied."

Normally the w.c. could only be used when the U-boat was in comparatively shallow water. *U.1206*, however, was fitted with the newly designed apparatus which would function at any depth. It was more complicated and more difficult to use than ever. Beneath the normal pan was attached a pressurised cistern which could be opened and closed by means of a special sliding device, and, most important of all, could be emptied outwards by compressed air by means of a special locking system capable of overcoming the pressure of the water outside, even at great depths.

After an interlude of leisurely but reasonable proportions Schlitt decided that the time had come to set the machinery in motion. As a precaution he read through the official "Instructions" which had been issued to all U-boats. It was a typical naval instruction of appropriate length. But Schlitt was taking no chances. He read it right through a second time.

"Ha!" he thought. "Too easy."

It was, however, by no means easy. Schlitt must have been a little ham-fisted in his procedure. He puffed and grunted and fumbled about but nothing happened. He thought that perhaps, after all, he'd better send for one of the artificers who had obtained his W.C.B.A. on the special course. While he was struggling with the levers and generally messing about, the door suddenly opened. The chief engineer, fearing the worst, had on his own responsibility sent Moebius, W.C.B.A., to his commander's succour. The wretched fellow could not know, of course, that the commander had not yet closed the sliding valve which cut off the actual pan itself. Full of zeal, he leapt to it and opened the ejector valve. A column of water as thick as a man's thigh burst in, thundering and foaming. The commander and his specialist assistant were first deluged by the anything but fragrant contents of the lower cistern and then by a cascade of salt water. The water burst in with such tremendous force that both men were hurled back, helpless.

"Close the ejector!" Moebius managed to yell. "Close the ejector!"

He tried, in the miniature whirlpool around him, to move forward. Blinded by the water, he fumbled gropingly, trying to find the valve. But he had no luck. The sea continued to pour in with such force that Moebius was hurled back again and again. The U-boat at the time was at a depth of 300 feet, and it was with a proportionate force that water was shooting through the contraption.

Realising what was happening, the chief engineer in the control-room swiftly took over. Without waiting for orders he brought the U-boat up to periscope depth. That would, at least, reduce the water pressure sufficiently to enable Moebius to close the ejector valve. But in the meantime the seawater had penetrated into the interior of the boat. It had seeped through the floor plates and penetrated into the battery compartment. White gases started to rise.

Lieutenant Schlitt was suddenly conscious of a paralysing numbness in his head. He grew dizzy, and he at once realised what was happening.

Chlorine gas!

Schlitt saw his men start fighting for breath, choking and gasping, and some of them vomiting. The deadly white wisps swept ghostlike in ever gathering numbers through the boat, and his shipmates looked like shadowy spirits in some supernatural cavern.

Unless something happened quickly, *U.1206* was lost. "Blow the tanks, chief! Take her up! Whatever may be there up above, take her up," Schlitt managed to gasp as his knees gave way beneath him.

The chief engineer blew the tanks. Schlitt crawled to the conning-tower ladder and laboriously dragged himself up it. With a last effort, he opened the hatch. Fresh air came pouring noisily into the U-boat. The ventilators sucked out the poisonous gases.

Two aircraft cruising in the vicinity sighted the U-boat and attacked at once. Before the crew had time to man the A.A. guns a hail of bombs was descending upon them. *U.1206* received no direct hit, but near misses damaged her so severely that she was no longer capable of submerging.

U.1206 was lost. Schlitt threw in his hand.

"Abandon ship!" he ordered.

What had started as a rather ludicrous predicament had developed into a serious material loss and had culminated in tragedy. For not all the crew escaped from the doomed U-boat. The chlorine gas had taken its toll.

CHAPTER XXXIV

CHIVALROUS TO THE BITTER END

Situation Report.
Shrouded in the mists of uncertainty, the year 1945 dawned to find
the German U-boat Arm stronger than ever before, with 426 U-boats
at its disposal. There was still a small ray of light on the horizon,
which gave rise to a hope that some more propitious diplomatic basis
for negotiations to end the war might yet be found. The sinkings of
enemy shipping began once more to rise. In all operational areas, the
U-boats, now fully experienced in the efficient employment of their
Snort, were evading detection by hostile air reconnaissance. In January
eleven ships (57,000 tons) were sunk. In February, fifteen more
(65,000 tons) were sunk.
"It has become evident," the enemy admitted, "that, while we have
driven the German U-boats underwater and have thus greatly reduced
their offensive powers, the Snort with which the U-boat is now equipped
has completely nullified the effectiveness of the radar location equip-
ment which we have been using since 1943 with such conspicuous
success." In February A. V. Alexander, the First Lord of the
Admiralty, warned the House of Commons that, notwithstanding the
encouraging successes achieved during the last two years, the A/S war
could not by any manner of means be regarded as ended. "It is both
significant and disturbing that, in spite of their severe losses in 1943,
in spite of the loss of many of their bases and other ancillaries, the
Germans still seem to be capable of renewing the fight in the Atlantic."
As yet not one of the new big electric U-boats, Type XXI, had
been in action. But the fact remains that Britain's misgivings were
by no means illusory.

*   *   *

A Snort-fitted U-boat had just returned from the vicinity of
Gibraltar. The commander affirmed that he had been able to
operate off the Straits of Gibraltar for ten days without once having
been endangered in any way by enemy radar. On the other hand,

he said, his offensive potentialities had been greatly reduced by the low underwater speed of the old type.

All the U-boats which returned in March reported successes. Doenitz was of the opinion that the remaining U-boats, which were still overdue, must also have been in action and must have sunk their share, too. The British would, of course, keep silent about the activities of these latter, in order to prevent the Germans from ascertaining the full extent of the effectiveness of the Snort types.

In March Lieutenant Hechler returned to base from operations off the east coast of England. His U-boat was one of the smaller Type XXIII electric U-boats, designed for operations in coastal waters. Having sunk a British merchantman which his high underwater speed had permitted him to attack in an area which was most rigorously patrolled by innumerable aircraft and surface vessels, Hechler had evaded all enemy attempts, either to detect his position or to attack him, by proceeding submerged at high speed out of the area in which the enemy was searching for him.

In April the U-boat successes again rose. At long last the first of the big Type XXI U-boats had completed their period of training and were declared fit to proceed on operations. Their commanders were for the most part old U-boat aces, experienced and proven men like Schnee, Topp, von Schroeder and Emmermann.

That these new types, whose entry *en masse* into the struggle had been promised by Doenitz for November 1944, should only now have become available, at the eleventh hour, was not due solely to the havoc caused in the dockyards and the factories by air raids. It was only when the new U-boats were commissioned that it became apparent that, for these new types, existing tactics would have to be reviewed, completely re-modelled and—most important of all—thoroughly tested. Since November 1944 Topp and Emmermann had been at great pains to gather and evaluate statistical data on the performance and characteristics of the first of the new types which had been allotted to the Trials Command. In spite of the critical situation, a whole fleet of target craft, convoy ships and aircraft had been placed at the disposal of the Command for carrying out exercises in the Gulf of Danzig and most realistic "convoy battles" had been organised.

It was during these exercises that it was for the first time realised that the new types were quite unstable when lying on the surface—they had, after all, been designed and constructed solely as underwater craft. On the surface they were like fish that had been pitched ashore. The net result was that some of the less experienced commanders fell victim to ramming attacks. Also every now and then collisions occurred at night, sometimes with other, friendly U-boats and sometimes with hostile merchantmen and patrol vessels; in this way more than one U-boat already declared fit for service found itself limping back to the dockyards instead.

Then, when at last Doenitz considered that the moment had arrived when he could send the first new U-boats on operations, the ports in the Gulf of Danzig came under Russian threat and had to be evacuated; all the essential craft for the carrying out of the U-boat tactical exercises had to be withdrawn and employed in rescuing German civilians from the threatened territories of Kurland and East Prussia and for the evacuation of German troops. The U-boats had to be transferred to the German ports in the western Baltic and to Norway. It had now become more important to save lives than to fight battles.

*   *   *

As has already been stated, the Allies had not remained unaware of the new U-boat menace which now confronted them. A network of spies, composed mostly of Poles, had obtained information about the new types and passed them to the enemy—and that in spite of the most rigorous security measures.

On the one side, the security measures were so strict that even the commanders of old type U-boats were forbidden to go aboard the new electric and Walter U-boats; on the other, in the shipbuilding yards round Danzig, where the component parts of the new U-boats were assembled, "reliable" foreign workers were employed. Comment is superfluous.

What Doenitz had feared for a long time and what he had tried to forestall by swift construction of bomb-proof U-boat pens now happened. Speer had given priority to the construction of similar shelters for the protection of the new jet fighter aircraft, and the Allies concentrated their air raids, now more massive than ever before, on the unprotected U-boat building and fitting-out yards. Everywhere, on the slipways, in the assembly shops and in the equipment basins, new U-boats nearing completion and about to be commissioned were reduced to scrap.

At sea, too, the redoubled efforts of the enemy led to increased losses. The British Press announced with great satisfaction that U-boat losses in April amounted to thirty-three—exactly as heavy as those incurred in May 1943.

In the interests of historical accuracy it must be stated that this high total included U-boats lost during the precipitated transfer to Norway after the collapse of the East Prussian front. These U-boats were by no means fully operational, and most of them still lacked Snorts. Of the Types XXI and XXIII not one single U-boat was lost. But Allied aircraft had laid so many mines in the waters of the western Baltic that passage through them was almost as dangerous underwater as it was on the surface.

*   *   *

In nautical mythology Thetis is the wife of Neptune. In the U-boat war it was the name given to a device designed to distort, mislead and confuse the enemy's radar. Developed by the Germans, it consisted of nothing more than a long, floating tube, closed at each end, with strips of tinfoil fastened to its upper end. Over the centre of the tube, which was weighted at the lower end, was fixed a rectangular piece of synthetic cork, the function of which was to keep the tube vertical in the water with the tin-foil attachment upwards. The synthetic cork was such that after a specific period it became waterlogged, and Thetis would then sink, its mission accomplished. This, however, did not deceive the British for very long. The self-destroying device did not always function properly, and patrol vessels were able to pick up a few of these miniature Trojan horses which had taken the field in the U-boat war. This, of course, gave the game away but it did not prevent Thetis from continuing to function effectively. Even so, it was only a supplementary improvisation and it did not lead to any radical and lasting incapacitation of the enemy's radar, and it certainly did not put them out of business.

On the other side, the British scientists were grappling with the problem of finding some means of defence against these Snort U-boats. In the very last weeks of the war they produced the Sonobuoy.

This device, which floated like a buoy, consisted of a tubular length of hollowed wood into which was built a small but very efficient wireless transmitter. In order to facilitate identification of the individual buoys, these transmitters used different frequencies. The portion of the buoy exposed above the surface of the water was painted with a brightly coloured ring, the colour used denoting the frequency used by that particular transmitter.

The Sono was to be dropped by aircraft in the principal operational areas, by means of a small parachute. In the lower half of the buoy was an underwater hydrophone secured to the end of a long cable. When the buoy struck the water, the hydrophone was automatically ejected from the bottom of the buoy and then remained hanging at the end of its cable at a depth of anything from forty-five to sixty feet. The hydrophone would then pick up the propeller noises of any submerged U-boat in the vicinity. The hydrophone effect reacted on the transmitter in the buoy. This in turn transmitted a clear signal on a fixed frequency to the patrolling aircraft. Knowing the position of the buoy and working on the strength of the signal received the aircraft would be able then to pinpoint the position of the submerged U-boat with a fair degree of accuracy and to attack it with depth charges.

It would appear that the Sonobuoy was the only reliable device the enemy had at the time with which to get on the track of the new type of U-boat. The British authorities asserted that it was a very reliable apparatus. They were convinced that if a sufficient number of Sonobuoys were distributed over any given area, even a change of course would not help a U-boat, once it had been detected, to shake off a pursuer. But, in fact, the Allies achieved no practical success during the last days of the war with this device, which at that time was still in the experimental stage.

The Sonobuoy also was an improvisation, no more and no less effective than the German Aphrodite and Thetis devices.

*　　　*　　　*

U.1227 (Lieutenant Altmeier) had just returned from operations off Gibraltar.

"This Snort contraption is first class. Without it we probably should never have got there, and we certainly wouldn't have got back," he declared. This confirmed the opinion of other U-boat

305

commanders who had returned safely from the same, heavily patrolled operational area, in which until quite recently no German U-boat had been able to remain.

Nothing out of the ordinary had occurred during the voyage. It is perhaps worth mentioning as typical of the haste with which the U-boats had been re-equipped, that *U.1227*, whose crew had still to be initiated into the working of the Snort, suffered her first breakdown immediately after leaving her base in Norway.

They managed to put the defect to rights, thanks to determination rather than skill or proper equipment.

Some days later a convoy hove in sight, fourteen ships, heavily escorted. No one was particularly surprised. It was what they had been expecting. Even so, Altmeier managed to pick out one of the escorting destroyers. Immediately after his torpedo had been discharged, he ordered a few "Bolds" to be launched in order to confuse the enemy's Asdic; as everything remained singularly quiet up above, he rose cautiously to periscope depth.

The torpedoed destroyer had sunk. Altmeier saw an escort vessel, all its lights ablaze as though peace reigned supreme, hastening to the spot to pick up survivors.

A sitting target for a U-boat?

"We could get that fellow for a snip!" murmured Altmeier.

"Why don't we, then, Sir!" asked the navigator, who was standing close beside him and who alone heard what he said.

"Why? Well—you can see for yourself what's going on over there. I just can't—not for all the tea in China."

Altmeier stepped back, and the navigator glued his eye to the periscope.

"He's right," grunted the navigator to himself. "It's just not done." And he made way for the commander. Altmeier thought it would be better to disappear into really deep water. The convoy meanwhile had steamed on. To get ahead of it again he would have had to surface. And though neither Altmeier nor his crew were lacking in courage and enterprise they equally showed no desire to commit suicide. The good old days when a U-boat could surface safely and get ahead of its prey were gone for good.

Having completed her rescue work, the destroyer dropped a few depth charges in token of her gratitude. They looked suspiciously like left-handed shots, pitched just for form's sake, for all the world

as though the British commander had known that the Germans
would not attack him while he was on his errand of mercy.

A few days later, more ships . . . another convoy? Swinging
masts, one . . . two . . . three . . . four.

No—not a convoy this time, but a group of six destroyers, one
of the deadly "Submarine Killer Groups".

Sboron, the senior engine-room artificer had just stretched himself on his bunk, when his engine-room petty officer, Herrsch,
woke him up.

"Time to get up, Sir. The balloon's going up any minute now."

Sboron looked at his assistant's face, grave but with no trace of
fear. Herrsch, as serious as that! That old blackguard, who always
had some damn silly joke to crack—without even a grin on his
face? His train of thought was interrupted by the shrill note of the
"noise-buoy" being towed by the approaching destroyers. So that's
what it was! A killer-group!

Sboron leapt from his bunk and then staggered back again, for
U.1227 was very sharply down by the bows, and Altmeier was all
set to take her down to the 600-foot limit as quickly as he could.
Depth charges began to come down, rumbling like a chorus of a
thousand kettle-drums.

The shuddering and shivering of the ship transferred itself to
the men, too.

WUUU . . . MMM!

Another—directly over the ship. An appalling crash like the
eruption of a thousand volcanoes, a noise as though the heavens
themselves had fallen in. Then came a shrill hissing noise, followed
by a tearing explosion.

Sboron saw some men grabbing at their life-saving gear. "Quite
useless at this depth," passed through his mind. Then he noticed
how some of the lads were ducking their heads every time a depth
charge went off, however far away. Also quite useless. It was, of
course, more or less a reflex action, just like the soldier ashore sticks
his nose into the mud when a shell bursts. But with this difference,
that if the soldier reacts instinctively and with real agility, his
movement may perhaps give him a chance to save his own life.
But a submariner must take his courage in both hands and keep
his nerves as steady as a rock. There is no cranny into which he can
creep for shelter. On his own he can do exactly nothing for his own

protection. Here, below the surface of the sea he is a member of a team, a link in the chain. And if the chain breaks he and all the other links break with it.

Over the intercom came the quiet, sonorous voice of the commander.

"Gentlemen! Gentlemen, there is nothing whatever to get excited or het up about. And now, please, let me have damage reports."

There was plenty of damage, but Altmeier got home, safely and complete with U-boat.

*   *   *

At about the same time, a sister ship, *U.1228*, also returned to base. Neumann, her chief engine-room artificer, was decorated with the German Cross in gold.

He and one other mechanic had remained on their feet when the rest had been bowled over like flies by the fumes which permeated the whole ship when the Snort head cut under the surface. With great presence of mind he pushed the lever forward and stopped the diesel.

He had saved the boat and all her crew.

CHAPTER XXXV

THE U-BOATS SURRENDER

Situation Report.

Let us anticipate the events of the last few weeks of the war and listen to what Doenitz, whom Hitler named as his successor, has to say with regard ot the final phases:

"Militarily speaking, the war was already irretrievably lost by the beginning of 1945. But capitulation then would have brought about the equally certain and total destruction of the German State and people and the implementation of the Yalta Agreement. A continuation of the struggle was essential in order to give the German race the best possible chance of survival. If we had capitulated at the beginning of 1945—then,

"(a) Some two million more German soldiers would have fallen into Russian hands than in May.

"(b) Some six to seven million more German nationals would have been delivered into the hands of the Russians.

"On the other side of the balance sheet, there would have been:

"(a) No more casualties at the front.

"(b) No more casualties through air raids.

"(c) No more destruction of property.

"If the troops and the civilian population in the East were to be rescued, a continuation of the struggle in the West was essential, for the Anglo-Saxon powers would certainly not have concluded a separate peace, and a cessation of hostilities on the Western Front would have been swiftly followed by the collapse of the front in the East. That we had to endure further losses of life, among both soldiers and civilians in the air raids, was a very painful necessity.

"My instructions to suspend hostilities in the West and to fight on in the East were rendered feasible by the fact that by that time the Western Front and Eastern Front had come so close to each other, that within a few days it became possible to achieve the object underlying my instructions—namely, to transfer soldiers and civilians from the East into the Western Zone. In any case surrender at the beginning of 1945 was not possible since Hitler would not hear of it."

When these facts are borne in mind, the decisions taken and the arguments on which they were based will bear the scrutiny of historians in the future. The question of the extent to which the entry of the new U-boats into the struggle during the last months would have affected the issue is one which has remained unanswered. Whether, during the last months of the war there was any real necessity to send the old type U-boats into action and to destruction, is a question which does not come within the scope of this book.

During the last black and fateful weeks of the Reich Doenitz organised naval brigades, to support the desperate efforts of the armies fighting in East Prussia and the Warthegau to stem the avalanche of Red fury and destruction. With great skill and determined energy he accomplished the evacuation of East Prussia and Kurland; and by thus throwing pell-mell into the fight, the faithful naval crews and the steadfast and undismayed personnel of the mercantile marine, he saved hundreds of thousands of encircled German soldiers and civilians from Russian captivity.

Doenitz also sent the last remaining surface ships of the navy into action. They bombarded the Russian positions in the vicinity of the threatened ports in East Prussia, Danzig and Kurland, and with the accurate and incessant fire of their heavy guns they covered the greatest rescue operation in history.

To Admiral Doenitz the news that Hitler had appointed him as his successor came as a complete surprise. Later he declared: "It was at once quite clear to me that it was my primary duty to end the war as quickly as possible and to save as many German lives as I could. I decided therefore to try and gain time in the East in order to be able to evacuate as many people as possible from East to West."

With this object in view Doenitz sent Admiral von Friedeburg, the naval C.-in-C., to Field Marshal Montgomery on the evening of 2 May. Attacked incessantly by fighter bombers and involved in a car accident as well, von Friedeburg did not arrive at Montgomery's headquarters before the morning of 3 May.

Von Friedeburg offered Montgomery the immediate capitulation of all troops in East Friesland and Holstein.

Montgomery: "I demand that this be extended to include capitulation in Holland and Denmark."

Von Friedeburg got in touch with Doenitz, who at once agreed, and this partial capitulation came into force on the morning of 5 May. The

U-boats had been ordered to cease operations some time before.

It was characteristic of Field-Marshal Montgomery's sense of fairness that he ordered an immediate cessation of aerial bombardment over the territories concerned as soon as these negotiations began.

More intricate were the negotiations with General Eisenhower, to whom Doenitz sent Admiral von Friedeburg and General Jodl on 6 May to negotiate further capitulation. Eisenhower insisted stubbornly on total capitulation, but eventually allowed himself to be persuaded to grant a respite of forty-eight hours, during which period he agreed to allow troops retreating from the east and civilians to enter the western zone.

On 7 May came capitulation on all fronts. It was signed on 8 May and came into force at 00.00 hours on 9 May.

*   *   *

U.826 was among those that surrendered. She had left her base in Norway on 6 March to proceed on operations for the first time. Later, after the war, her chief engineer, Lieutenant Reuter, wrote as follows:

"While we were prisoners we were very amused indeed to hear that the Americans had heralded a six-week underwater voyage which they had made in one of the captured Snort U-boats as a unique, world-shattering and outstanding performance. The American Press celebrated the fact as a triumph for American technique and science! All I can say is that we submerged on 6 March and did not surface again until we surrendered on 9 May. To my way of reckoning, that comes to sixty-four days, or nine weeks! Even then we had used barely half of our fuel oil, and we could with the greatest comfort and ease have remained submerged for another eight weeks. Fuel consumption, when the Snort is in use, is astonishingly low.

"On this, her first and last patrol, *U.826* used the Snort in all weathers.

"During the whole of her voyage *U.852* was not once attacked. She remained at sea as a perfect submersible craft invisible to the enemy. Only twice, once on the outward voyage and once on the way back, did she blow tanks, and then only enough to bring the jumping wire above the surface, in order to transmit a signal."

To return, however, to 9 May. When the news of the capitulation was received *U.852* was in the narrows between Iceland and the Faroes. The crew were neither surprised nor depressed by it.

Orders had also been received to destroy all secret matter. It was all packed in weighted cases and later, when the U-boat surfaced, thrown overboard, with the exception of the engine-room handbooks.

A signal from Doenitz, "To all concerned," was then received. In it Doenitz said that though he would give no orders on the subject, he hoped that all U-boats would proceed to a British port. If the U-boats surrendered, the message went on to say, it was hoped that as a result many thousands of German lives would be saved.

Lübke (*U.852*) called his officers to a conference, which lasted for three hours. Should they make for Ireland? Or Spain? Or even South America? The deciding factor, however, was that last sentence of Doenitz's signal.

"Had we but known what was coming," wrote Reuter later in his diary, "nothing on earth would have induced us to surrender to the British."

And so, unaware of what the future held in store for them, they prepared the U-boat for surrender. The torpedoes were withdrawn from their tubes, and the pistols replaced in their containers, and Lübke made a signal giving his position.

The answering signal did not come from a German station. Instead, a British station came on the air. The British ordered the Germans to haul down the German flag. *U.852* received instructions to proceed at nine knots to Loch Eriboll. Lübke felt the blood surge to his head as he read the rest of the message:

"In the place of the German ensign, a black flag will be flown."

A black flag! The flag of a pirate!

A torn old bed-sheet was found and was smeared with oil and soot.

There are no such things as tears in a U-boat—whatever the danger and whatever happens, even when shipmates fall dying on all sides. But now the men turned aside. They hung their heads and avoided looking into each other's eyes. Lübke, too, withdrew into the solitude of his cabin, while the chief engineer fumbled and pored with unseeing eyes over a batch of papers.

The black flag had not yet been hoisted; and then suddenly what they had been fearing occurred. A Sunderland came flying directly towards the U-boat. The crew remained tense, expectant, ready for any eventuality.

"To hell with that order! Action stations!"

Never had the men leapt with such speed to man their guns. Never had they seen their commander look so grimly determined. The crew of the British aircraft sensed that something was afoot. The 'plane kept its distance and flew round the U-boat in a wide circle, signalling with a morse lamp.

U.852 kept on her course to Loch Eriboll. During the afternoon a corvette hove in sight. Training all its guns on the U-boat, it made a signal: "Follow me." The corvette steamed ahead and led *U.852* through the minefield.

CHAPTER XXXVI

WHERE IS PROFESSOR WALTER? WHERE ARE THE GERMAN WONDER U-BOATS?

Situation Report.

The war is over. By its end 1,174 U-boats (including training ships) had been commissioned. Of these 781 were lost, 721 as the result of direct enemy action, and the remainder in collisions, accidents, etc. And of the total no less than 505 were sunk by British A/S forces at sea and in the air. The remaining 63 U-boats—the difference between the total of 721 destroyed and 658 destroyed actually at sea—were destroyed in the dockyards or in the U-boat bases.

Of the surviving U-boats, 221 were sunk by their own crews, 156 were handed over to the Allies and 26 were broken up or taken over by Japan. At the end of 1944, 880 ocean-going ships and 2,200 coastal craft were being employed by the Allies in the struggle against the U-boats; and hundreds of aircraft, capable of penetrating far out into the Atlantic, were patrolling the danger zones everywhere, where German U-boats appeared. An immense force, in the air and at sea, had been built up to master the U-boat menace.

Ships of the Allied convoys sailed more than 200 million sea-miles, while the British A/S forces fought no less than 13,200 actions against U-boats. The British and Canadian Air Forces alone flew one hundred million miles in 850,000 flying hours, in more than 120,000 sorties against the U-boat Arm.

*   *   *

"The U-boats of 23 Flotilla will proceed forthwith to Kiel."

Thus ran the order received by the Flotilla commander, von Bülow, at the end of January 1945 aboard the depot ship *Deutschland* in Danzig. Among others, the order affected the U-boat commanded by Lieutenant Daehne, who, as a midshipman some years previously had taken part in the rescue of the three survivors from the *Bismarck*.

"Class A U-boats will take over as many provisions as possible," continued the order; and this, too, affected Daehne, for his U-boat which had arrived in Kiel was in category A—U-boats fit for operations.

Group B consisted of U-boats still fit for restricted operations, to which precise instructions were to be issued later.

In Group C were included all U-boats unfit for service. These, like the special U-boats which it was not desired to hand over to the enemy, were all to be sunk.

The rest of the German Navy and the last of the German merchantmen were being employed in an attempt to save those cut off in the eastern territories from captivity. What the men of these ships accomplished defies description. Two million souls were rescued.

During these tragic days Daehne was on the way to Norway. In the Belt he received a W/T signal.

"The scuttling of all U-boats is to be completed by 06.00 on 9 May."

"Well—that gives us plenty of time," said Daehne to his officers.

"And, damn it, gentlemen, if it's got to be done, I suggest it should be done where we can step ashore on German soil!"

His officers agreed.

Daehne set course for Flensburg.

Spirits aboard were low, and minds were in a state of confusion. An order of things which they had regarded as rock-like had begun to totter.

"Sink the ship—what the hell!" exclaimed Daehne, breaking the heavy, gloom-laden silence. "I'm damned if I can do it. The order's bloody nonsense!"

"You won't find such a thing in any manual," ventured one.

"No—and you won't find any precedent for it in history either," chimed in another.

Daehne and his officers simply did not know what they ought to do. The whole crew were utterly bewildered.

During the night 8/9 May 1945 some thirty U-boats of all types and one destroyer gathered together off Steinberg in the Geltinger Bay. On Daehne's ship, as on all the others, the periscope was up, and from it fluttered the German ensign.

From Steinberg pinnaces and motor boats were approaching fussily, and there was a hurried and nervous scurrying to and fro. Staff officers clambered aboard the individual U-boats and repeated once again the strict orders with regard to the sinking of the ships. The first, hesitant sunrays of this lovely May morning illumined a dramatic scene. One after the other, the U-boats slowly sank. With colours flying, the dark grey wolves of the sea disappeared one by one, unvanquished, into the depths. Here in Kiel Bay, off Travemünde, Wesermünde and elsewhere along the whole German coast millions worth of treasure disappeared beneath the waves.

For those, who had remained true to their service till the bitter end, who, in the words of the British, had fought till the last moment with seamanlike discipline and admirable determination, their whole world was breaking to pieces about them.

Daehne's ship was the last one remaining afloat in this watery graveyard. A pinnace approached at high speed and with foaming bows. Across the water came the urgent shouts of staff officers....

"Hurry! Sink that boat at once!"

Every fibre in his being urged Daehne to ignore the call. Up to the last second he had hesitated to fulfil this order, which after all was clear and categorical enough. He struggled desperately to reach a decision, to find some way out. But what way out could there be for a fighting man, to whom obedience to an order is automatic, even when the order is contrary to his own convictions and feelings! "Prepare to abandon ship! At speed!"

Daehne, Lieutenant Detleffsen, the chief engineer, and Hegenbarth, the chief engine-room artificer alone remained aboard. Together and in silence they placed the demolition charges. Some of them they fastened to the warheads of the torpedoes.

"If we've got to do it, we'll do it properly," muttered Daehne grimly. And then he himself set light to the time fuses.

"Seven minutes! Out you go, both of you!"

"I'm staying where I am," Daehne heard Hegenbarth mutter behind him. He turned swiftly and stared into the steady, stony face of his petty officer.

"Don't be a fool, Hegenbarth," he snapped. "You won't stop the wheel of fate that way. Come on! Off with you." Gently Daehne tried to push Hegenbarth before him. But the petty officer stood like a rock.

"No, Sir. The war's finished. I'm staying aboard. I believed in our cause and I served it faithfully. It's not only the world I believed in that's falling to pieces. My parents have been slaughtered by the Russians. I'm staying where I am."

"I know how you feel. But we all of us believed in all good faith in our cause, and we did our duty. What was false, history alone will reveal. But that a great deal was false is proved by this ending."

Hegenbarth's only answer was a tired shrug of the shoulders. Then he turned swiftly and in a flash had disappeared through the hatch. Daehne realised that further argument was useless. There was only one thing he might do. He could give the man an order. Yet never had an order passed so unwillingly from his lips. Daehne clambered into the conning-tower.

"Petty Officer Hegenbarth," he said sternly, "I order you to leave the ship. And be quick about it, or the whole lot of us will be blown up."

No answer. To penetrate further into the ship would have been suicidal. To try and persuade Hegenbarth seemed equally hopeless. Dähne turned and with his chief engineer left the ship. He was still not sure that he had done the right thing, and for yet another moment he kept the pinnace waiting. It was a painful moment. Another few miserable minutes and the torpedoes would go off and would blow the pinnace to pieces. The officer in charge had been unaware of what had been happening. And when, after the two U-boat officers had stepped aboard, Hegenbarth appeared once again on the conning-tower, it was he who raised the alarm. "Good God!" he shouted, "There's still someone aboard." Daehne merely nodded, and then shouted to Hegenbarth, "Come on, Hegenbarth, for goodness' sake." The petty officer merely touched his cap, but did not move. Above him the red cloth of the German ensign fluttered in the early morning breeze.

On Daehne's orders the coxswain of the pinnace let in the clutch of the engine, and the little boat rapidly gathered speed. It was not a moment too soon, if they were not all to be blown sky-high.

All eyes were fixed on Hegenbarth, who still stood like a statue on the conning-tower.

Once again he saluted his shipmates in the pinnace, then he turned, saluted the colours, and as he did so the whole U-boat was enveloped from end to end in a ruddy cloud of flame, water, fragments and steam. A terrific explosion once again rent the stillness of the morning; and then those in the pinnace heard the water come roaring and crashing down again. And then all was quiet.

A small part of the U-boat's stern was still visible and then it, too, disappeared. *U.349* had started on her last journey, And with her went Hegenbarth.

Daehne did not know which moved him most, his grief at the loss of his boat or his admiration for the end of a man, broken by the sight of the death of his beloved and deadly weapon and the end of a myth which he had served in good faith, unquestioningly and with a clear conscience in the cause of his fatherland.

*   *   *

He was followed very shortly by another such man, one of the finest of German naval officers, the last Commander-in-Chief of the German Navy, Admiral von Friedeburg.

When Hans Georg von Friedeburg signed the capitulation he did so with the same sense of duty that had made him serve his country as an officer in two world wars. It was without a shadow of doubt the most painful duty that the admiral had ever been called upon to perform.

23 May, 1945

British troops and British armour had surrounded the Mürvik enclave, where the "Reich Government" had established itself in the Naval Sports School.

Like all other officers of Supreme Headquarters of the Armed Forces, Admiral von Friedeburg had been informed by the Allied Control Council that he was to regard himself as a "prisoner of war".

"Please get ready to move." This order sounded very like an arrest.

The decision which he had reached a long time before now seemed to him to be not only justified but also to be the only way of avoiding disgraceful and humiliating treatment.

Arriving at his headquarters, he took leave of his youngest son and through him sent last messages of greeting to his wife and his eldest boy. He was now prepared and determined to end his life.

Admiral von Friedeburg retired to his bathroom and took poison.

*   *   *

And one of the last shots fired during these days of chaos ended the life of an officer who had defied death at sea a hundred times: Captain Wolfgang Lueth, holder of the Knight's Cross with Oak-leaves and Swords.

318

Fearing that certain groups might be planning a *coup de main*, Lueth, as Commander of the Naval School at Flensburg-Muervik, gave strict orders that any person failing to halt when challenged was to be immediately fired upon.

One evening Lueth himself was crossing the grounds in the gathering gloom. Deeply distressed at the fate that had overtaken his country and his brothers in arms, he was plunged in thought and oblivious of his surroundings. He did not even hear the sentry's challenge. And the latter, as ordered, opened fire.

The first shot was fatal.

Captain Wolfgang Lueth was the last sacrifice, victim of a shot fired by a German hand.

On the soil of his shattered and vanquished country Wolfgang's life was extinguished as though the future had no further use for him, a shining example of a German naval officer, a humane man, kind and ever thoughtful of those under him, of whom he was wont to say: "All you have to do is to look after them and give them your affection."

*   *   *

No sooner had the capitulation come into force than the hunt was on, among all the Allies, for one solitary German. French, Russian, American and British Secret Intelligence services were searching for Professor Helmuth Walter. His name did not stand at the head of that list of 'wanted' men, which included those of senior members of the Government and the Armed Forces. To catch this fellow Walter was of no less importance to the Allies than was the capture of Himmler, who had gone to ground somewhere or other. It was not as a war criminal that they sought him; the man they were after was Walter, the inventor and constructor of the German wonder U-boats. A full-scale wooden model of Type XXVI was found by the Americans in a Blankenberg factory, while the British had seized off Cuxhaven *U.1407*, a Type XVIIb Walter boat—the large, high seas type—complete in every detail and ready to proceed on operations.

Among the British naval officers detailed to hunt for German Walter U-boats was Commander Chapman. In the mud off Cuxhaven he came across one of the two boats of this revolutionary type which had been blown up and scuttled.

319

The U-boat was raised and with Lt. Commander John Harvey, a submarine commander, in charge, it was towed over to England by an old German tug.

"It was a bit of luck," said a British officer to Heller, the U-boat engineer, during an interrogation session, "that these U-boats never came into action. There was nothing we could have done about them. If they'd been operational two years ago, the invasion would have been impossible, and the Germans would once again, and this time decisively, have taken the offensive in the Atlantic. We should have been overtaken by a catastrophe just as surely as the U-boats were in 1943—Now what about sound location?"

Heller's mind went back to the U-boat trials. He had never ceased to wonder why the hydrophones had failed to function when *U.793* had done her trials over the measured mile. "The two U-boats stationed at each end of the mile can't possibly have been in a blind spot," he had repeated again and again to himself.

But all that was long ago.

Now, when the British officer posed a question on this very point, Heller pretended that he did not see much point in it. But, what was the fellow driving at?

"Well—what about the underwater location, Captain?" he answered aloud. "They all functioned, as regards the Walter boats, more or less as we expected, both the hydrophones and the Asdic."

"Ree-ally?" said the British officer, staring hard at Heller. "All right, you can go. You're free."

*   *   *

At the International Military Tribunal in Nuremburg, the German U-boat Arm was declared "not guilty", in spite of every endeavour of the jurists and all the mass of detailed evidence produced.

On 6 October, after promulgation of the finding, Admiral Doenitz declared:

"The conduct by Germany of the war at sea stands unblemished and immaculate. Every German sailor can hold up his head proudly. And, in the welter of accusations, both justified and unjustified, that have been hurled at the German people and German's conduct of the war, that is something of inestimable value.

"Compared with this victory won in the fight for the repute of the Navy, my own personal fate is of no significance at all."